Planning Community Mental Health Services for Women

D0555521

The policy of moving mental health care back into the community is intended to provide a more appropriate and flexible range of services adapted to the needs of those who use them. However, the number of mental health settings which meet the particular needs of women are few. In this book, contributors working in a range of settings show how services and clinical practice can be informed and modified by a better understanding of women's diverse needs and experiences.

Planning Community Mental Health Services for Women looks at what women want from services, and the differences between their perceived needs and what they have often received. It offers models of good practice and describes innovative services focusing on women.

This book encourages a collaborative approach to service planning and provision. It is relevant to all professionals working with women in the community and particularly useful to those who are developing local services.

Kathryn Abel is an MRC Fellow at the Institute of Psychiatry, London. **Marta Buszewicz** is a Research Psychiatrist and Honorary Senior Registrar at the Institute of Psychiatry, London. **Sophie Davison** is a Clinical Research Fellow in Forensic Psychiatry at the Institute of Psychiatry, London. **Sonia Johnson** is a Lecturer in Community Psychiatry at the Institute of Psychiatry, London. **Emma Staples** is a Senior Registrar in Psychiatry at the Maudsley Hospital, London.

Planning Community Mental Health Services for Women

A multiprofessional handbook

Edited by
Kathryn Abel, Marta Buszewicz,
Sophie Davison, Sonia Johnson
and Emma Staples

London and New York

First published 1996
by Routledge
11 New Fetter Lane, London EC4P 4EE

Simultaneously published in the USA and Canada
by Routledge
29 West 35th Street, New York, NY 10001

Routledge is an International Thomson Publishing company

Selection and editorial matter © 1996 Kathryn Abel, Marta Buszewicz, Sophie
Davison, Sonia Johnson and Emma Staples; individual chapters, the contributors

Typeset in Times by Datix International Limited, Bungay, Suffolk
Printed and bound in Great Britain by TJ Press (Padstow) Ltd, Padstow, Cornwall

British Library Cataloguing in Publication Data
A catalogue record for this book is available from the British Library

Library of Congress Cataloguing in Publication Data
Planning community mental health services for women:
  a multiprofessional handbook / edited by Kathryn Abel . . . [et al.].
  p. cm.
  Includes bibliographical references and index.
  1. Women – Mental health services.   2. Community mental health services
  – Planning.   3. Women – Mental health.   4. Women – Mental health
  services – Great Britain.   5. Community mental health services –
  Great Britain – Planning.
  I. Abel, Kathryn, 1961–RC451.4.W6P53   1996
  362.2'2'082–dc20   95-38887
                                                                              CIP

ISBN 0–415–11455–1 (hbk)
ISBN 0–415–11456–X (pbk)

Contents

Contributors

Kathryn Abel: MRC Fellow and Honorary Senior Registrar, Institute of Psychiatry; Bethlem and Maudsley Trust, London.

Martin Blanchard: Consultant in Old Age Psychiatry, Royal Free Hospital, London.

Mary Burd: Prince of Wales Fellow in Mental Health, RCGP, and Head of Clinical Psychology Services in Primary Care, Tower Hamlets Healthcare Trust, London.

Marta Buszewicz: Research Psychiatrist; Honorary Senior Registrar, Institute of Psychiatry; Bethlem and Maudsley Trust, London.

Fiona Caldicott: President, Royal College of Psychiatrists, London; Medical Director, South Birmingham Mental Health NHS Trust.

Jane Cook: Clinical Nurse Specialist for Homeless People, Primary Care for Homeless People Team, Islington, London.

Roslyn Corney: Professor of Psychology, University of Greenwich, London.

Christopher Dare: Senior Lecturer in Psychotherapy and Consultant Psychotherapist, Institute of Psychiatry; Bethlem and Maudsley Trust, London.

Sophie Davison: SHSA Clinical Research Fellow in Forensic Psychiatry, Institute of Psychiatry, London.

Elaine Gadd: Senior Medical Officer, Department of Health, Wellington House, London.

Khalida Ismail: Registrar in Psychiatry, Bethlem and Maudsley Trust, London.

Sonia Johnson: Lecturer in Community Psychiatry, PRISM (Psychiatric Research in Service Measurement), Institute of Psychiatry, London.

Elizabeth Kuipers: Senior Lecturer in Psychology, Institute of Psychiatry, London.

Gill Livingston: Senior Lecturer in Psychiatry, Whittington Hospital, UCLMS, London.

E. Jane Marshall: Senior Lecturer; Consultant Psychiatrist, National Addiction Centre; Bethlem and Maudsley Trust, London.

Gillian Mezey: Consultant Forensic Psychiatrist and Honorary Senior Lecturer, St George's Hospital, London.

Maggie Mills: Psychologist and Psychotherapist, Shanti, West Lambeth Community Care Trust, London.

Mary Nettle: User Consultant, Gloucestershire.

Gillian Parker: Nuffield Professor of Community Care, Department of Epidemiology and Public Health, University of Leicester, Leicester.

Rachel E. Perkins: Head of Psychology Services to Rehabilitation Services and Continuing Care, Pathfinder Community and Specialist Mental Health Services, Springfield Hospital, London.

Andrea Phillips: Mental Health Service User, Swindon MIND, Swindon.

Andrea Pound: Director of Psychology Services, St Clement's Hospital and Tower Hamlets Healthcare Trust, London.

Liz Sayce: Policy Director, MIND, National Association for Mental Health, London.

Marcia Scazufca: Clinical Psychologist and Doctoral Student, Institute of Psychiatry, London.

Elizabeth Stanko: Reader in Criminology, Brunel University, Middlesex.

Emma Staples: Senior Registrar in Psychiatry, Bethlem and Maudsley Trust, London.

Geraldine Strathdee: Head of Service Development, Sainsbury Centre for Mental Health, London.

Fiona Subotsky: Consultant Child and Family Psychiatrist, Bethlem and Maudsley Trust, London.

Estela Welldon: Consultant Psychiatrist and Honorary Senior Lecturer in Forensic Psychotherapy, University College, London; Portman Clinic, London.

Foreword

I was delighted to be invited to open the conference on women's mental health which led to the writing of this book. Any attempt to improve the quality of women's lives through addressing their mental health problems is very relevant and the recent movement of mental health care to the community means that this book comes at an especially pertinent time.

This development in care was designed to provide services which are more appropriate, accessible and flexible; therefore, providers of health care are increasingly required to consider the needs and choices of users of those services. In spite of a great deal of rhetoric, the number of mental health settings where needs of women are met in the community is lamentably few. Abuse, harassment and discrimination are still all too common in our mental health services. Consideration of the issues raised in this book will greatly assist any future attempt to reconfigure the service to be more responsive to the needs of women.

There may well be obstacles to the setting up of such a service. The continuing male domination, both of the consultant grade in psychiatry and of senior health service management, has meant that many female patients do not feel understood. In addition, there is a greater readiness of general practitioners to refer male patients for specialist mental health care, in spite of the greater prevalence of mental disorder in women. The relatively poor attendance of male mental health workers at the conference was striking.

Our resources for the provision of mental health services are limited and, therefore, must be used as efficiently as possible. There are, of course, dangers in setting up services which are very specifically targeted so that it may become increasingly difficult to ensure that they are used cost-effectively. The increasing debate about single-sex wards illustrates this point very well, as does the difficulty of ensuring that appropriately skilled staff are available. This makes the evaluation of women-only services most important.

The challenge for clinicians and managers is to guarantee that women receive a service which is both appropriate and timely for them as individuals, and also that women have some choice in determining the nature of their treatment. I trust that this book will help both mental health service users and services planners and providers to work together to meet this challenge.

Fiona Caldicott
September 1994

Chapter 1

Introduction

Sonia Johnson and Marta Buszewicz

Recent central policy and local planning in the UK have been based on a commitment to moving mental health services into the community. Although the level of resources available continues to be criticised, this move holds considerable promise for the development of services that meet users' needs better. The wider, more flexible and more accessible range of services that is possible in the community offers great scope for the development of ways of working that are more helpful to women with mental health problems.

Psychiatry has been vociferously criticised for lack of attention to the social basis of women's mental health problems and for failure to meet their needs. Chesler (1972) and Showalter (1987) are among those who have presented psychiatry as essentially opposed to the interests of women. They suggest that it has been used to pathologise and ostracise women who deviate from traditional gender roles or who are distressed by their powerlessness. Whilst many of these arguments have considerable force, they have relatively little to say to the woman who is currently incapacitated by distressing psychological problems, or to the clinician seeking appropriate ways to help her.

This book begins from the premise that individual clinical responses to women's distress remain relevant, and that it is difficult to envisage social conditions in which there would be no women seeking professional help for mental health problems. However, many of the criticisms levelled against mental health services seem valid, and they need to be taken into account if we are to develop appropriate services. By discussing how clinical practice may be informed and modified by a better understanding of women's diverse needs and experiences, this book is intended to contribute to the building of a bridge between clinical and social views of women's mental health.

The book originated from the Third International Conference on Women and Mental Health, organised by the editors at the Institute of Psychiatry in London. The theme was the provision of community mental health services for women, and discussions at the conference gave rise to many interesting and innovative ideas that had been explored little in the published literature.

In succeeding chapters, these ideas about a variety of aspects of community care for women at all stages of life are outlined and developed. Contributions are based on a variety of theoretical perspectives and professional and personal experiences. However, a number of themes and principles recur in many of the chapters.

First, services must be equally accessible to all groups of women and men, and women must receive a share of resources that is in proportion to their needs. Currently, there is evidence that women are less likely to be referred to specialist services than men who present with comparable mental health problems. Problems with childcare or fears of losing custody of children may produce barriers to asking for help, as may the greater stigma attached to problems such as substance misuse or violent behaviour in women. Experiences of harassment or intimidation by other service users, or even by staff, may prevent women from remaining engaged with services. All the individual attitudes and all the aspects of service organisation that may prevent equity in distributing health care resources according to need must be considered.

Second, there are many ways in which social factors may contribute to women's distress. Marriage has been found to be associated with depression among women more than among men, and motherhood may adversely affect mental health. Women are particularly likely to experience poverty, which is associated with an increased risk of mental illness. Discrimination and lack of access to power may render women vulnerable to poor self-esteem and depression. Because of these factors, it is very important that the problems for which women seek help should be evaluated in their social context. Rather than seeing women as inherently vulnerable, clinicians need to understand the social roles and experiences that may be important in the genesis of their distress. With the move to the community, patients' environments and social networks have become more accessible and visible to clinicians, so that it is easier to take them into account in assessing problems and planning treatment.

Third, for equitable provision to be achieved, the full range of interventions required to meet women's needs must be available. There is evidence that some of the problems that are especially prevalent among women are not given a high priority. Emotional disorders following rape, domestic violence and childhood sexual abuse are widespread among women, but have only recently begun to be significant targets for service provision. Women predominate among those presenting in primary care with depression and anxiety. There is a variety of treatments from which this group may benefit, including psychological as well as drug treatments, but the range of interventions available locally is often very restricted. Among people with severe mental illnesses, such as schizophrenia, women are more likely than men to be married or cohabiting or to have young children, and they often experience considerable difficulties in sustaining these roles. However, support in parenting and in managing sexual and domestic relationships is not often a major focus for community mental health teams.

Fourth, clinicians and service planners need to take account of the diversity of women's experiences, needs and wishes. Psychiatric texts often treat women as an homogeneous category: they assume that it is unproblematic to generalise about women's needs and vulnerabilities. Good clinical practice should be informed by an understanding of the great variety in living situations, relationships, employment experiences, ethnic origins, attitudes and values that increasingly characterise women in the UK. There is a pressing need to consider those women for whom previous generalisations fit especially badly, such as black women, single parents and lesbians.

A fifth essential element in developing appropriate mental health services is consultation with users and carers, and with the voluntary sector organisations who represent their interests. The best-intentioned attempts to establish appropriate services may not succeed if they do not fit users' own views of what they need. Both in individual clinical consultations and in the overall planning of services, the best hope for good community service provision lies in establishing an open dialogue between professionals and users, in order to allow a genuinely collaborative approach to treatment and service planning.

Lastly, we need to understand how to provide interventions in the community that do not compound the social difficulties that have contributed to women's mental health problems. For example, if low self-esteem and limited access to social power contribute to mental ill health, this may be exacerbated by very passive and dependent patient roles, in which women relinquish more control of their lives. For women who have been victimised, treatment in settings such as mixed in-patient wards, where they may be vulnerable to further victimisation, is perilous. Treatment in the community also presents hazards where women's mental health problems have been caused or exacerbated by their difficult social situations – hospital admission or residential care can at least offer respite from these pressures.

Underlying each of the contributions to this book are these concerns with equity, with an understanding of the role of social factors in women's psychiatric disorders, with the diversity of women's mental health needs, and with the need for extensive dialogues between users, carers, clinicians and planners. Most of the book is made up of discussions of women's needs and of clinical practice. A background is provided in Chapter 2, where current knowledge about the prevalence of psychological symptoms and disorders among women in the UK is outlined, and factors which may make certain women especially vulnerable to mental health problems are discussed. Subsequent chapters examine women's needs at various stages in their lives, and consider how the experiences of particular groups of women affect their mental health and their contacts with services. Current models of good practice are important to those developing local services: descriptions of innovative services focusing on women are therefore included wherever possible. In the last five chapters, there is a particular emphasis on the practical aspects of establishing and maintaining appropriate services for women.

Each chapter includes an outline of the theoretical background and a comprehensive reading list, but the book is mainly intended as a practical guide for planners, providers and users of services. The handbook format will allow readers to begin with particular chapters of interest to them, before looking at the book as a whole. There is therefore some overlap of general information, but we have aimed to keep this to a minimum and have cross-referenced to other chapters where necessary. Most chapters begin by describing the mental health difficulties that may affect women in the group with which the chapter is concerned and discuss the factors that may exacerbate these difficulties, or that are important in treatment. Chapters conclude by making practical suggestions for ways of making services more helpful to women users. Within this framework, some chapters have a more theoretical bias, whilst others emphasise service provision more strongly.

This book is relevant to all those involved in the provision of mental health services and we hope that both men and women will read it. We anticipate that it will be useful for a wide variety of disciplines.

The Appendix includes the names and addresses of any organisations to which chapters refer. We have decided not to provide a more extensive list of relevant organisations working in each field, as this might rapidly become out of date, and we feel reluctant to include organisations of which we have no direct experience. However, contact addresses are included for some of the major national organisations that are active in campaigning for the interests of women with mental health problems. These organisations should be able to give interested readers more detailed information about relevant local organisations.

Finally, it is important to emphasise that this book is based on a clinical point of view, and aims to contribute to debate about how to provide appropriate mental health services. However, the effects of social pressures on women, their greater reporting of certain symptoms, and their greater use of some psychiatric services should not be seen as exclusively clinical problems. There are also political and public health implications that are crucial. It is never likely to be adequate to respond *only* in clinical ways to mental health problems that originate partly in women's socialisation, in their lack of social power, in stressful combinations of roles, and in experiences such as rape and sexual abuse. If we view women's mental health problems exclusively as disorders of biology or of individual psychological development, we run the risk of legitimising inactivity in seeking social, political and educational ways of alleviating the stresses that contribute to them. For this reason, as well as for good clinical practice, it is important for researchers and clinicians to seek to understand and raise awareness of the social background to women's difficulties.

REFERENCES

Chesler, P. (1972) *Women and madness*, New York: Doubleday.
Showalter, E. (1987) *The female malady: women, madness and English culture, 1830–1980*, London: Virago.

Chapter 2

Women's mental health in the UK

Sonia Johnson and Marta Buszewicz

An important initial step in planning appropriate mental health services in the community is the examination of the prevalence of mental health problems in the population to be served. In this chapter, we set out the background for discussions of service provision in subsequent chapters by describing the range and reported prevalence of mental health problems among women in the United Kingdom. National information of this kind is useful in considering what service needs may exist at a local level, although local information and individual assessments of needs are also important. There are substantial differences between men and women in their patterns of psychiatric service use and their reported psychological symptoms. This chapter describes the social factors that may contribute to differences between the sexes and that should be considered in planning how to meet women's needs for services.

HISTORICAL PERSPECTIVE

Before the nineteenth century it is unclear whether more women or men were resident in institutions for the mentally ill. However, from about 1830, significantly more women than men were admitted to psychiatric asylums in Britain. It is often difficult to compare the diagnoses of that time with those used today, but several writers have pointed out that many women were referred to physicians or admitted to institutions for what might be seen as socially unacceptable behaviour, e.g. pregnancy outside marriage, 'sexually forward' behaviour or reluctance to undertake 'normal' womanly tasks within marriage or the home (Showalter, 1987; Ussher, 1991). They argue that during the Victorian era women's social roles were very clearly defined and limited, and that any deviation might be defined as 'madness'.

THE CURRENT PICTURE

This historical perspective makes it clear that, at least in the past, definitions of mental illness have often depended on social context. In the last thirty years, a great deal of effort has been made to produce consistent and reproducible diagnoses, although these remain somewhat in a state of flux.

Studies of the prevalence of mental disorders in the community

Studies estimating the number of people with significant psychiatric or psychological symptoms within the community have nearly always shown a marked predominance of women, both in the UK and in other Western countries. Bebbington *et al.* (1981) interviewed adults in the community in Camberwell, South London, and showed that 14.9 per cent of women were affected by conditions identified by the psychiatric questionnaire used, compared with 6.1 per cent of men. Of these, two-thirds displayed a level of symptoms greater than or equal to that found in people referred to outpatient clinics. Subjects were not asked about alcohol or drug abuse. Nearly all those identified were suffering from depression and anxiety (also called neurotic disorders), and within this group women outnumbered men in a ratio of 2:1. This and other studies have shown that women are more likely to get depressed between the ages of 20 and 50.

One of the problems in assessing the level of disorder or of need in a community is whether or not all the relevant groups are being considered. This is illustrated by the Epidemiological Catchment Area Programme, a community survey of 10,000 individuals over three sites in the USA (Robins *et al.*, 1984). When alcohol abuse, drug abuse and antisocial personality, all of which are more common in men, were included, the numbers of women and men found to have a psychiatric disorder were virtually equal. Whether or not these should be considered psychiatric problems is open to debate and will be discussed further later.

A community survey of 10,000 people in the UK (OPCS, 1994) looked primarily at the occurrence of neurotic disorders. Participants were asked about symptoms in the week before the interview. Again, the results showed a marked predominance of women in all the categories of neurotic disorder; the most common disorder being mixed anxiety and depression. Between the ages of 20 and 54, 22 per cent of women were affected compared with 12 per cent of men. There was a predominance of men admitting to alcohol and drug abuse and equal (small) numbers of both sexes reporting a history of psychotic illness.

The eating disorders have the most marked female predominance: around 90 per cent of people with anorexia nervosa are female. Community estimates suggest a prevalence of anorexia of between 0.1 per cent and 1 per cent in adolescent girls, rising to 7 per cent in vulnerable populations such as ballet and modelling students. The prevalence of bulimia nervosa in adolescent girls and young women is thought to be around 1 per cent (Russell, 1993).

Presentation to services

Women present more to their general practitioners, both with physical and with psychological complaints. Possible reasons for this are discussed below. However, the predominance of women is less marked among referrals to the specialist services (Goldberg and Huxley, 1992). This indicates a bias towards the referral of men to secondary care services, and appears to apply particularly to younger men.

Sashidaran *et al.* (1990) interviewed women referred to hospital care, as well as women found to have significant psychiatric symptoms on screening in the community. They found that, although those in the hospital group tended towards the more severe end of the spectrum, and were older and more often single, the untreated community group also had significant morbidity. This raises questions about the effectiveness of present strategies for detecting and treating women with psychiatric disorders in the community.

Hospital populations

Despite the apparent bias towards referring men to secondary care, women occupy more psychiatric in-patient beds than men, and this has been the case for the past 150 years. Although the number of patients in long-stay institutions has continued to fall, this has not altered the overall female: male ratio. The main diagnoses in the hospital in-patient population are very different from those in the community, with far more people affected by psychotic disorders.

As can be seen, there is a large female majority in the category 'organic psychotic conditions' which includes the dementias. Women predominate here largely because they form the majority of the elderly population. There are also large female majorities in the affective psychoses, which include depressive psychoses, and in neurotic and personality disorders. The greater

Table 2.1 In-patient cases by main diagnosis, NHS hospitals, England 1991–92

Diagnosis	Female	Male
Total (excluding mental retardation)	**114,969**	97,424
Organic psychotic conditions	**29,712**	17,957
Schizophrenic psychoses	14,524	**19,430**
Affective psychoses	**24,336**	12,272
Other psychoses	**18,765**	17,510
Neurotic and personality disorders	**20,771**	14,503
Alcohol dependence syndrome	5,488	**13,091**
Drug dependence	1,373	**2,661**

Source: Hospital episode statistics, vol. 1, England, financial year 1991–92, Government Statistical Service, Department of Health, London: HMSO.

number of women surviving into old age is also likely to be a factor in the female majorities in these categories, but is unlikely to account for them entirely. Numbers of admissions will be influenced by the willingness of the family and the community to find other ways of coping with the problem. As women are often the carers, it may be that men are looked after for longer at home. Older women, tending to outlive their husbands, are more likely to be living alone and therefore to be admitted. Rates of admission for single people are higher than for the married in both sexes.

Community and day services

Sex differences in service use have been discussed little in the extensive recent literature on community mental health services. In the USA, women seem to be in the majority in most day-care and out-patient settings (Gift and Zasto-way, 1990). However, men generally outnumber women among the popula-tions served by assertive outreach and home treatment teams, which tend to target people with schizophrenia and other psychotic illnesses. Test *et al.* (1990) suggest that the seriously mentally ill women who use these services have different characteristics and experiences from their male counterparts – for example, they are much more likely to be caring for children or to be involved in a sexual relationship. They argue that these differences create specific needs among the female clients of community teams, and that these are currently very rarely addressed. In the UK, Perkins and Rowland (1991) found that 60 per cent of users of a rehabilitation-oriented day hospital were men. In their study, female users tended to receive less intensive input and to be engaged in less demanding activities than men with a similar level of functioning.

Suicide rates

Although more women commit acts of self-harm such as overdosing or cutting there is a male excess in completed suicides at all ages.

POSSIBLE CAUSES FOR GENDER DIFFERENCES

Thus considerable sex differences emerge, both in patterns of symptoms reported in community surveys and in use of mental health services. Why this should be has generated heated debate. The social explanations put forward are of great interest in considering women's needs, as they draw attention to the ways in which women's roles and experiences influence their mental health. Much of the literature on these sex differences has focused on depression and anxiety, as these are disorders for which women seem to be at higher risk, and where especially strong arguments may be put forward for social factors having an aetiological role. The following discussion therefore refers particularly to these disorders. However, women suffer from a wide range of mental health problems. Their experiences and environments will shape the onset, course and presentation of any psychological disorder they experience. These social factors will also play an important part in determining what sort of services they find acceptable and helpful.

Sex differences have been explained in two main ways. Some have suggested that there are no real differences between men and women in levels of symptoms. Apparent differences have instead been explained in terms of variations in the way distress is expressed, or in terms of diagnostic bias. Others argue that there *are* real differences in psychological symptoms, and propose that a variety of biological and social factors may underlie these differences. In the following sections, we summarise these various explanations.

Do real differences in levels of psychological distress exist?

It has been argued that the reported excess of psychiatric symptoms in women is a misleading product of the way in which the boundaries of psychiatric disorder happen to be defined. Winokur (1979) suggests that women express their distress as depression, whilst men more frequently disguise it with drink and drugs or channel it into antisocial behaviour. If substance abuse and antisocial behaviours were classified as psychiatric disorder, then the difference observed in overall rates of psychiatric disorder between men and women would vanish. The lists of symptoms used to diagnose depression may also omit some that are most likely to accompany depressed mood in men, such as irritability, recklessness or anger (Wilhelm and Parker, 1993). Therefore, men and women may experience psychological distress to a similar degree, but women may be more likely to be perceived as 'mad', whilst men are perceived as 'bad'. This makes a speculative assumption that psychological distress is the general basis of antisocial behaviour and drug-taking.

Some authors have argued that the fact that women are more likely than men to be diagnosed as having a mild or moderate depressive disorder or anxiety, is mainly a result of bias among clinicians, making them more ready to perceive women as depressed. In a widely cited study, Broverman *et al.* (1970) suggested that clinicians operated a double standard in their views of what characterised good mental health in the two sexes. The characteristics of healthy males were seen as very similar to those of healthy adults. In contrast, healthy females were seen as more submissive, excitable, subjective, emotional and easily hurt than the healthy adult. The researchers suggested that women find themselves in a double bind. If they behave as clinicians expect healthy women to behave, they will be deviating from standards of mental health for adults. This may make clinicians more likely to label them as mentally ill.

Recent studies have not always replicated these findings, but Potts *et al.* (1991) found some bias towards the over-diagnosis of depression in women and its under-diagnosis in men. Overall, it appears that clinicians' views of what constitutes normal, healthy behaviour for women may well influence diagnosis, treatment and rehabilitation in potentially problematic ways. However, diagnostic bias is unlikely to be the whole explanation for sex differences in depression as, even in community surveys, women report more psychological symptoms.

A final way of understanding why women might be diagnosed as having mental disorders more often than men, even if their levels of distress are in reality equivalent, is that they may more readily articulate feelings of distress or seek help with such feelings. Briscoe (1982) found that women were more likely than men to report both positive *and* negative feelings. She speculated that this might be because social constraints make men less likely than women to express their feelings. Several authors have found that women tend to present more with psychological symptoms to their GPs, although Williams *et al.* (1986) found evidence that the majority of the difference in presentation was likely to be due to women coming on behalf of others and then taking the opportunity to discuss themselves. In her study of civil servants, Jenkins (1985) found that women *without* minor psychiatric morbidity visited their GPs more and had more certified sick leave. However, among those who were suffering from significant psychological symptoms, the likelihood of visiting their GPs was similar for men and women. This suggests that, although women may present more to GPs, this is unlikely to account for their forming the majority of those with significant psychological symptoms.

BIOLOGICAL MODELS FOR SEX DIFFERENCES

Biological explanations have a long and sometimes disreputable history of being used to explain a variety of psychological differences between men and women (Ussher, 1991; Showalter, 1987). Feminist theorists have often regarded these forms of explanation as dangerous, arguing that purely biological explanations for the increased prevalence of depression in women may discourage investigation of the social difficulties they experience. Two forms of biological theory will be discussed: genetic and hormonal.

When all psychiatric disorders are considered, the evidence for a biological contribution to psychiatric disorder is strongest for the more severe mental disorders, where the sex distribution is more equal. For example, the evidence for a genetic contribution to mood disorders is strongest for manic depressive illness, where the sex ratio is close to equal. However, for unipolar depression, where women predominate, there is little evidence for a genetic link (Paykel, 1991). Thus it seems unlikely that women's greater vulnerability to depression can be explained in exclusively genetic terms.

Hormonal causes seem most likely to be implicated in mental illness occurring in women shortly after childbirth, when there seems to be a clear increase in the onset of major psychosis. However, the evidence for a link between other disorders and the postpartum period is more tenuous (see Chapter 3). Some have also suggested that there are psychological symptoms associated with the pre-menstrual period, the contraceptive pill and the menopause, and hormonal explanations have been proposed for these. Recent summaries of available studies by Weissman *et al.* (1993) and by Paykel (1991) suggest that the evidence remains inconclusive, but there is currently no clear support for these factors as major contributors to psychiatric disorders in women. However, as Ussher (1992) argues, perhaps the most significant contribution of reproduction to women's distress is that women themselves often attribute their symptoms to menstruation, childbirth and the menopause. Thus biology remains central to the ways in which women understand their own feelings.

SOCIAL EXPLANATIONS FOR SEX DIFFERENCES

Social explanations for the differences in psychiatric diagnoses have taken two major forms. First, it is possible that socialisation into the female gender role and the experience of being a woman in our society create low self-esteem and make women in general more vulnerable to depression. Alternatively, being a woman may not in itself be a risk factor for psychological symptoms, but the particular social roles or experiences of certain groups of women may be associated with such symptoms. We will discuss both these theories.

Negative stereotypes and low self-esteem

One way of understanding women's apparently greater vulnerability to mental illness is that it results from the ways in which they learn to view themselves in societies where they occupy a generally disadvantaged position. Many studies have compared the views that girls and boys have of themselves during childhood. Not all studies find differences, but the evidence overall suggests that lower self-confidence, greater dependence on the opinions of others and a tendency to blame themselves for failures may develop quite early in girls (Ruble *et al.*, 1993). From childhood, women may develop lower self-esteem through being taught to be less independent, to see themselves as less competent and to have lower expectations than men. Studies on self-esteem in adulthood suggest that these sex differences may persist (Hong *et al.*, 1993). Women's negative views of themselves may be reinforced in adulthood by negative stereotypes and negative images of women in our culture, particularly their representation as passive and dependent, and by their experiences of discrimination and powerlessness.

The work of George Brown and his group fits with the idea that low self-esteem may be important in depression in women. In their Islington study of women with children living at home, a negative view of themselves and poor support from close relationships were the two main factors which made women more likely to become depressed after experiencing a negative event (Brown *et al.*, 1990a). Women who had some positive views about themselves were more likely to recover quickly from episodes of depression (Brown *et al.*, 1990b). Thus if persistent discrimination in a society means that the experience of being a woman generates low self-esteem, one might predict that this would also create susceptibility to depression.

For eating disorders, in which the most marked female predominance is found, a variety of theories have been put forward explaining the disorders in terms of women's response to lack of social power, and to the expectations associated with the feminine role as it is currently defined.

Social roles and vulnerability to depression

Another way of understanding apparent gender differences in psychological symptoms is in terms of the social roles that particular groups of women occupy. Studies of female and male civil servants (Jenkins, 1985), and of women and men entering the teaching profession (Wilhelm and Parker, 1989) indicate that, if other factors such as educational attainment, social class, marital status and professional status, are matched, similar rates of depression are found in men and women. These findings seem to support the idea that it is not being female *per se* that is the source of depression: rather the differences found in the community may need to be explained in terms of the psychological effects of the roles occupied by some groups of women, such as mothers, housewives or informal carers, or by some combination of these.

Marriage and children

Important early work in this field demonstrated much higher rates of depression in married women compared with those who were unmarried (Gove and Tudor, 1973). In contrast, single men had higher rates of psychological distress than those who were married – hence the suggestion that marriage was good for men's mental health, but disadvantageous for their wives. Some subsequent studies have shown similar findings (Bebbington *et al.*, 1981), but the picture appears to be more complicated than initially thought.

Women who are employed and married appear to be less depressed than those who stay at home, indicating a protective effect of having more than one source of self-esteem (Gove, 1972; Cochrane and Stopes-Roe, 1981). However, having children, particularly if under school-age, appears more often to have a negative effect on women's mental health (Elliott and Huppert, 1991). It has therefore been suggested that it may be having children

rather than marriage which is detrimental, possibly by increasing both demands and potential life events (Bebbington *et al.*, 1991). Cleary and
Mechanic (1983) found that having a young child greatly increased the psychological symptoms reported by women who were also working, and that the
increased stress involved in childcare appeared to counteract the beneficial
effect of being employed.

Having several roles but limiting the associated demands seems to be
beneficial. Elliott and Huppert (1991) found that being employed was better
for middle-class mothers who could also afford reasonable childcare and
Brown and Bifulco (1990) found that working-class mothers who worked
part-time appeared least likely to become depressed, compared with those
working full-time or staying at home. Other work by Brown's group has
emphasised the importance of the quality of the marital relationship.
Women who lacked a close confidante were much more likely to become
depressed (close confidantes were not necessarily husbands or partners).

Recently, studies have been less clear about whether single women are in
fact less likely to become depressed than those who are married, although
the protective effect of marriage remains for men. Those of both sexes who
are separated, divorced or widowed appear to have a greater likelihood
of depressive symptoms than either single or married groups. This is of
particular importance given changing social structures and the rising divorce
rates. Rates of neurotic disorder are higher in all single parents than in those
living in a family unit with another adult (OPCS, 1994). Divorced women
and separated men have even higher rates of symptoms.

Employment

Overall, being in paid employment appears to be beneficial for both men
and women, but the effect is more marked for men. The initial concept,
following Gove and Tudor's work (1973), was that 'bored unemployed housewives' were the most likely to get frustrated and depressed. However, despite
dramatic social changes over the last thirty years, resulting in much larger
numbers of women being involved in some paid employment, the increased
prevalence of women suffering from depressive symptoms persists.

More recent work has shown that in some cases, working outside the
home appears to be associated with an increased risk of depression in
women. This is more likely if they are involved in poorly paid or menial
work, or as part of a difficult life with responsibilities for children and home
as well as an unsupportive relationship. Evidence for this comes from Parry
(1986), who found that working outside the home was beneficial for women
if they had good social support structures to help with their domestic responsibilities, but otherwise it could be detrimental. Rosenfield (1989) found that
work appears beneficial for women if it increases sources of self-esteem and
sense of control. It can, however, be detrimental if it increases the number

of demands that a woman feels are made on her and is accompanied by a sense of having little control in either her work or home life. Interestingly, she also found that if men became more involved in domestic tasks their reporting of symptoms of sadness and anxiety increased (Rosenfield, 1992). However, other studies have shown no adverse effect on men as a result of their wives' employment.

Being unemployed has been clearly shown to have a detrimental effect on the mental health of men, and Cochrane and Stopes-Roe (1981) found that women with unemployed husbands are likely to report high levels of depression. Several workers have shown a marked adverse effect of unemployment on women's mental health, but this may depend on how crucial the job was as a source of financial and other reward.

Poverty and social class

Most studies have shown higher rates of neurotic disorder in those of lower social class in both sexes. Women, even if working, are disproportionately represented among the lowest wage-earners, as well as having low-status jobs with less power. Because their involvement in childcare limits their ability to get employment, they are also over-represented in the poorest and most deprived segments of the population.

Women as carers/supporters

In addition to looking after children, women predominate as carers of the mentally ill, elderly, physically disabled and those with learning difficulties. Twigg and Atkin (1994) have reviewed literature on the consequences of the caring role and describe a range of possible adverse effects, including poorer mental health. Some evidence suggests that informal caring may have more adverse effects on women than on men. Women seem to subordinate their needs more to those of the person they care for, whilst receiving less support from the available services.

Effect of multiple roles

It is therefore probably not the presence or absence of particular roles in women's lives that predispose some of them to more distress, but a particular combination of roles. There is evidence that multiple roles can be good for women's mental health. Women who have several roles, but who also have social support and financial security, are less likely to get depressed than either women with few roles or sources of self-esteem/power, or those with multiple roles with many demands and little support (Thoits, 1986).

Ethnicity

There are substantial gaps in knowledge about the mental health of women in general and this applies even more to the ethnic minority populations in the UK. The main focus in literature about the mental health of these communities has been on the controversy about higher rates of schizophrenia reported among Afro-Caribbeans. Patterns of other psychological symptoms have been explored little, and discussion of the service needs of the Asian, Afro-Caribbean and African communities remains limited. Reported findings have often been inconsistent, and this may be because local social and political factors have considerable effects. One clear finding that suggests a need for action is an elevated rate of suicide nationally among young Asian women (Soni-Raleigh and Balarajan, 1992).

Women's experiences and psychiatric morbidity

A further form of social explanation proposes that women are more vulnerable to psychological morbidity because they are more likely to have certain experiences that may cause depression. Experiences that may be particularly important in understanding women's mental health problems are childhood sexual abuse, rape and domestic violence.

The last ten years have seen a greater awareness of childhood sexual abuse, and several studies have suggested that it is a risk factor for various psychiatric disorders in adulthood (Mullen *et al.*, 1993). Associations are thought to include depression, eating disorders, deliberate self-harm and difficulties with relationships. There is as yet little work that assesses how far the apparently greater prevalence of experiences of abuse among women might account for differences between men and women in patterns of psychiatric morbidity. Cutler and Nolen-Hoeksema (1991) have tried to estimate to what extent childhood sexual abuse might explain sex differences in depression. Their calculations suggest that it might account for a substantial proportion, though not all, of the greater prevalence of depression in women. Rape and domestic violence may also contribute to increases in psychiatric morbidity in women: this possibility has as yet been investigated little.

CONCLUSION

Examination of gender differences in patterns of mental health problems and of service use reveals a complex picture, but the finding of a greater prevalence of reported symptoms of depression and anxiety among women than among men has been consistently replicated, both in community studies and in treatment populations. It has also been reported by a number of authors that women have a greater overall prevalence of psychiatric disorder. However, the classification of substance abuse and antisocial personality disorder as forms of psychiatric disorder leads to very similar overall rates being found in men and women. It is interesting that the problems that more commonly affect women have traditionally been regarded as core forms of psychiatric disorder, whilst more debate remains about the difficulties that are more prevalent among men. This may reflect a greater willingness to view distress and difficult behaviour among women as a form of 'madness', whilst men tend to be seen as morally deviant.

The question of why women and men seem to have different patterns of psychiatric disorder remains unresolved. Investigation is hampered by the fact that multiple confounding factors are almost invariably present. For example, the social and biological effects of being a woman cannot be examined in isolation from one another.

One possible explanation is that men's and women's internal states are, in reality, very much the same, but that there is some form of bias in observation or reporting of symptoms, although clinician bias is unlikely to account for a high proportion of the differences observed. However, the important possibilities remain that men and women express distress in different ways or have different levels of willingness to admit to symptoms. The relationship between 'real' and reported emotions is very difficult to investigate.

If real differences do exist, there are a variety of ways of explaining these. These may not be mutually exclusive: indeed it seems likely that several factors contribute. Suggested explanations include biological differences and lower self-esteem resulting from female socialisation. A further very important possibility is that sex differences may not be the result of women in general having a greater vulnerability to neurotic disorders, but rather that particular social roles and experiences, which are more prevalent among women, may be associated with mental health problems. Likely candidates are motherhood, other caring roles, poverty, lack of paid work outside the home, and the stresses resulting from occupying multiple roles with limited social support. Experiences of victimisation such as domestic violence, rape and childhood sexual abuse may also be important. A common factor that may be identified in all these is an experience of powerlessness, and it is possible that this interacts with poor self-esteem and social isolation to produce depression. However, selection bias produces important difficulties in disentangling the evidence about social roles: for example, in considering the evidence about marriage, one needs to remember that the factors influencing whether individuals get married may be different for men and for women.

Finally, in discussing gender differences, we have largely confined ourselves to considering depression and anxiety, as this is the area where a large literature has accumulated. However, the various social factors we have discussed are likely to have a more general importance in considering women's mental health problems. Experiences of victimisation and stresses due to social roles are likely to shape the onset and course of a variety of problems, including eating disorders, substance abuse and personality difficulties. Even where they are not causal, social stresses may also contribute to the difficulties of women suffering the full range of mental health problems, including psychotic illnesses, and they should be taken into account in considering how to help all these women.

REFERENCES

Bebbington, P., Hurry, J., Tennant, C., Sturt, E. and Wing, J. (1981) 'Epidemiology of mental disorders in Camberwell', *Psychological Medicine* 11: 561–581.

Bebbington, P.E., Dean, C., Der, G., Hurry, J. and Tennant, C. (1991) 'Gender, parity and the prevalence of minor affective disorder', *British Journal of Psychiatry* 158: 40–45.

Briscoe, M. (1982) 'Sex differences in psychological well-being', *Psychological Medicine Monograph Supplement 1.*

Broverman, I.K., Broverman, D.L., Clarkson, F.E., Rosenkrantz, P.S. and Vogel, S.R. (1970) 'Sex role stereotypes and clinical judgements of mental health', *Journal of Consulting and Clinical Psychology* 34: 1–7.

Brown, G.W. and Bifulco, A. (1990) 'Motherhood, employment and the development of depression; a replication of a finding?', *British Journal of Psychiatry* 156: 169–179.

Brown, G.W., Bifulco, A. and Andrews, B. (1990a) 'Self esteem and depression 3. Aetiological issues', *Social Psychiatry and Psychiatric Epidemiology* 25: 235–243.

—— (1990b) 'Self esteem and depression 4. Effect on course and recovery', *Social Psychiatry and Psychiatric Epidemiology* 25: 244–249.

Cleary, P.D. and Mechanic, D. (1983) 'Sex differences in psychological distress among married people', *Journal of Health and Social Behaviour* 24: 111–121.

Cochrane, R. and Stopes-Roe, M. (1981) 'Women, marriage, employment and mental health', *British Journal of Psychiatry* 139: 373–381.

Cutler, S.E. and Nolen-Hoeksema, S. (1991) 'Accounting for sex differences in depression through female victimisation: childhood sexual abuse', *Sex Roles* 24: 425–438.

Elliott, B.J. and Huppert, F.A. (1991) 'In sickness and in health: associations between physical and mental well-being, employment and parental status in a British nationwide sample of married women', *Psychological Medicine* 21: 515–524.

Gift, T.E. and Zastoway, T.R. (1990) 'Psychiatric service utilization differences by sex and by locale', *International Journal of Social Psychiatry* 36: 11–17.

Goldberg, D. and Huxley, P. (1992) *Common mental disorders*, London: Routledge.

Gove, W.R. and Tudor, J. (1973) 'Adult sex roles in mental illness', *American Journal of Sociology* 78: 812–835.

Hong, S., Dianca, M.A., Dianca, M.R. and Dollington, J. (1993) 'Self esteem: the effects of life satisfaction, sex and age', *Psychological Reports* 72: 95–101.

Jenkins, R. (1985) 'Sex differences in minor psychiatric morbidity', *Psychological Medicine Monograph Supplement 7.*

Mullen, P.E., Martin, J.L., Anderson, J.C., Romans, S.E. and Herbison, G.P. (1993) 'Childhood sexual abuse and mental health in adult life', *British Journal of Psychiatry* 163: 721–732.

OPCS Surveys of Psychiatric Morbidity in Great Britain (1994) 'Bulletin no.1: the prevalence of psychiatric morbidity among adults aged 16–64 living in private households in Great Britain', London: OPCS.

Parry, G. (1986) 'Paid employment, life events, social support and mental health in working-class mothers', *Journal of Health and Social Behaviour* 27: 193–208.

Paykel, E.S. (1991) 'Depression in Women', *British Journal of Psychiatry* 158 (suppl. 10): 22–29.

Perkins, R.E. and Rowland, L.A. (1991) 'Sex differences in service usage in long-term psychiatric care: are women adequately served?', *British Journal of Psychiatry* 158 (suppl. 10): 75–79.

Potts, M.K., Burnam, M.A. and Wells, K.B. (1991) 'Gender differences in depression detection: a comparison of clinical diagnosis and standardised assessment', *Journal of Consulting and Clinical Psychology* 3: 609–615.

Robins, L.N., Helzer, J.E., Weissman, M.M., Orvaschel, H., Gruenberg, E., Burke, J.D. and Regier, D.A. (1984) 'Lifetime prevalence of specific psychiatric disorders in three sites', *Archives of General Psychiatry* 41: 949–958.

Rosenfield, S. (1989) 'The effects of women's employment: personal control and sex differences in mental health', *Journal of Health and Social Behaviour* 30: 77–91.

—— (1992) 'The costs of sharing: wives' employment and husbands' mental health', *Journal of Health and Social Behaviour* 33: 213–225.

Ruble, D.N., Greulich, F., Pomerantz, E.M. and Gochberg, B. (1993) 'The role of gender related processes in the development of sex differences in self evaluation and depression', *Journal of Affective Disorders* 29: 97–128.

Russell, G.F.M. (1993) 'Eating disorders', in D. Bhugra and J. Leff (eds), *Principles of social psychiatry*, Oxford: Blackwell.

Sashidaran, S.P., Surtees, P.G., Kreitman, N.B., Ingham, J.G. and Miller, P.M. (1990) 'Affective disorders among women in the general population and among those referred to psychiatrists: clinical features and demographic correlates', *British Journal of Psychiatry* 157: 828–834.

Showalter, E. (1987) *The female malady: women, madness and English culture, 1830–1980*, London: Virago.

Soni-Raleigh, V. and Balarajan, R. (1992) 'Suicide and self burning among Indians and West Indians in England and Wales', *British Journal of Psychiatry* 161: 365–368.

Test, M.A., Burke, S.S. and Wallisch, L.S. (1990) 'Gender differences of young adults with schizophrenic disorders in community care', *Schizophrenia Bulletin* 16: 331–344.

Thoits, P.A. (1986) 'Multiple identities: examining gender and marital status differences in distress', *American Sociological Review* 51: 259–272.

Twigg, J. and Atkin, K. (1994) *Carers perceived: policy and practice in informal care*, Buckingham: Open University Press.

Ussher, J. (1991) *Women's madness: misogyny or mental illness*, Hemel Hempstead: Harvester Weatsheaf.

—— (1992) 'Research and theory related to female reproduction: implications for clinical psychology', *British Journal of Clinical Psychology* 31: 129–151.

Weissman, M.M., Bland, R., Joyce, P.R., Newman, S., Wells, E.J. and Wittchen, H.U. (1993) 'Sex differences in rates of depression: cross national perspectives', *Journal of Affective Disorders* 29: 77–84.

Wilhelm, W.K. and Parker, G. (1989) 'Is sex necessarily a risk factor to depression?', *Psychological Medicine* 19: 401–413.

—— (1993) 'Sex differences in depressogenic risk factors and coping strategies in a socially homogeneous group', *Acta Psychiatrica Scandinavica* 88: 205–211.

Williams, P., Tarnopolsky, A., Hand, D. and Shepherd, M. (1986) 'Minor psychiatric morbidity and general practice consultations: the West London Survey', *Psychological Medicine Monograph Supplement 9*.

Winokur, G. (1979) 'Unipolar depression: is it divisible into autonomous sub-types?', *Archives of General Psychiatry* 36: 47–52.

Chapter 3

Motherhood and mental illness

Andrea Pound and Kathryn Abel

INTRODUCTION

The psychological impact of motherhood has long been recognised by women all over the world. By contrast, health care professionals have been slow to take note. Although severe mental illness in relation to childbirth was described in the mid-nineteenth century, only in the 1950s did it become the focus of scientific study. Much of the current debate focuses on questions of classification: should psychological illness in childbearing women be considered a separate, well-defined entity, with a clearly identified aetiology and treated as such, or are childbirth and motherhood 'natural' life events whose psychological sequelae are to be expected as following any other life event?

To those involved in care and service planning, discussion that is confined to issues of classification is unhelpful. Whatever the origin of their problems, mothers with young children have markedly different needs from other groups of women. In this chapter, we briefly describe the types and extent of psychiatric disorder associated with the postnatal period, before moving on to a fuller discussion of the practical and clinical issues facing health carers in their attempt to understand and respond to the needs of the mothers and children involved. We conclude with suggestions for good service provision, as well as examples of good clinical practice.

EPIDEMIOLOGY

Postnatal mental disorder covers three symptom categories (see Table 3.1):

- Maternity 'blues': a mild, self-limiting mood change with marked tearfulness which occurs in most women during the first postnatal week and lasts a matter of days.
- Postnatal depression: may have atypical symptoms such as disturbed sleep at the beginning of the night and mood disturbance worst in the evenings; may be indistinguishable from depressive disorder at other times.

Table 3.1 Summary data for postpartum psychological syndromes

	Blues	Depression	Psychosis
Numbers	1 in 2 women	1 in 10–20 women	1 in 500 women
Timing	4 to 10 days postnatally	Within 90 days	Within 14 days
Duration	Days	Maybe years	Usually weeks

Note: For review see O'Hara and Zekoski, 1988.

• Postpartum psychosis: most commonly manic in presentation with prominent perplexity, confusion and disinhibition occurring within two weeks
of giving birth; probably a distinct entity from other psychotic illness.

Official classification systems, such as ICD-10, only recognise mental disorder that begins within six weeks of delivery as specifically related to childbirth. In addition, to date no classificatory system makes mention of the
psychological sequelae of other peri-reproductive problems, such as miscarriage and pregnancy itself; whilst fertility treatment and termination are
of increasing relevance to the care of women's mental health. This may have
an important impact on planning of services for mothers.

Childbearing and motherhood are two related, but separate events. If we
are to plan for women simply on the basis of 'classifiable' childbirth-related
illness, we shall miss the vast majority of illnesses that are associated with
the process of motherhood: of all women, those with young children are
more likely to suffer mental ill health. Also, it should not be forgotten that
women can suffer from all known psychiatric disorders during their childbearing years, and if any mental illness coincides with childbearing or having
young children, then this will surely have an important influence on the
individual woman's experience.

However, those planning mental health services for childbearing women
undoubtedly need to know the extent of the psychological burden of childbirth and motherhood, and more importantly whether special provision
should be made for women at this time. Epidemiology provides only partial
information from which to estimate the prevalence of postnatal mental disorders. For other mental disorders related to reproduction, information is
extremely scant.

There seems little doubt that an increase in psychotic illness occurs postnatally. Although the exact figures vary, most studies suggest a rate of postnatal psychosis of between 1 and 2 per 1,000 live births.

It is less clear whether there is an increase of non-psychotic illness, such as
depression, in the postnatal period. One group found an increase in the
prevalence of all mental disorders in women for as long as two years following a birth (Kendell *et al.*, 1976, 1981). Another found that depressive illness
is twice as common in the postnatal period (Oates, 1988), while a third

suggests that women are significantly more depressed early in pregnancy and particularly for the first three months after delivery (Kumar and Robson, 1984). Other studies found no increase in non-psychotic illness in the post-natal period, compared to women with young children outside the postnatal period (Nott, 1982), but continued to describe a hugely increased risk of depression in the first month after delivery (Cox *et al.*, 1993). It has also been observed that many women who become depressed for the first time in their lives after childbirth continue to seek help years later.

Thus, although postpartum non-psychotic illness does not seem to be a distinct entity related to childbirth, the place of illness occurring in the very early postnatal period seems unsure. There are a number of possible reasons for this. Many studies are hospital based and may underestimate the prevalence of disorder in the community, by including only those women who have been identified and referred.

Cooper and Murray (1995) suggest that there are two different populations of women who become depressed after childbirth. They found that women who became depressed for the first time postnatally were more likely to experience future depression only in relation to motherhood and postulate that, for this group, their illness is specifically related to motherhood and its demands. The second group of women were no more likely to become recurrently depressed after childbirth than at any other stressful time in their lives. For them, motherhood appears to act as a non-specific stressor. Cooper and Murray suggest that previous studies have been too small to distinguish these groups.

It is estimated that a hospital liaison service may expect sixteen referrals per 1,000 live births. This is probably a gross underestimate of the problem, as rates of 14–15 per cent for depressive illness, or seven new cases of depression per week, can be expected from an obstetric service delivering 2,500 children per year. A clearer picture of women's actual needs is required from user-informed, community-based research.

RISK FACTORS FOR POSTNATAL MENTAL DISORDERS

Cooper and Murray (1995) propose distinct risk factors for women whose first depression is postpartum, and suggest that biological factors may be more relevant here. However, psychosocial risk factors associated with any depression, e.g. socioeconomic status and lack of a supportive relationship, may have different meaning and impact on women at this time. These are discussed in more depth later in the chapter. Other risk factors may include age and parity. Younger women and those with more children may be at greater risk of depression. Finally, risk factors exclusive to women at this time include previous infertility or abortion and some suggest that the 'blues' may predispose one to subsequent depression. Obstetric stressors do not seem to predispose women to blues or depressive illness.

In contrast, postpartum psychosis seems to be distinct from other psychiatric illnesses in women, and is associated with specific risk factors. It appears that young mothers having their first child and those who have a Caesarean section are at greater risk of psychosis than other women. The risk for recurrence of psychotic illness is around 1 in 7. Also, it is well described that family or personal history of psychotic illness in a mother increases her risk of developing postpartum psychosis.

The 'blues' and puerperal psychotic illness can only be explained fully by postulating specific factors relating to childbirth. Hormonal changes are most likely to be partially responsible for mood changes although, to date, there is little convincing evidence to confirm this. Treatment studies with hormone replacement have been unsuccessful in preventing recurrence of psychosis in at-risk women and do not seem to prevent the 'blues'.

THE EXPERIENCE OF MOTHERHOOD

The changing environment of motherhood

Women in modern Western societies receive little preparation for motherhood compared with the extensive preparation they receive for entry into the workforce. There is also little support from the general culture to aid their transition into the maternal role (Stern and Kruckman, 1983). Most traditional societies have elaborate rituals to prepare the woman for birth and to emphasise her new status after the birth, and postnatal depression on the scale found in the West seems to be relatively rare. Rationales for special conditions for postpartum women vary, from a belief in their being polluted and needing a period of purification to their being in need of rest and of time to care for the new baby. In either case, the woman is usually secluded, rests in bed, receives special food and gifts, is the focus of protective and celebratory rituals, and is cared for by relatives or traditional midwives. Birth in our society usually takes place in a large, impersonal hospital, surrounded by medical gadgetry, followed by a rapid return home to the job of caring for the household and older children, with minimal time for adjustment to her new situation or to focus on the new baby (Priya, 1992). Even compared with a few decades ago in this country, when 'lying in' lasted 10 to 14 days, this is a novel situation. Families are also more isolated than in the past and there is less structural support for family bonds, and less close community supervision of behaviour in the family.

Other social changes also impact on the young mother. The small size of the modern Western family means that there is rarely opportunity to learn the skills of childrearing from observation; they have essentially to be learned afresh in each generation. Almost no preparation is provided within the education system for parenting, or indeed for marriage, and young parents therefore set out on this major life task with a minimal knowledge of children's needs. The health care system places strong emphasis on the physical health of the pregnant woman and the unborn child however, and there has been a welcome increase in preparation for labour and delivery resulting in less fear and dread and less need for intrusive obstetric intervention (Kitzinger, 1989). Education in childcare in pregnancy however, is often limited to one or two sessions on breast-feeding and bathing the baby. *It is not clear whether this is because the task of parent education is seen as too onerous for public services to take on, or because parenting is seen as an innate skill that does not need to be learned.*

In addition, class differences in attitudes towards childrearing are wider than in the recent past, arising particularly from class differentials in levels of unemployment. Middle-class, educated women are likely to have postponed their first pregnancy, often into their early or mid-thirties when they have completed professional training or established themselves in a secure career. Less educated women, with less satisfying work, or unemployed women generally have a greater investment in the maternal role, which may realistically be their only available career. They are, however, often even less well prepared, have their first babies at a younger age and are often in much poorer circumstances in terms of income, housing and environment (Gavron, 1966). In one study of young mothers aged under 20, both they and their partners had few educational qualifications and were usually unemployed. Most were providing adequate care for their children but in very impoverished conditions and their families were unlikely to be able to provide extra financial support as middle-class families might do (Phoenix, 1991).

One of the major factors differentiating middle- and working-class women is the high level of depression in working-class mothers, especially those living in run-down inner-city areas. Since depression is associated with increased child disturbance, it is paradoxically and tragically the most child-centred women in the population who are likely to experience the most difficulty and disappointment with their children, despite all their high hopes. It is not that these women do not care for their children, rather that they find themselves without the resources, internal and external, to cope with motherhood and its demands.

The transition to motherhood

Although each pregnancy involves some readjustment and even turmoil, the first pregnancy in particular involves a major re-evaluation of the self, especially in relation to one's own mother and to one's identity as a woman. Much will depend on whether the pregnancy is welcome or unexpected or whether there is a secure marital relationship, but a certain degree of ambivalence about the anticipated change of role and especially the loss of autonomy is almost universal and again the general culture provides little psychological support at this stage. 'Morning sickness' and severe fatigue in early pregnancy are also often discounted in the workplace, although they are very unpleasant symptoms which are difficult to treat. Moreover, 10 per cent of women become depressed in early pregnancy, especially when there are doubts about the pregnancy or marital problems (Kumar and Robson, 1984). Rigid concepts of the perfect, all-giving, sacrificial mother intensify the conflict. Well-adjusted women in one study were more anxious in pregnancy than less well-adjusted women, perhaps as an index of 'working through' of unconscious conflict, and were less idealising of mothers in general (Breen, 1975).

Rafael-Leff (1985) has identified two main types of mother, the 'facilitators' and the 'regulators'. Essentially, the facilitator adapts to the baby, seeing herself as a part of the great chain of mothers, while the regulator expects the baby to adapt to her, and emphasises her individuality and separateness. Most women are a mixture, producing a tension between meeting their own and their baby's needs which the more extreme types do not feel. Women whose self-esteem and identity are highly invested in their career may feel considerable anxiety about giving up their work, at least for a time, and find the relative isolation and lack of intellectual stimulation of domestic life difficult to tolerate, despite a genuine commitment to their child. Younger, more vulnerable women who have a major investment in the birth may feel elated and excited at the new social status their pregnancy has given them, but in reality may be very unprepared for the care of a child. There is rarely any attempt by services to identify at-risk women in pregnancy and to offer extra support, although one American study reported good outcomes from a programme of instruction in the maternal role, the management of stress and self-care, especially if the husband was also involved (Gordon and Gordon, 1959).

DEPRESSION AND MOTHERHOOD – THE CIRCLE OF DEPRIVATION

Social class

Mild to moderate neurotic depression is most common in working-class women with three or more children at home, where there is no close confiding relationship and where there has been a recent disturbing life event (Brown and Harris, 1978). Some studies have shown that between 30 and 40 per cent of working-class mothers of young children are clinically depressed at any one time (Richman et al., 1982). A poor relationship with one's own mother and a dysfunctional relationship with a current partner emerge in numerous studies as risk factors for the development of postnatal depression. A third factor appears to be a high level of interpersonal sensitivity, (e.g. shyness, need for approval and being easily hurt), and this element may be particularly significant in sustaining the depressive state (Boyce et al., 1991).

An inner structure of 'worthlessness and helplessness' has been suggested to explain the association of poor care in the mother's own childhood, unsatisfactory marriage and depression. The importance of the husband's personality strengths in providing security and support to a partner in her transition to motherhood is also a significant factor in outcomes (Birchnell, 1988).

Whilst a supportive relationship is very important for the new mother and the success of the parenting, this is a time of particular risk for the marital relationship. Particular problems at this time stem from the fact that fathers are often even less prepared for the increased burden of parenthood than are mothers, and that conflicts over domestic and work roles increase after the birth of the child. Differing expectations may lead to dissatisfaction and a sense of lack of support, even in relationships where the partner attempts to be supportive (Belsky and Kelly, 1994). Furthermore, it has been suggested that diminishing affection for each other and increased ambivalence on the woman's part towards her husband or partner may occur in up to 50 per cent of new parents. Working-class marriages seem to deteriorate more than middle-class ones on the arrival of children, another factor which makes working-class mothers more vulnerable to depression than their middle-class counterparts. In poorer areas, where the quality of life is lower, where women are likely to feel even less supported and where services are overwhelmed by the demand, little is available in terms of marital support and preparation for parenting at a local level. Parenting preparation should begin in adolescence as part of the national curriculum and there are already several well-researched courses suitable for this age group (Whitfield, 1994).

The environment

Despite the continuing debate as to the biological or social origins of depression in the postpartum period, for many women, depression arising at this time is the first such episode in their lives and seems to sensitise them to further episodes in the context of other stressful experiences. A woman with a young child is likely to feel more vulnerable and exposed than usual. She needs both emotional and material support which may not be forthcoming from the infant's father. The increase in divorce and single-parent families in recent years means that many young mothers have no partner at all. At a time when she is 'losing emotional supplies' it could be argued that she is in need of more care herself. Depressed mothers of young children are likely to be living in poor environments, often in bleak inner-city estates with high levels of vandalism and violence and no safe play space for children. Such conditions affect self-esteem and level of life satisfaction, as well as providing a poor environment for the child's development, or for building up networks of mutual support among neighbouring families.

MATERNAL DEPRESSION AND PARENTING SKILLS

The symptoms of depression, including social withdrawal, irritability, impaired concentration and low mood all have a marked impact on social relationships. Since the mother of a young infant generally constitutes the major part of its social environment, it is unsurprising that maternal depression has been shown to have an effect on emotional and cognitive development in the early months. Mothers of 2–3-month-old babies who are currently depressed show more negative mood and less focus of attention on the infant than non-depressed women, especially when interacting with boy children. Children with mothers who suffered from depression postpartum are also likely to be insecurely attached at 18 months of age and to perform less well on tests of infant development (Murray *et al.*, 1993). Working-class mothers of 2–3-year-old children in South London showed few differences in gross measures of time spent on play and level of involvement, but spent more time preoccupied and withdrawn from their children and from any productive activities. They spent more time in physical play and cuddling, possibly because it was comforting to themselves, but the cognitive aspects of the interaction were more limited. They used fewer questions, suggestions, explanations and distractions and ignored more initiations by the child, especially low-level demands. The children showed more disobedience and control issues were often dealt with in a hopeless kind of way, with the mother often giving in after a long battle of wills (Pound *et al.*, 1988). However, some mothers, even though deeply depressed, were able to sustain a warm and satisfying relationship with their child who was often their only comfort in an otherwise harsh world. These children were usually found to be developing satisfactorily.

MATERNAL DEPRESSION AND THE CHILDREN

Young children of depressed mothers have two to three times the rate of 'marked disorder', such as behaviour problems, sleep and eating disorders, of children of well mothers (Cox *et al.*, 1987; Richman *et al.*, 1982). Older children show poorer social functioning at school, are more rivalrous with other children and have difficulties in concentrating and in learning to read. A major risk in later childhood and adolescence is of the children themselves developing depressive illness or other disorders such as substance abuse, especially where parental depression has been prolonged (Billings and Moos, 1985). Girls are more likely to become their mothers' comforters and boys to get into a conflicted relationship, but in either case are likely to miss out on cognitive stimulation and support for their own development. However, some children survive and show great strength of character in the face of adversity. It appears that those children who are able to sustain a positive relationship with their mother and feel they have a helpful role to play in the family are able to overcome their situation and have a better outcome. Moreover, the most important factor for children is to feel loved and cared for by the parent and so warmth and lack of criticism emerge in various studies as overcoming the otherwise negative effects of maternal depression.

The strong association between maternal depression and childhood disturbance goes a long way towards explaining the persistence of both, since they are likely to reinforce each other in a vicious circle. It is very easy then for mothers to blame their unruly and disobedient children and for children to blame their irritable and preoccupied mothers for their distress, when both are, in fact, victims of the same unhappy circumstances. The circular nature of the problem, whereby mothers cause disturbance in children and vice versa, means that without some outside intervention, in many cases it could persist over a number of years. Well-supported families with close kin nearby and those where the father shares responsibility and sustains a good relationship with the child when the mother is unwell, will be able, in time, to break this vicious circle. Poorly supported families, including single-parent families, families with high levels of marital discord and those living in difficult economic and housing conditions are more likely to need outside help in order to move on to a happier state of affairs.

Other psychiatric conditions

A mother suffering episodes of mania and depression (bipolar disorder) may create particular problems because of the disturbance to family life arising in the manic phase when relationships can become very strained and the patient may need in-patient care. However, there is some evidence that children of bipolar mothers are at less risk of developing disorder than children of mothers with unipolar depression, probably because it is a less chronic condition (Downey and Coyne, 1990). One serious effect of the illness is a high level of divorce, which can leave the children of the family very isolated and coping alone with the disturbing and often frightening symptoms of the acute episodes.

Schizophrenia tends to develop later in women than in men, usually between the ages of 25 to 30 years, by which time about one-third of sufferers have already had at least one child. They are also vulnerable to psychotic episodes in pregnancy or postpartum, particularly after the birth of the first child. In the past, children of schizophrenic mothers were likely to be placed in long-term care, and in many cases were exposed to numerous placements and a very unsettled childhood. At the present time, about two-thirds of such children are likely to stay with their mothers, often being looked after by their fathers while their mothers are hospitalised or very unwell. Some of these children seem to survive the disruption of acute episodes without serious psychological effects, but some psychotic symptoms, such as paranoia, may place children at risk from extreme isolation or from becoming involved in their symptoms, e.g. poor diet because of fear of poisoning (Webster, 1990).

Maternal personality disorder has emerged as one of the most damaging conditions for children's development, especially when it is of an aggressive type and involves direct hostility to the child. However, there is little research on outcomes for such children, though it could be anticipated that they are likely to be either cowed and over-submissive or identified with the angry parent and likely to develop a behaviour disorder. Similarly, there is little work on the effects of maternal anxiety states, obsessive-compulsive disorders and other types of psychiatric disorder on children. In general, involvement of the child in the parent's symptomatology is likely to lead to a more negative outcome than if the child has a neutral role and is seen as neither the cause nor the cure of the parent's ills.

SUPPORT FOR MOTHERS AND THEIR FAMILIES

Mothers with young babies and suffering from disorders severe enough to require hospitalisation, whether profoundly depressed or suffering from a psychotic episode, may be admitted to specialised mother and baby units. However, there are not enough of these units for one to be sited in every district, so frequently mothers and babies are placed instead on adult psychiatric wards with little provision for their special needs. A few services have developed a system of psychiatric consultation to obstetric units or of community care when there is judged to be no danger of harm to the infant or mother. This system has been found to be highly acceptable to patients and their families (Appleby et al., 1989; Oates, 1988). Children of hospitalised, acutely ill schizophrenic mothers can be protected from the ill-effects of residential care by the use of family aides in the home; these can also support the mother on her return from hospital and help restore her to her place in the family as she recovers (Webster, 1990).

The vast majority of mental health problems in mothers consists of neurotic depression. Better preparation for the parenting role has been shown to be effective in reducing postpartum distress and depression, but is at present rarely provided except by small, specialised projects. Brief counselling by health visitors given a short training has been shown to produce recovery in 70 per cent of women with postnatal depression compared to 38 per cent of untreated women, showing that the need for someone to listen is a key factor in recovery (Holden et al., 1989). Health visitors may also help to build up supportive networks by linking new mothers to more experienced mothers in the neighbourhood. Such modest interventions could be initiated within any health-visiting service, but the pressure of other demands such as care of the elderly and child protection work and the chronic shortage of staff has led to a diminished role for home visiting and more emphasis on group and community interventions (Goodwin, 1988). There is, therefore, a danger of some very depressed women slipping through the net and they and their children struggling on unknown to any public service.

THE ROLE OF ANTIDEPRESSANTS

Although women respond equally well to conventional antidepressant medication postnatally as at any other time, they are less likely to want it, fearing a detrimental effect on both their ability to breast-feed and generally to care for the infant. Early identification of depressed mothers may allow for other non-pharmacological interventions, although delaying medication in depressive illness may make the illness less responsive.

PRACTICAL ASPECTS OF SERVICE PROVISION

Funding

Most agencies would agree that part of the difficulty of service provision for mothers lies in whether or not monies are earmarked especially for them. Depressive illness occurs more frequently in women with children, not only in the postnatal period. However, in practical terms, new mothers will have special needs. Who is specifically responsible for new mothers is another question. This group cuts across the spectrum of health, social and education services and within services they cross disciplines, such that a woman may be visited by community obstetric, psychiatric or general nurses and health visitors.

Case identification

It remains unclear just how aggressive a primary health care team should be in prevention and case-finding. Many women do not seek help at this time, perhaps because they are too unwell to do so, or because mental illness stigmatises them, or because they have a real fear of their children being removed from their care. In addition, many women are unhappy with the services available: they may feel that current services are irrelevant; some resent seeing male practitioners; the access is often unsuitable for women bringing young children; and they may be reluctant to take medication, either feeling that it would be addictive or that they would not wake in the night in response to their babies. Similarly, cases are missed because of professionals' emphasis on physical problems at this time, or their assumption that low mood is either the 'blues' or a natural response to the event of childbirth. Women would probably be more willing to seek or accept help if their wants were taken into account by a more 'user-friendly' approach.

Management

Services should be local, accessible, involve multiple agencies, parents and partners where possible, and should attempt continuity of care-workers. In addition, as will be seen below, diversion of funds to, and increased awareness of, alternative care resources is vital at the community level. These include care groups, nurseries and play-groups and other voluntary organisations in which parents may become involved. Choice remains an essential component of all provision. Early referral to specialist services for particular needs should always be considered. In the following section, we outline some of the features of good existing services and how they are organised.

HIGH-QUALITY COMMUNITY SERVICES

Given limited resources, there probably needs to be a focus on those most at risk, i.e. younger mothers, single parents and those with poor relationships with their partners and difficult environments. Many of the severe, chronic cases of maternal depression are concentrated in particular housing estates, where depression can be seen as an indicator of the dysfunction of community, social and family systems. Focused initiatives by voluntary organisations can test out models of work which may then be developed on a larger scale by statutory services or through funding contracts with local authorities. In one project, participation of local people in identifying local needs led to the development of a local housing office, a centre for families with children under five, and a play centre for older children, the latter involving local people in their organisation. The family centre provides self-help courses, facilitates self-help groups and a volunteer reading scheme and organises clubs and outings as well as running a drop-in centre. This has led to the development of cohesive social networks and a sense of belonging in a formerly fragmented and isolated inner-London estate (Ryan, 1986).

DAY NURSERIES, PLAY GROUPS AND PARENT EDUCATION

The provision of day nursery care has been one common form of intervention for women who are depressed and/or having problems in parenting their young children. Day nursery care is seen as providing a more benign environment for the child and relieving the mother of the stress of full-time care, in line with a paternalistic philosophy of taking over from mothers who seem to be less competent or are in more difficult circumstances than usual. However, this is not without its problems. A number of studies have identified more anxious attachment, especially of the avoidant type when children have been in full-time day care in the first year of life (Belsky, 1988). Insecure attachment patterns in early childhood are highly associated with later behaviour problems, including aggression and non-compliance. There is less evidence regarding the value of full-time day care in the second year, but observation suggests that unless there is an effective system of small-group care with attachment of children to specific carers, toddlers become anxious and disorganised in group settings.

Mothers who are already feeling insecure and incompetent can become even more so faced with both apparently competent care staff and a difficult and unhappy child. Both for the sake of mothers and their young children, interventions need to reinforce the mother's sense of agency and effectiveness rather than take over her role. In fact, some public-sector day nurseries have transformed themselves into family centres, offering a far wider range of options for both parents and children and attempting to be aware of the mothers' as well as of the children's needs.

Pre-school play groups run on co-operative lines and involving parents in the day-to-day running of the group can provide a rich environment for children's social and cognitive development and opportunities for mothers to learn from observation of skilled play leaders. Increasingly, nursery schools and classes provide similar opportunities for parental involvement and for building up social networks for young families, avoiding social isolation and protecting against depression.

Over recent years, several organisations have also been set up to provide education in parenting; among these are 'Parent Network' and 'Exploring Parenthood' (see below for details). Both provide courses on parenting skills in addition to group work that allows parents to explore their feelings about their children and helps to free them from possible tensions in their relationships, often deriving from their own childhood experiences.

SPECIALISED SERVICES FOR FAMILIES AT RISK – 'HOME-START' AND 'NEWPIN'

'Home-Start' is a voluntary organisation which offers support, friendship and practical help to families with at least one pre-school child, who are experiencing difficulties with parenting, stress or depression. Volunteers, who are usually parents themselves, visit families in their own homes, helping to prevent family crisis and breakdown. There are now 180 local Home-Start schemes throughout the UK plus 60 in other countries, and Home-Start has been shown to be highly valued by both parents and referrers. Many volunteers have been supported formerly by Home-Start themselves. Having recovered from depression and gained in both parenting skills and self-confidence, they then choose to support other mothers (Van der Eyken, 1982).

'NEWPIN' is a similar organisation with a more intensive therapeutic orientation which originated in South London and is now spreading throughout the country. It offers a range of interventions, including volunteer befriending, a year-long personal development programme, which includes group therapy as well as lectures and workshops on child development, play, parenting skills, etc. Most 'NEWPIN' members have had very difficult lives, including childhood loss and abuse, disturbed adult relationships, severe depression and sometimes abusive relationships with their own children. Nevertheless, most not only recover from depression and anxiety, but also show improved self-esteem and parenting skills and a number have gone on to higher education or to train as 'NEWPIN' co-ordinators themselves (Pound *et al.*, 1988). Referral can be made by the mother herself or via other agencies. (See Appendix for addresses of the above two organisations.)

CONCLUSION

Postnatal mental illness, especially non-psychotic depression, is a common and painful condition for women, who receive little support for the extra demands made on them. Comparison between our own and other societies, where support for new mothers is formalised, highlights this shortfall. Large studies show that different groups of women experience depression in the postnatal period in different ways, depending on their social circumstances. For some women depression seems confined to the postnatal period.

We have shown how particular groups of women at high risk can easily be identified. Women in the most deprived circumstances experience more depression and it is these women for whom depression is most persistent. Other factors known to increase the probability of postpartum mental illness include the quality of the marital relationship and being a very young mother. Both maternal depression and marital conflict have a major impact on the interaction between mother and child, with potentially serious consequences for the child's emotional and cognitive development. Limited resources mean that health workers need to target interventions that are known to be effective, such as health visitor counselling, at high-risk groups of women. Failure to address the needs of women and their young children not only results in distress, but has lasting consequences for the families and society as a whole which we cannot afford to ignore.

CROSS-REFERENCES WITHIN THIS BOOK

Chapter 4   Girls in distress: an unconsidered issue
Chapter 13   Women as abusers

REFERENCES

Appleby, L., Fox, H., Shaw, M. and Kumar, R. (1989) 'The psychiatrist in the obstetric unit – establishing a liaison service', *British Journal of Psychiatry* 154: 510–515.
Belsky, J. (1988) 'Infant day care and socioemotional development: the United States', *Journal of Child Psychology and Psychiatry* 29: 397–406.
Belsky, J. and Kelly, J. (1994) *The transition to parenthood*, New York: Delacorte Press.

Billings, A.G. and Moos, R.H. (1985) 'Children of parents with unipolar depression: a controlled one-year follow-up', *Journal of Abnormal Child Psychology* 14: 149–166.

Birchnell, J. (1988) 'Depression & family relationships – a study of young married women on a London housing estate', *British Journal of Psychiatry* 153: 758–769.

Boyce, P., Hickey, I. and Parker, P. (1991) 'Parents, partners or personality? Risk factors for postnatal depression', *Journal of Affective Disorders* 21: 245–255.

Breen, D. (1975) *The birth of a first child*, London: Tavistock.

Brown, G.W. and Harris, J. (1978) *Social origins of depression*, London: Tavistock.

Cooper, P.J. and Murray, L. (1995) 'Course and recurrence of postnatal depression: evidence for the specificity of the diagnostic concept', *British Journal of Psychiatry* 166: 191–195.

Cox, A.D., Puckering, C., Pound, A. and Mills, M. (1987) 'The impact of maternal depression on young children', *Journal of Child Psychology and Psychiatry* 28: 917–928.

Cox, J.L., Murray, D. and Chapman, G. (1993) 'A controlled study of the onset, duration & prevalence of postnatal depression', *British Journal of Psychiatry* 163: 27–31.

Downey, G. and Coyne, J.C. (1990) 'Children of depressed parents: an integrative review', *Psychological Bulletin* 108: 50–76.

Gavron, H. (1966) *The captive wife*, London: Routledge & Keegan Paul.

Goodwin, S. (1988) 'Whither health visiting?', *Health Visitor* 61: 379–383.

Gordon, R.E. and Gordon, K.K. (1959) 'Social factors in the prediction and treatment of emotional disorders of pregnancy', *American Journal of Obstetrics and Gynaecology* 77: 1074–1083.

Holden, J.M., Sagorsky, R. and Cox, J.L. (1989) 'Counselling in a general practice setting: a controlled study of health visitor intervention in the treatment of postnatal depression', *British Medical Journal* 298: 223–226.

Kendell, R.E., Rennie, D., Clarke, J.A. and Dean, C. (1981) 'The social and obstetric correlates of psychiatric admissions in the puerperium', *Psychological Medicine* 11: 341–350.

Kendell, R.E., Wainwright, S., Hailey, A. and Shannon, N. (1976) 'The influence of childbirth on psychiatric morbidity', *Psychological Medicine* 6: 297–302.

Kitzinger, S. (1989) *The new pregnancy and childbirth*, London: Penguin.

Kumar, R. and Robson, K.M. (1984) 'A prospective study of emotional disorders in childbearing women', *British Journal of Psychiatry* 144: 35–47.

Murray, L., Kempton, C., Woolgar, M. and Hooper, R. (1993) 'Depressed mothers' speech to their infants and its relation to infant gender and cognitive development', *Journal of Child Psychology and Psychiatry* 34: 1083–1101.

Nott, P.N. (1982) 'Psychiatric illness following childbirth in Southampton: a case register study', *Psychological Medicine* 12: 557–561.

—— (1987) 'Extent, timing and persistence of emotional disorders following childbirth', *British Journal of Psychiatry* 151: 523–527.

Oates, M. (1988) 'The development of an integrated community-oriented service for severe post-natal mental illness', in R. Kumar and I.F. Brockington (eds), *Motherhood & mental illness*, London: Wright.

Phoenix, A. (1991) *Young mothers*, Cambridge: Polity Press.

Pitt, B. (1968) 'Atypical depression following childbirth', *British Journal of Psychiatry* 114: 1325–1335.

Pound, A. (1990) 'The development of attachment in adult life – the NEWPIN experiment', *British Journal of Psychotherapy* 7: 77–85.

Pound, A., Puckering, C., Mills, M. and Cox, A.D. (1988) 'The impact of maternal depression on young children', *British Journal of Psychotherapy* 4: 240–252.

Priya, J.V. (1992) *Birth traditions and modern pregnancy care*, Shaftesbury, Dorset: Element.

Rafael-Leff, J. (1985) 'Facilitators and regulators; participators and renouncers: Mothers' and fathers' orientations towards pregnancy and parenthood', *Journal of Psychosomatic Obstetrics and Gynaecology* 4: 169–184.

Richman, N., Stevenson, J. and Graham, P. (1982) *Pre-school to school: a behavioural study*, London: Academic Press.

Ryan, P.J. (1986) 'The contribution of formal and informal systems of intervention to the alleviation of depression in young mothers', *British Journal of Social Work* 16: 71–82.

Stern, G. and Kruckman, L. (1983) 'Multi-disciplinary perspectives on post-partum depression: an anthropological critique', *Social Science and Medicine* 17: 1027–1041.

Van der Eyken, W. (1982) *Home Start – a four year evaluation*, Leicester: Home Start Consultancy.

Webster, J. (1990) 'Parenting for children of schizophrenic mothers', *Adoption and Fostering* 14: 36–42.

Whitfield, R. (ed.) (1994) *Life foundations*, Nottingham: NES Arnold and National Family Trust.

Chapter 4

Girls in distress

An unconsidered issue

Fiona Subotsky

Our Polly is a sad slut! nor heeds what we have taught her.
I wonder any man alive will ever rear a daughter!
(John Gay, *The Beggar's Opera*, I, viii, vii)

INTRODUCTION

Typically the Child Guidance Clinic of the past saw more boys than girls as 'the identified patient'. This was probably because such clinics were often set up in conjunction with the Local Education Authority or Social Services, and the children presenting to those services were likely to have such problems as poor concentration, reading difficulties, antisocial behaviour and 'disruptiveness', and were possibly delinquent as well. All these problems occur more frequently in boys than girls (Rutter, 1989), and there is no doubt that they are associated with a high risk in later years of antisocial behaviour, and that there are therefore good reasons for trying to intervene (Robins, 1978).

However, in adult life, women have a much higher incidence of psychiatric disorders requiring the help of mental health services (OHE, 1989; Gorman, 1992). So how are the 'at-risk' women of the future being identified and helped? Very little attention has been given to this topic, even though the recently increased awareness of child sexual abuse has brought the needs of some girls to the fore.

Changing society, changing families

Twenty per cent of the population is now under the age of 16. The pattern of care for these children has altered markedly in the last two decades. For instance, the 1994 Social Trends reports (Church, 1994):

- the mean age of mothers has risen to 27.8 years for a first birth, the highest ever recorded;
- for every two marriages in the UK in 1991 there was one divorce;

- the proportion of births outside marriage more than doubled to almost 1 in 3, although three-quarters were registered by both parents;
- the number of undergraduate women has more than doubled since 1970;
- the proportion of women in at least part-time employment is increasing.

Thus, while mothers are more likely to have children without marriage and to become divorced, their children often have involved, or at least acknowledged, fathers. Mothers are older, better educated, and quite likely to have employment outside the home.

There is no evidence that girls are adversely affected by their mothers working outside the home – perhaps the opposite. Studies of working mothers have shown that while negative effects were often looked for, daughters seem typically to be more self-confident and to achieve better school grades than the daughters of non-working mothers (Hoffman, 1984).

Research on divorce indicates that it is often painful and distressing for children, and may have long-term effects, even when there seems to be superficial adaptation. However, there are differences between boys and girls. Girls seem to get on well with their custodial mother after divorce, whereas boys do not. Girls receive more adverse remarks from their fathers than boys, and also do not get on well with new step-fathers. Boys, however, do eventually adjust better if there is a step-father (Hetherington, 1989; Wallerstein and Blakelee, 1989).

THE BACKGROUND OF NEED: SUGAR AND SPICE

Knowledge of the epidemiology of childhood mental disorder is increasing all the time (Rutter, 1989). There are marked gender differences. Cohen *et al.* (1993) note that such data are important as they may be used to:

- help develop theories regarding aetiology and course of disorder;
- elucidate prognostic implications;
- determine whether some groups may be significantly under-served.

Their New York study's most recent findings regarding sex differences for particular diagnoses are summarised in Table 4.1.

Interestingly, identified need can also vary depending on the informant as well as the age of the child, as is shown by some of the findings of the Ontario Child Health Study (Offord *et al.*, 1989). For example, for girls aged 4 to 11, emotional disorder is noted more frequently by parents than for boys, but less frequently by teachers. Differences are more marked in the 12–16 age group, where emotional disorder and somatisation disorder are greater among girls than boys, and more commonly identified by teachers than by parents.

Table 4.1 Age and gender trends for individual diagnoses

Diagnosis	Prevalence by age and gender
Attention deficit/hyperactivity disorder	Prevalence nearly twice as high in boys as in girls up to age 17.
Conduct disorder	Twice as prevalent in boys as girls overall. *Girls peak rate at age 16.*
Major depressive disorder	Similar low rates in childhood for boys and girls; *a peak after puberty (at 14) for girls.* Older adolescents had the same rates.
Oppositional defiant disorder	Similar rates for boys and girls, rising from age 12, decreasing at age 16.
Overanxious disorder	Boys showed a decline in rate from ages 10 to 20 while *for girls higher rates were evident from age 12.*
Separation anxiety	Similar rate in boys and girls; declining from age 10.

The affective disorders of anxiety and depression seem to be particularly relevant to girls, especially in their teens. There have been studies focusing on this area. For instance, Cooper and Goodyer (1993) looked at mood disorders in 11–16-year-old girls in a community study and found 6 per cent prevalence for major depressive disorder in the last year: none of the girls was known to the mental health services. The main symptoms were depressed mood, social withdrawal and irritability.

Why are girls apparently more resilient than boys when younger, and less prone to conduct disorder when older? It remains very difficult to tease out the effects of 'nature' from 'nurture' as, from the beginning, parents and other caretakers treat boys and girls differently (Nagy Jacklin, 1989).

Werner's longitudinal Hawaiian study sheds light on how girls may be more resilient than boys under conditions of 'high-risk' upbringing. Two-thirds of children with four or more 'risk factors' such as perinatal stress, family discord or disruption, poverty and parental mental illness, had a variety of serious psychosocial problems by the age of 18. There were more girls in the group without problems; they had been temperamentally easier from a young age, and elicited more positive attention from others. This led them to positive relationships and interests outside the family, with friends, school and community activities which seemed to protect them from the detrimental environment of home (Werner, 1989).

It also remains unclear why teenage girls become vulnerable to anxiety and depression. Cohen *et al.* (1993) suggest that the prevalence curve for depression in girls can be most plausibly explained by an aetiological or triggering role of hormonal and/or social changes associated with puberty. Some studies indicate that young teenage girls are more self-conscious and have lower self-esteem than do boys (Rosenberg and Simmons, 1975), and are more likely than boys to believe it is hard to be a member of their own sex (Lewin and Tragos, 1987). Girls' greater capacity for developing confiding relationships may even put them at risk if these go wrong for them (Hill, 1993). There clearly needs to be more research focused on clarifying this vulnerability of teenage girls to depression and anxiety in order to know how best to intervene for treatment and prevention. It will also be interesting to see if the pattern alters with the current major social changes, such as the rise of feminist ideas, more thought having been given to girls' educational needs, and the improved employment prospects for young women as opposed to young men.

CURRENT MENTAL HEALTH CARE FOR CHILDREN: LOCAL PROVISION AND UTILISATION

All investigations of child psychiatric disorder in the community have found a considerable mismatch between need and provision of services.

(Evans and Brown, 1993)

In the UK, many of the old-style multi-agency, multidisciplinary child guidance clinics in the community have been disrupted by the withdrawal of local authority staff towards other priorities, and by the uncertainties of the new health 'commissioning' process (Kurtz and Wolkind, 1994). Needs are not being systematically addressed – let alone by gender – and service provision is variable. Children with mental health problems are seen by a variety of professionals, many of whom have no specific training in the field.

Fewer girls present to child mental health services

In the old Camberwell Health District area, there are three child psychiatric clinics primarily serving the local community – two in the community and one based in a general hospital – as well as a specialist centre.

The numbers of new cases in each clinic, which vary little from year to year, characteristically show more boys than girls being referred to child mental health services. There are, however, differences between clinics, and these may be explained by referral patterns and special projects. One of the clinics, partly funded by the Education Authority, has many referrals from schools in connection with poor behaviour, attainment and attendance, which are all commoner in boys, and this clinic has the lowest proportion of female new cases (30 per cent). Referrals for the 'assessment of special educational needs' involve even fewer girls (19 per cent) (Subotsky, 1990). The hospital-based clinic and the other community-based clinic, on the other hand, each have girls making up approximately 40 per cent of new cases. This may be because the hospital-based clinic receives more GP and general hospital referrals, has a special programme for children referred by 'Victim Support' and takes all the 'parasuicides'. The other community clinic is situated within a health centre and has recently specialised in offering therapy for sexually abused girls. Subotsky and Brown (1990) found that a still higher percentage of girls was seen in an 'outreach' clinic into general practice (see Chapter 13).

The age and stage make a difference

The proportion of girls seen by child psychiatric services varies with age (see Table 4.2). The move towards the more 'adult' pattern of mental health referral can be seen with the increasing proportion of girls in the oldest age group.

Table 4.2 Percentage of girls seen by age group

	<5yrs	*5–11*	*12–16*
General hospital clinic	39	37	61
Specialist child psychiatry department	33	31	45

Girls present with different diagnoses and symptom patterns

At the specialist department, girls presented with similar numbers of emotional disorders overall. Emotional disorder was absolutely more common in girls over 13, and anorexia nervosa much more common (86 per cent of 81 cases). Boys presented with more conduct and mixed disorders and with more pervasive developmental disorder (Richards, personal communication).

Major symptom-pattern differences are shown in Table 4.3. Again, there is a picture of greater symptoms of anxiety and unhappiness for girls.

Table 4.3 Symptoms more common in girls

	Girls (per cent)	*Boys* (per cent)
Suicidal ideas, attempts or threats	12	5
Anxiety	31	21
School refusal or phobia	24	16

MAJOR PROBLEM AREAS FOR GIRLS: RECOGNITION OF NEED AND APPROPRIATE PROVISION

It is interesting to speculate on fashions in diagnosis. The recent use of standardised symptom-oriented questionnaires has led to acknowledgement that children and adolescents can develop conditions that are the same as the major affective disorders of adulthood (Harrington, 1992). Curiously, Harrington's paper, on 'The natural history and treatment of child and adolescent affective disorders', does not even mention the prevalence in girls. Nevertheless, the increasing recognition of depression, panic disorder, and post-traumatic stress disorder in young people may facilitate the referral of girls in need to child mental health services. It is possible that this may reduce the necessity for extreme presentations such as parasuicide or anorexia.

PARASUICIDE

It has been estimated that 19,000 to 20,000 adolescents under the age of 19 years take an overdose every year in England and Wales. The rate for each age rises – to a peak for girls in late adolescence. At all ages there are more girls than boys (Hawton and Fagg, 1992). Relationship difficulties are the most frequently associated problem, and alcohol and drug misuse are also common. Adolescents also 'self-harm' in other ways. Follow-up studies of wrist-slashers indicate that the later outcome is poor and that repetition is addictive (Tantam and Whittaker, 1992).

Prevention

There have been studies of community interventions to reduce suicide and parasuicide, and some efforts to set up educational programmes in school have been successful (Gunnell and Frankel, 1994). Although evidence is as yet lacking, it seems that improved access to the specialist services such as child psychiatry and the Samaritans would be likely to be helpful, as would be training for those in most contact with teenage girls, such as teachers, school doctors and nurses, and general practitioners. It would be worthwhile raising public awareness that paracetamol, far from being 'safe', can lead in overdose to extremely unpleasant, potentially fatal consequences.

Management

Most districts attempt to offer an assessment by a social worker or member of the child psychiatric team to a young adolescent who has taken an overdose, but 'self-harmers' seem to be under-recognised and referred by casualty departments. Ideally the girl should be admitted until it is possible to interview both her and her family, separately and together. If assessment is not available at the time, then there is often a default to a later offered appointment.

It is still unclear:

- how to assess reliably for later risk of parasuicide or of suicide;
- what is the best form of intervention;
- what the later psychosocial morbidity is (Kingsbury, 1993).

Nevertheless, there is a good opportunity to affect the acute situation using a crisis-counselling model, to help improve the usually difficult family relationships, and to offer advice for the considerable proportion of girls who are in local authority care. It is therefore important to have available emergency psychiatric assessment, ready access to family therapy of a short-term focused kind, and longer term therapy or counselling for girls who would seem likely to benefit from this kind of approach. Good collaborative links between the hospital, child mental health services, schools and social services need to be maintained for the management and treatment to work well. There is otherwise a strong possibility of such cases falling through the gaps; collaborative audit of treatment and outcome might well help to improve this. There is little role for antidepressants, which may not be safe and do not seem to be very effective in this age group (Harrington, 1992).

CHILD SEXUAL ABUSE

In the last twenty years it has become recognised that child sexual abuse, often within the family, occurs much more frequently than was previously realised. A UK study by Baker and Duncan (1985) indicated that one in eight girls and one in twelve boys experienced some kind of sexually abusive experience in childhood. Apart from the obvious immediate psychological distress in childhood, it is becoming clear that a history of childhood abuse correlates with an increased risk for a wide range of mental health problems in adulthood (see Chapter 10). The more serious the abuse the greater the association with psychopathology in adult life – which can even overcome the otherwise protective effects of a more stable and advantaged childhood background (Mullen et al., 1993).

Prevention

A number of preventive educational programmes have been developed, especially in the USA. These have improved the safety skills and knowledge of children, but no study has produced data showing that education actually reduces the occurrence of sexual abuse. However, some 'disclosures' have been enabled, thus offering the opportunity for secondary prevention.

Difficulties for programmes include:

- whether to offer a narrow or broad definition as to what constitutes abuse;
- complex rules about, e.g., 'who can touch' are often not understood by children;
- a specific plan is needed for appropriate 'telling'.

There can be avoidance of the really emotively threatening aspects such as parental abuse, and the emotions aroused by sexuality. Few efforts seem to have been made to involve parents (Repucci and Haugaard, 1989). Glaser (1991) remarks: 'We risk developing programmes that make adults feel better but do not protect children.'

Perhaps, now the subject has come out into the open, there is an opportunity for an interruption to the inter-generational cycle of abuse. Certainly, it is our clinic's experience that many mothers are recalling their own experiences and looking for help in trying to prevent or stop the same thing happening to their own children. Both statutory and voluntary provision geared to child sexual abuse 'survivors' can be of help, as well as child and family mental health services. However, a focus is clearly even more necessary on the potential and actual perpetrators – an area that needs much more study to provide clues to successful prevention.

Again, links between agencies can nearly always be improved, so that children – as victims or as perpetrators – can be identified and helped as effectively as possible.

Management and treatment

Once child sexual abuse has been identified as a high probability, the first steps are usually primarily management of the situation, rather than 'treatment' of the psychological consequences. Reasons for this are that

- there is likely to be a denial of various aspects of the problem by the family;
- there are likely to be the constraints of various legal proceedings and processes;
- many agencies are likely to be involved.

In the first place, support needs to be identified for the child and family so that the further necessary investigations and court hearings may be as untraumatic as possible. Usually this needs to be provided by social services, which is the key agency responsible for child protection, but health, police, legal and voluntary services have responsibilities to ensure good collaboration and co-ordination. Prosecution of a perpetrator is not done primarily in the interest of the victim, and can be re-traumatising. Good practice would include keeping the girl and her current carers well informed of the progress of any case, and if court attendance is necessary then she should be advised about procedures and allowed the maximum flexibility in giving evidence – such as the use of video screens (Westcott and Davies, 1993).

While 'counselling' is often requested by parents and professionals who know that a girl has been abused, this is sometimes confused with access to a trusted adult in whom the girl could confide if there seemed to be the possibility of a repeat of the abuse. In addition some girls, at the time at which the abuse is discovered, do not wish to go over the experience again in any way, and coercion must be avoided. There needs to be provision for the girl to 'call in' help at a time, perhaps much later, when she feels she needs it. On the other hand, the mother especially is often very distressed, and may recall similar incidents in her own life which she needs to work through. Everson *et al.* (1989) recommend that, as parental support is an important protection at times of stress, less effort should be expended on the degree of the mother's culpability over the abuse and more on trying to show mothers how they can help their children to recover.

Treatment for the girl herself needs to be tailored to the individual need. There is no 'post-abuse syndrome' as such. Nevertheless there are common experiences, and there has been some considerable experience of providing therapeutic groups both for children and for parents. These can counteract isolation, help to raise low self-esteem and allow for secondary prevention by way of education (Furniss *et al.*, 1988).

While some agencies provide systematic, educational groups for women and child 'survivors', many workers in child and adult mental health agencies find themselves treating what turns out to be the aftermath of child sexual abuse. This is demanding and stressful work, and needs good training and access to supervision and discussion with colleagues.

EATING DISORDERS: ANOREXIA NERVOSA AND BULIMIA

Although overt anorexia nervosa is considerably rarer, anorexic-type eating disorders have been found in about 3 per cent of adolescent girls, and abnormal eating behaviour in about 20 per cent (Rutter, 1989). While anorexia nervosa most commonly arises in 16 to 18-year-old girls (Szmukler *et al.*, 1986), child psychiatrists are recognising increasing numbers of cases commencing in childhood.

Prevention

Early recognition and prompt treatment are particularly important in younger children because of the risk of impaired physical growth and sexual development in those cases persisting through puberty and into adult life (Russell, 1985). The outcome with the youngest cases may also be very poor (Walford and McCune, 1991). Salmons *et al.* (1988) suggest that primary prevention of eating disorders should focus on education in positive attitudes to individuality of shape and sensible eating choices. Current social trends, however, such as earlier sexual activity, and the continued pressure to be thin, may make this an uphill task.

Management and treatment

There are drawbacks to the in-patient treatment of anorexia for children. First, provision with sufficient expertise may only be available in 'adult' ward settings, with the lack of a child-centred milieu, and the likelihood of contact with more severely and chronically ill women. Second, the experience may be perceived as unnecessarily coercive, with long-term detrimental effects on the patient–therapist relationship. Third, a prolonged time in hospital may serve to undermine parental authority (Walford and McCune, 1991).

If weight-loss is not life-threatening, then children with anorexia may be adequately managed without in-patient admission. Family therapy seems to have the advantage over individual therapy for younger anorectics – possibly because it helps parents overcome their sense of failure and gain control over their child's eating (Russell *et al.*, 1987).

What is clear from outcome research at specialist centres (e.g. Crisp *et al.*, 1991) is that active therapies including admission, family and individual treatment and group therapy can all be effective. What needs to be understood, however, when planning services, is that anorexia and bulimia are not easy to treat and that therapists need to have considerable expertise and experience. As with other child psychiatric disorders, a range of therapeutic skills needs to be available, with admission as a last resort, either to a paediatric ward or to an adolescent psychiatric unit.

YOUNG TEENAGE PREGNANCY AND MOTHERHOOD

Evidence over the last thirty years suggests that teenagers are having their first sexual experiences at ever younger ages. The conception rate among 13 to 19-year-olds is 9.1 per 1,000 and roughly half the pregnancies are aborted (Babb, 1993). Under-16s are the least likely in their sexual activity to be aware of the risks, to seek contraceptive advice, to get appropriate advice when sought and to use it effectively when received. They are the least likely to be in stable relationships, the most in need of parenting themselves, and the least able to realistically envisage the consequences of bringing up a child (Ineichen and Hudson, 1994). Studies have shown that adolescent mothers:

- are less responsive to their infants' needs than older mothers;
- have less realistic developmental expectations for their children;
- are cognitively less prepared to parent;
- are more likely to engage in negative interactions with their infants.

There is thus a greater risk of these young mothers abusing their own children (Haskett *et al.*, 1994).

Prevention and intervention

Under-16s can be effectively targeted through systematic provision of sex education in schools and through the provision of accessible contraceptive and advisory services in the community. This can be at youth clubs as well as in health centres and specialist family planning centres. Locally, education services and community health services are best placed to collaborate to ensure good practice. This is particularly important in areas of low socioeconomic status which tend to have both a high teenage pregnancy rate and a low proportion of such pregnancies being terminated (Smith, 1993).

Young teenagers who are pregnant need early access to specialist clinics, and to advice on whether to continue their pregnancy. Many of these girls have had difficult early experiences, including abuse, but referral to child mental health services may not be acceptable or practical. An alternative would be for such a clinic to get in regular consultative advice for staff training and support on issues such as how to deal with disclosures of sexual abuse, excessive consumption of drugs or alcohol, repeated pregnancy and termination, or complicated emotional reactions to termination. Education authorities need to have efficient arrangements to encourage pregnant school-girls to continue their schooling both before and after the birth, as such girls may well have been poor attenders before.

It has been shown that home visiting programmes, such as by health visitors, can help prevent child physical abuse and neglect, especially for disadvantaged girls who continue with their pregnancy (MacMillan *et al.*, 1994).

OTHER VULNERABLE GROUPS

Bullying

Surveys have shown that bullying among children is very common, with perhaps 10 per cent of primary-school pupils being bullied per week (Olweus, 1993). Boys are more likely to bully than girls, but both boys and girls suffer bullying (Whitney and Smith, 1993). However, the experience of a special 'bullying' telephone helpline was that 65 per cent of the callers were girls, and just over half the bullies were reported to be girls. It seemed that children are reluctant to tell about their bullying, and adults do not always respond helpfully or intervene effectively. For prevention, a variety of methods, from whole-school methods to individual counselling may be necessary (Lafontaine, 1991). For the victim, support from an available yet anonymous helpline seems useful, but systematic sympathetic and effective listening and action in schools are even more important. For a few more clearly upset children, who may be more vulnerable due to other circumstances, specialist counselling from child mental health services may be helpful.

Major trauma

Recently, there has been a growing awareness of the importance of trauma, both serious and single, or repeated and prolonged, in affecting the emotional adjustment of children and adolescents. While girls may not be over-represented among the victims of group disaster, they may be vulnerable to a range of traumas from bullying to sexual abuse and gang-rape, and treatment experience from other situations can be of benefit. Group treatments usually involve education and 'debriefing' (e.g. Stallard and Law, 1993). Crisis intervention for an individual girl may comprise helping her to communicate her experience, and understand what she has undergone (Pynoos and Eth, 1986). Our experience with encouraging referrals of children from the local victim support service is that early intervention with the family in support is usually sufficient during the crisis period when court cases may be pending. Individual help may be necessary at a later stage according to individual needs.

CONCLUSION

Much child mental health provision has been 'gender-blind'. Youth provision has tended to be dominated by and for the troublesome – i.e. the boys. However, the separate needs of girls are becoming increasingly recognised. It is clear that girls, especially in adolescence, are prone to emotional disorders, and there are a variety of situations that may make this more likely. Looking at the specific needs of the girl may shed light on where treatment could be better refined and targeted. Werner (1989) suggests that appropriate interventions for prevention should include attempts both to reduce the exposure to stress-related life events and to increase the protective factors – communication and problem-solving skills, and sources of emotional support.

Many agencies, such as social services, voluntary agencies, the police, GPs and hospitals, are likely to come across girls in more serious situations of crisis, risk or disturbance. They should develop systems to ensure good communication, and comprehensive and complementary provision. In the crisis situation, protection is the first responsibility. The next is ensuring good childcare if necessary. Beyond that, there should also be available programmes of support or therapy, as appropriate.

There need to be sufficient resources available to ensure that intervention can be timely and of sufficient quality and quantity, as responding on a crisis-only basis cannot offer the continuity necessary. Child guidance units and voluntary agencies should have open referral systems to facilitate accessibility. Female staff should be available, as they may be preferred by girls as confidantes where individual therapy is indicated, especially after sexual abuse. There should be a range of treatments available. Family therapy, for example, may be the treatment of choice for some situations, especially anorexia nervosa.

Schools often provide social and personal education. It is helpful if there are designated people such as school counsellors or school nurses to whom girls can bring specific worries. Better sexual education and accessible contraceptive advice would also be helpful for both girls and boys. Community health and education services are well placed to collaborate in developing good services.

There are opportunities, with the provision of good services for girls, to lessen the burden of psychological disturbance and distress in adulthood, and to help to break the inter-generational cycle. Therapeutic interventions can be effective, but more research is needed to further elucidate which are most helpful to girls in need.

CROSS-REFERENCES WITHIN THIS BOOK

Chapter 6   Planning services for black women
Chapter 10   Women with drug and alcohol problems
Chapter 11   The impact of childhood sexual abuse

REFERENCES

Babb, P. (1993) 'Teenage conceptions and fertility in England and Wales 1971–1991', *Population Trends* 74: 12–17.

Baker, A. and Duncan, S. (1985) 'Child sexual abuse: a study of prevalence in Great Britain', *Child Abuse and Neglect* 9: 457–467.

Church, J. (1994) *Social trends 24. 1994 edition*, Central Statistical Office, London: HMSO.

Cohen, P., Cohen, J., Kasen, S., Velez, C.N., Hartmark, C., Johnson, J., Rojas, M. and Streuning, E.L. (1993) 'An epidemiological study of disorder in late childhood and adolescence – I. Age and gender-specific prevalence', *Journal of Child Psychology and. Psychiatry* 34: 851–867.

Cooper, P.J. and Goodyer, I. (1993) 'A community study of depression in adolescent girls. I: Estimate of symptom and syndrome prevalence', *British Journal of Psychiatry* 163: 369–374.

Crisp, A.H., Norton, K., Gowers, S., Norton, K., Gowers, S., Halek, C., Bowyer, C., Yeldham, D., Levett G. and Bhat A. (1991) 'A controlled study of the effect of therapies aimed at adolescent and family psychopathology in anorexia nervosa', *British Journal of Psychiatry* 159: 325–333.

Evans, S. and Brown, R. (1993) 'Perception of need for child psychiatry services among parents and general practitioners', *Health Trends* 24: 53–56.

Everson, M.D., Hunter, W.M., Runyon, D.K., Edelsohn, G.A. and Coulter, M.L. (1989) 'Maternal support following disclosure of incest', *American Journal of Orthopsychiatry* 59: 197–207.

Furniss, T., Bingley-Miller, L. and Van Elburg, A. (1988) 'Goal-oriented group treatment for sexually abused adolescent girls', *British Journal of Psychiatry* 152: 97–106.

Glaser, D. (1991) 'Treatment issues in child sexual abuse', *British Journal of Psychiatry* 159: 769–782.

Gorman, J. (1992) *Stress on women: out of the shadows*, London: MIND.

Gunnell, D. and Frankel, S. (1994) 'Prevention of suicide: aspirations and evidence', *British Medical Journal* 308: 1227–1233.

Harrington, R. (1992) 'Annotation: the natural history and treatment of child and adolescent affective disorders', *Journal of Child Psychology and Psychiatry* 33: 1287–1302.

Haskett, M.E., Johnson, C.A. and Miller, J.W. (1994) 'Individual differences in risk of child abuse by adolescent mothers: assessment in the post-natal period', *Journal of Child Psychology and Psychiatry* 35: 461–476.

Hawton, K. and Fagg, J. (1992) 'Deliberate self-poisoning and self-injury in adolescents: a study of characteristics and trends in Oxford, 1976–89', *British Journal of Psychiatry* 161: 816–823.

Hetherington, E.M. (1989) 'Coping with family transitions; winners, losers and survivors', *Child Development* 60:1–14.

Hill, P. (1993) 'Recent advances in selected aspects of adolescent development', *Journal of Child Psychology and Psychiatry* 34 (1): 69–99.

Hoffman, L.W. (1984) 'Work, family, and the socialization of the child', in R.D. Parke (ed.), *Review of child development research* 7: 223–281.

Ineichen, B. and Hudson, F. (1994) 'Teenage pregnancy', *National Children's Bureau Highlight* No. 126.

Kingsbury, S.J. (1993) 'Parasuicide in adolescence: a message in a bottle', *Association for Child Psychology and Psychiatry Review and Newsletter* 15 (6): 253–259.

Kurtz, Z. and Wolkind, S. (1994) *Services for the mental health of children and young people in England: a national review*, London: South Thames RHA.

Lafontaine, Jean (1991) *Bullying: the child's view*, London: Calouste Gulbenkian Foundation.

Lewin, M. and Tragos, L.M. (1987) 'Has the feminist movement influenced adolescent sex role attitudes? A reassessment after a quarter of a century', *Sex Roles* 16: 125–135.

MacMillan, H.L., MacMillan, J.H., Offord, D.R., Griffith, L. and MacMillan, A. (1994) 'Primary prevention of child physical abuse and neglect: a critical review. Part I', *Journal of Child Psychology and Psychiatry* 35 (5): 835–856.

Mullen, P.E., Martin, J.L., Anderson, J.C., Romans, S.E. and Herbison, G.P. (1993) 'Childhood sexual abuse and mental health in adult life', *British Journal of Psychiatry* 163: 721–732.

Nagy Jacklin, C. (1989) 'Female and male: issues of gender', *American Psychologist* 44 (2): 127–133.

Offord, D.R., Boyle, M.H. and Racine, Y. (1989) 'Ontario child health study: correlates of disorder', *Journal of American Academy of Child and Adolescent Psychiatry* 28 (6): 856–860.

OHE (1989) *Mental health in the 1990's; from custody to care?* London: Office of Health Economics.

Olweus, D. (1993) *Bullying at school: what we know and what we can do*, Oxford: Blackwell.

Pynoos, R.S. and Eth, S.S. (1986) 'Witness to violence: the child interview', *Journal of the American Academy of Child Psychiatry* 25 (suppl. 3): 306–319.

Repucci, N.D. and Haugaard, J.J. (1989) 'Prevention of child sexual abuse: myth or reality', *American Psychologist* 44 (10): 1266–1275.

Robins, L. (1978) 'Sturdy childhood predictors of adult antisocial behaviour: replications from longitudinal studies', *Psychological Medicine* 8: 611–622.

Rosenberg, F.R. and Simmons, R.G. (1975) 'Sex difference in the self-concept in adolescence', *Sex Roles* 1: 147–159.

Russell, G.F.M. (1985) 'Premenarchal anorexia nervosa and its sequelae', *Journal of Psychiatric Research* 19: 363–369.

Russell, G.F.M., Szmukler, G.I., Dare, C., et al. (1987) 'An evaluation of family therapy in anorexia nervosa and bulimia nervosa', *Archives of General Psychiatry* 44: 1047–1056.

Rutter, M. (1989) 'Isle of Wight re-visited: twenty-five years of child psychiatric epidemiology', *Journal of the American Academy of Child and Adolescent Psychiatry* 28 (5): 633–653.

Salmons, P., Lewis, V. J., Rogers, P., et al. (1988) 'Body shape dissatisfaction in school children', *British Journal of Psychiatry* 153 (suppl. 2): 27–31.

Smith, T. (1993) 'Influence of socioeconomic factors on attaining targets for reducing teenage pregnancies', *British Medical Journal* 306: 1232–1235.

Stallard, P. and Law, F. (1993) 'Screening and psychological debriefing of adolescent survivors of life-threatening events', *British Journal of Psychiatry* 163: 660–665.

Subotsky, F. (1990) 'Assessment for special education in a child guidance unit', *Psychiatric Bulletin* 14: 16–18.

Subotsky, F. and Brown, R. (1990) 'Working alongside the general practitioner: a child psychiatric clinic in the general practice setting', *Child: care, health and development* 16: 189–196.

Szmukler, G., McCance, C., McCrone, L., et al. (1986) 'Anorexia nervosa: a psychiatric case register study from Aberdeen', *Psychological Medicine* 6: 49–58.

Tantam, D. and Whittaker, J. (1992) 'Personality disorder and self-wounding', *British Journal of Psychiatry* 161:451–464.

Walford, G. and McCune, N. (1991) 'Long-term outcome in early-onset anorexia nervosa', *British Journal of Psychiatry* 159: 383–389.

Wallerstein, J. and Blakelee, S. (1989) *Second chances*, New York: Bantam Press.

Werner, E.E. (1989) 'High risk children in young adulthood; a longitudinal study from birth to 32 years', *American Journal of Orthopsychiatry* 59 (2): 72–81.

Westcott, H.L. and Davies, G.M. (1993) 'Children's welfare in the courtroom: preparation and protection of the child witness', *Children and Society* 7 (4): 388–396.

Whitney, I. and Smith, P.K. (1993) 'A survey of the nature and extent of bullying in junior, middle and secondary schools', *Educational Research* 35 (1): 3–25.

Chapter 5

Planning community mental health services for older women

Gill Livingston and Martin Blanchard

INTRODUCTION

In the 1990s, older people remain a very disadvantaged minority group, and many professionals and planners still show little interest in older people with mental illnesses. Innovative community service models are few and research on the needs for mental health care of older people remains very limited. A cultural change is currently needed, with carefully designed policies and incentives to stimulate interest and optimism.

In considering how well community mental health services meet the particular needs of women, this pervasive lack of interest in the needs of older people is of great concern. The adequacy of services for the elderly may be regarded as a 'women's issue' for several reasons.

First, the great majority of users of these services *are* women. This is in part because women predominate among older people in general, and among the very old in particular (OPCS, 1987). It also results from women's apparently greater vulnerability to the conditions which account for most psychological morbidity in older people, such as dementia and depression (Livingston *et al.*, 1990).

Second, social deprivation is a very important factor in perpetuating and exacerbating the mental health problems of older women, and in increasing the need for services. Poverty, poor living conditions and isolation are problems that older people in general frequently experience, but to which older women are especially susceptible (Victor and Vetter, 1986). Women are more likely than their male peers to be living alone in old age, and the proportion of women living alone increases with ageing, mainly as a consequence of widowhood. A recent report has shown that nearly twice the proportion of older women (compared with older men) have incomes at or below the poverty line. The current generation of older women may still be suffering consequences of the lack of concern about women's economic independence earlier in the century – for example, working women were not generally expected to maintain pension schemes of their own after marriage. Widowhood or divorce may then have left them to survive on a very meagre income.

Finally, the state of mental health services for older people has far-reaching effects on women not only as users of these services, but also as carers. Most care for mentally ill older people is currently informal, and the majority of carers are wives, sisters and daughters. If they are not adequately supported by the statutory services, or if the running down of residential resources means that their relatives have to be maintained in the community longer than is really sustainable, the burden and the morbidity these carers themselves experience may become very great.

Thus the planning of adequate community services for older people is an issue which must be very much on the agenda for those who are concerned with identifying the unmet mental health needs of women. In this chapter, we first outline the needs that community services ought to meet, and the ways in which these are changing. We then describe the current state of policy and planning in community mental health services for older adults, and the difficulties that arise in the delivery of these services. We outline some principles and identify some service models that may usefully guide future community service planning. Finally, ways in which women may be particularly affected by the move to the community are considered, and the opportunities and risks offered by this shift are then discussed.

NEEDS FOR CARE AND THE POPULATION STRUCTURE

The planning of mental health services needs to be preceded by the identification of needs in the population. In the twentieth century, the number of people aged over 65 has increased by 400 per cent. Over the next few decades, the proportion of the population who are aged over 65 will continue to increase slowly, but numbers aged over 85 will increase much more rapidly: a natural increase of a million people aged over 85 is forecast between 1985 and 2041.

The implications of this expected shift in the age distribution of the population are important for the provision of mental health services through both health and social services, particularly with regard to meeting the needs of women. Women make up the majority of all older people, with currently about three older women for every two older men. Among the very old this predominance becomes still more marked – over the age of 75 this number shifts to two women for every man, whilst of those aged over 80 there are about seven women to every two men. Among the very old, women living alone are the largest group.

Disability increases with age, so that by the age of 85, 752 per 1,000 men and 852 per 1,000 women have some degree of disability. Much of this disability is directly due to, or associated with, mental health difficulties. Many in this age group have both physical and mental disabilities.

Demographic factors, such as gender and current marital status have an important influence on the impact on health services of increasing disability. For example, unmarried women aged over 75 have twice the average length of stay in hospital of married men in the same age range. Many of the men living independently of formal services are dependent on women, as it is usually the female partners who become carers in order to allow a shorter hospital stay. Therefore, community mental health service planning must also take into account the known increase in morbidity in those caring for the mentally ill. Utilisation of social services is also very much affected by the demography of the population, so that the heaviest service users are those who are very old, living alone or disabled: the vast majority of these are women.

In summary, those involved in planning community mental health services for elderly women should take into account the numbers and structures of the older population. It should be noted, however, that population needs should be continually reviewed, as current projections are based on the assumption that the birth and death rates will remain stable – this is in fact unlikely to be the case. Other factors that may well change include patterns of mental illness and treatments available. First, there were improvements in child nutrition following the observation of nutritional deficiencies in those conscripted for military services during World War I: these may mean that subsequent generations are better nourished and their brains may be less vulnerable to organic mental illness. Second, new drugs are being developed that may be effective in slowing or even reversing the progression of dementia. Third, it is often observed by clinicians that older people currently tend to report themselves as overall fairly well, even after responding positively to a list of symptoms which include being unable to enjoy themselves in any way, pessimism, loss of appetite, inability to sleep, frequent crying and suicidal ideation. Often they do not request any help, and much of their morbidity goes either undetected or untreated. This may be a characteristic of ageing, but is more likely to be a cohort effect, in which education and experience have led to a 'stiff upper lip' and low expectations. As people who are currently younger adults age, it is likely that their expectations will be higher, although their morbidity may be the same or lower.

Unknown factors in populations, morbidity, treatment and expectations thus make planning future services an inexact science. Information regarding present morbidity can be used only to help inform assessment of future needs – continual reassessment of these needs will be necessary.

MENTAL ILLNESS IN OLDER WOMEN

In old age the overall picture of mental illness shifts, so that depression and dementia become the commonest major illnesses. In older people, depression is usually accompanied by marked negative thoughts about themselves, the world and the future, which may be more prominent than expressed low mood. Depression of clinical severity reduces functioning, decreases recovery from physical illnesses and may be associated with suicidal ideation or completed suicide. There are many surveys of rates of depression in the over-65s living at home. Most of these find prevalence rates between about 11 per cent and 17 per cent, and rates are higher among women than among men. Risk factors for depression include living alone, not being currently married, loss (including bereavement), and physical ill health. Most of these factors occur more commonly in the very old. Despite this, depression is no more common in the very old than in older people generally. It has been suggested that this is accounted for by the increasing losses of old age being compensated for by added experience, which leads to resilience. Community studies of the natural history of depression have found that a third still remain depressed around three years later and only 20 per cent have recovered completely.

Dementia is again more prevalent in older women than in older men. The most important risk factor for dementia is increasing age, and education may be protective. While the rates of dementia vary according to the populations surveyed and the instrument used, in general the prevalence of dementia doubles for every increase of 5 years after the age of 65. Overall, around 5 per cent of the over-65s and 20 per cent of those aged 80 and over have dementia (Jorm et al., 1987).

Various less common mental health problems create needs for services in older women (Livingston and Hinchliffe, 1993). Paranoid illnesses of late life, where people firmly hold fantastic beliefs that are not culturally appropriate, predominantly occur in women. The prevalence in the over-65s is around 2 per cent. The development of this condition is particularly associated with impaired vision and hearing: improvement with medication and with greater social contact is common. Generalised anxiety disorders are usually associated with depression. Phobias, however, often occur in the absence of other mental illness. After retirement, older people seem to be able to avoid many of the triggers for their phobias simply by decreasing their activity and therefore their exposure. This may explain why older people with phobias rarely seek help from the services. Some recent research suggests that alcohol abuse may be a significant unrecognised problem among older people: more research is needed.

Thus a variety of disorders generate needs for mental health care among older people, and most of these disorders are commoner among women. Mental illness in older people often leads to a loss of capacity for independent living, as well as great personal distress. The illness can thus burden carers and health and social services, as well as the affected individual. Both the personal and the socioeconomic costs are very high.

CARERS OF ELDERLY PEOPLE

While responsive formal services are an essential part of community care, the main support of most older frail, disabled, mentally and physically ill people comes from family, friends and neighbours. Wives, sisters and daughters are the main informal supporters of the older people, and they are often alone in providing care. Most older people with mental illness live outside institutions, and the government policy of providing care in the community means that this will increasingly be the case. The priority to be given to the needs of carers is now explicit in community care legislation, but there are no guidelines as to how this is to be achieved. Apart from attendance allowance (1994 rates were £28.95 per week for day or night help, and £43.35 per week if both were required), there is no financial recompense for the personal, social and financial hardships incurred. The large contribution that informal carers make to the economy is not generally discussed.

About 75 per cent of people with dementia live with others, or have a helpful relative close by. However, 60 per cent of older people with depression live alone. Carers of confused or dementing older people are themselves likely to be in older age groups, with an average age calculated as 74 years. Up to a third of older people are carers at some time, providing the most intimate and arduous personal care, usually to a highly dependent spouse. Distress in carers is particularly associated with any disabilities the carers themselves have which limit their activities, with the severity of the behavioural and interpersonal problems of the dependent person, and particularly with lack of normal conversation between carer and care receiver (Murray, 1995).

There is increasing evidence that women, and especially wives, experience more subjective burden, distress and lack of satisfaction from the role of carer than do men. Despite this, men receive more practical help with caregiving, and this is associated with a reduction in their subjective burden. For women, however, receiving formal support may be associated with high stress. This negates the common assumption among service providers and carers of both sexes that women are more natural carers as they are more competent at domestic and personal care tasks.

Another possible consequence of carer distress may be the abuse of the person they care for. An estimated 500,000 older people may be at risk of abuse (physical, psychological, sexual and financial). In a recent study of 64 incidents of abuse from two London boroughs, 51 out of 64 (80 per cent) of those abused were women, and the majority were over 80 years old (Department of Health and Social Services Inspectorate, 1992). In particular, those at highest risk of abuse in the USA and Britain have been found to be white women aged over 75 years, who have a mental or physical disability and who live with or are cared for by their adult child. Abuse is also associated with problem drinking in the carer and with long-term poor-quality relationships.

Unfortunately, a lack of resources currently leads to people living alone being prioritised by social services, leaving carers with all the personal and domestic care tasks. Day centres, sitting services and residential respite care are service models which provide some relief for carers: however, day centres have limited opening hours, and sitting services are normally available only during the day. In general, the availability of respite care is increasing, but it does remain in very short supply.

Carer support groups exist in various settings. The Alzheimer's Disease Society (ADS) is a nationwide organisation for carers of people with dementia (see Appendix for address). It provides support and information, as well as representing and acting as an advocate for carers. However, those looking after people with dementia often find it difficult to attend meetings in the few free hours they have available.

USE OF HEALTH SERVICES

The general practitioner is the service most frequently used by older people, about 30 per cent of whom would have seen their GP over a period of a month. It has been estimated that this number has now risen to around 40 per cent, as GPs have a new contractual obligation to screen all patients aged 75 or over annually. However, the role of GPs in detecting and managing the mental health needs of older people has been questioned. A study in the early 1960s found that they often failed to diagnose dementia or depression in older patients. More recent studies, however, have not substantiated these findings: they suggest that, if anything, GPs over-diagnose older patients as depressed, but then do not act on this diagnosis in any way. Where they do act on the diagnosis, there are a variety of possible referral pathways, including district nurses, psychiatrists, social workers, geriatricians and community psychiatric nurses.

Another cause for concern is the treatment of mental illness in older people by prescription of benzodiazepine drugs, such as valium. This is particularly prevalent among women. The number of prescriptions rises with age, and whilst in general current benzodiazepine prescribing in the UK has fallen, this decrease has not been reflected in older people. A recent survey (Cullen et al., 1994) has suggested that 60 per cent of older people prescribed such tranquillisers were still taking them two years later. As benzodiazepines can cause confusion – as well as being addictive – in older people, it is important that they are only initially prescribed for short periods of crisis, and the high prevalence of long-term use of benzodiazepines may constitute a significant health problem for older women.

Both mental and physical health services are working ever more closely with social services, and use of one cannot be divorced from use of the other. Whilst around 9 per cent of older people are visited by nurses at home over a period of a month, approximately 60 per cent of people over 65 use social services within the same time period. Those people who are multiple-service users tend to be the old, the isolated, and the physically or psychiatrically ill. Those with depression tend to be in contact with the health services, but may not be receiving any formal recognition or treatment for their condition. Those with dementia, on the other hand, tend to be in contact with social services rather than the health services. Once older people start to use services, they usually continue to do so (Cullen *et al.*, 1994).

PROVIDING MENTAL HEALTH SERVICES FOR OLDER WOMEN

Public policy in the 1980s and 1990s

In the 1980s, several central principles were formulated that guided government policy. These included:

- giving priority for health and social services to people who were confused or demented;
- keeping them in their homes and supporting them by informal carers wherever possible;
- the costs associated with their disabilities being borne increasingly by individuals;
- reducing NHS long-term beds, with a virtual freeze on local authority homes;
- using public monies to subsidise private care.

However, it has become clear that older people with mental illnesses are an expensive group to care for, and that they may need intensive support which they often do not receive. Thus, moves have subsequently been made to contain costs and promote a rational allocation of resources. The legislation underlying the policies of the 1990s is set out in the NHS and Community Care Act, which was implemented in 1993. This has made 'needs assessment' one of the cornerstones of social policy: views are to be sought from the patient and carer, and a care package administered by a care manager is then to be formulated. Difficulties have already arisen because of insufficient staffing to assess needs, too few formal carers, and problems arising from lack of co-ordination between services. There is still separation between medical and social services, between the medical specialities, and between in-patient and community health services.

The NHS and Community Care Act brought with it the concept of the purchaser–provider division in health and social services. The main tasks of the purchasers are to assess accurately the health needs of their local populations, to set quality standards, and, in the case of social services, to purchase from private services as well as local authorities. The hidden morbidity and unmet needs of carers and patients ought therefore to be addressed, but there is already evidence that some difficulties are arising. Most of the community care budget handled by local authority purchasers will not be 'ring fenced', and therefore protected explicitly for this use. It is also often found that not enough money has been budgeted to provide the financial incentive for the private sector to provide specifically for mental illnesses in the old. Purchasers need to co-operate in order to negotiate seamless services from the public and private care providers. Only with such co-operation can the power of consumers to choose be used, and the non-profitable aspects of care be included in care packages. A further difficulty is that needs assessment is a slow process which sometimes hampers the fast delivery of care. There is a greater demand than was originally anticipated, and care management therefore needs additional personnel.

One of the priorities of another government initiative, the Health of the Nation (1991), is a reduction in the suicide rate. Completed suicide is particularly prevalent among older people, and in this group it is usually associated with a depressive illness. This ought to lead to extra efforts and resources to identify and manage depression among older people.

Community psychiatry

Government policy, user groups and most professionals suggest that living in the community is best for most older people with mental health problems. In particular, people with dementia are sensitive to the environments in which they live, and function best in familiar and appropriate environments. The needs of older people are often multiple, so that good co-ordination is needed between services. Other important principles of care in this group are to retain dignity, and maximise independence and activity so as to enhance quality of life.

The overall current picture is of unrecognised psychiatric needs and lack of action, even when mental health difficulties are diagnosed. However, some principles that should underlie good practice may be identified, and a number of models of good practice are in place: some of these principles and models will now be described.

Multidisciplinary teams for mental health care for older people have been developed within the old-age psychiatry services. Referral to these teams comes not only from general practitioners, but may also come from hospital doctors, social workers, community nurses, relatives, friends and other carers. Each member of the team may undertake assessments, will liaise with the team and act as a keyworker. These teams aim now to perform the majority of initial assessments and to carry out most of the management within the home. This multidisciplinary model is still not in place everywhere, and where it is, there is usually a shortage of workers.

An important service model which may strongly influence the way that professional carers operate is the Kent Community Care Project. From this work has developed a model of 'care management' which involves:

(a) a principal support worker who holds the budget and allocates it on behalf of the patient; and
(b) the home-care worker, who is paid to undertake a wide range of domestic and personal care tasks, rather than, for example, employing a home help to clean the house and a district nurse to assist with bathing.

The role of social services

The social worker acts as a provider of services including home helps and home carers, meals on wheels, incontinence laundry services, day care and some respite care. The domiciliary services offered seem to be particularly valued by users, but, again, there are not enough of them. Flexibility of services tends to be the exception rather than the rule. Nevertheless, it is important that carers are made aware of all the services available locally. Across the country, there needs to be a reduction in the variability in standards of services, with evaluation and improvements in the organisation and level of care. Some of those who most need services still do not receive them. A major difficulty in most current and proposed models of social care is the shortage of practical support, especially in the evenings and at nights and weekends. These are issues which have begun to be addressed but will require a reassessment of the allocation of resources if adequate services are to be made available. Models suggested for making best use of limited resources include the construction of total-care packages by the private sector, or competitive tendering of individual components of services, with the social services acting as care purchasers.

Pressures on community care

The numbers of long-stay hospital beds have been declining, despite the fact that many people with dementia eventually require long-term psychiatric nursing care, and that the number of people with this condition is increasing. If this continues, there may eventually be no facilities to care for the most difficult and behaviourally disturbed older people with long-term mental illness. The Department of Health advocates a policy where there is co-operation between health services, social services and the private sector, so that a mix of long-term beds are provided appropriate to needs. A situation where the NHS ceases to be a provider of long-stay beds could mean that a hole develops in the safety net of community care, because each provider could choose not to accept those with the most complex and difficult-to-cope-with needs. In order to prevent this, some form of NHS provision is needed. This does not have to be large, as many of those with severe dementia do not manifest these behavioural complications. Without such long-stay NHS provision, there is concern that when community provision is insufficient, acute assessment beds may be used inappropriately for long-stay patients whom no community residential setting will accept, leaving nowhere for patients who need such acute assessment.

Admission to residential care

A number of risk factors for admission for residential care have been identified, and include:

- level of cognitive impairment;
- significant behavioural or interpersonal problems;
- absence of an informal carer;
- the main carers being in favour of residential care;
- poor physical health of carers;
- packages of care which have not included respite care.

The general shortage of residential places often means that admissions have to wait until crises occur, rather than taking place when people with dementia, their carers and professionals feel it to be appropriate. Thus there are fears that breakdowns in community care may become the main route to admission. Further research is needed into the question of when admission to long-stay facilities should occur, including study of patterns of admission, life expectancy, quality of life and people's preferences.

Models of good practice for older people with mental health problems

The Admiral Nurse service has been set up in some parts of London by the Joseph Levy Charitable Foundation. Admiral Nurses are specially trained nurses whose work focuses on the carer of a person with a dementing illness. They aim to help carers to acquire a greater understanding of the nature and prognosis of dementia, to help them to deal with the symptoms of dementia and to improve access to other support services. Evaluation suggests that carers appreciate and value this service.

Recent research indicates that primary-care nurses can assess and care-manage depressed older people. Depressed older people under their care make greater improvements over three months than those receiving regular GP care. Training packages that enable primary-care nurses to perform this role are currently being developed (Blanchard et al., 1995).

Another form of intervention has targeted those carers of people with dementia who have high levels of psychological stress. This stress, as well as the behavioural difficulties of the person with dementia, can be alleviated over a three-month period by the implementation of individually tailored intervention packages by a research doctor. These packages have been devised to help the carer cope with stress, to provide some respite, and to reduce behavioural complications of dementia. Improvements persisted when seen after a further three months (Hinchliffe *et al.*, 1995).

Innovative community schemes have also tried to fill the gap between the level of support usually supplied in sheltered accommodation and a move to residential care. These are the 'very sheltered housing programmes', and they illustrate the fact that dementia is rapidly becoming an important housing issue.

Wide implementation of those innovations that have been shown to be effective for the older mentally ill is required. Evaluation of other new ideas is also needed, so that changes in service provision are based on rational judgements rather than administrative convenience or current fashion. Effectiveness must be judged in terms of the people a service fails to contact as well as those it does treat.

Costs and consequences

Dementia and depression among older people incur considerable costs. Residential care in hospital is usually thought to be the most expensive option, followed by residential care and then care in the community. However, cost is only one side of the equation, and must be balanced by effectiveness. Some researchers believe that additional resources for people with dementia would be most effective if they were used to support the carer at home. Other researchers report contradictory findings as to whether specially designed support for people with dementia at home can be cheaper than hospital provision or residential care. One innovative home-care scheme turned out to be almost three times as expensive as services that would otherwise have been provided – this appears to suggest that it is not total costs that vary greatly between settings, but rather the level of care. When community care is as comprehensive as residential care, it is probably as, or more, expensive. It is often the family's labour in caring that results in lower costs.

The place for change in medical services

Recent changes in health policies are intended to address the problems posed by the *status quo*. However, the future problems that will result from the continued ageing of the population are not at present being addressed at a policy level.

The expected availability of drugs to improve cognition in dementia in the near future will result in the need for more medical resources to identify and treat early dementia. These drugs will inevitably have only limited effectiveness, so that important resource and ethical decisions about their use will be needed.

It is theoretically possible to reduce the severity and perhaps the prevalence of mental illness among older people by reducing the numbers of secondary dementias. This could be done by improving the management of physical disorders associated with old age, such as high blood pressure, diabetes and thyroid diseases. It should also be possible to reduce iatrogenic mental disorder by increased education in prescribing.

Health education for older people may be an important component of improved mental health care, empowering them to present psychological symptoms to their general practitioners.

CARING FOR ELDERLY WOMEN IN THE COMMUNITY: OPPORTUNITIES AND RISKS

Thus, overall, a policy commitment has been made in the UK to caring for older people with mental health problems in the community. Application of these policies has been patchy and often under-resourced, but some principles and some helpful service models have been identified. As discussed at the beginning, the state of services for older people with mental health problems is of general importance for women because they predominate among those with needs for these services, as well as among carers. Some of the opportunities and risks associated with the move to the community may also be especially relevant for women.

The move to the community has the potential to meet the particular needs of older women better in various ways. First, older women are particularly likely to live alone, and are thus often very reliant for help on the statutory services. Without well-developed community services, these women have little prospect of receiving the care they need whilst being able to remain in their own homes.

Second, social factors such as isolation and poverty are especially prevalent among older women, and contribute to their mental health problems. Working in the community gives professionals better opportunities to recognise and assess these social factors and to take steps to alleviate them, such as arranging practical help with poor accommodation or helping older women to increase their social networks.

Third, care in the community holds out the promise of allowing service provision to be tailored to individual needs. Younger people often tend to see older people as a homogeneous group with uniform needs and interests, and forget the enormous diversity of their experiences. This may be particularly the case for older women: men are at least identified in terms of their former occupations, whereas the tendency to perceive older women in terms of a generic 'old lady' stereotype may be strong. Some residential and day services have thus tended to strip older women of their identities and to assume common wishes and interests. If the stated aims of community care policies are realised, choice among a range of services may considerably increase the degree to which older women's diverse experiences and preferences are taken into account.

However, community care does also present some particular risks for women. First, if residential care is run down without adequate community services becoming available, those isolated older women for whom no informal carers are available may be particularly vulnerable to severe neglect and inability to cope. Second, where particular social situations, such as abusive relationships or isolation, cause or exacerbate mental health problems, care in the community may lead to older women being left in these problematic circumstances longer than might previously have been the case. Finally, the costs of caring for informal carers, who are predominantly women, may be great, and they need to be taken into account in any cost–benefit evaluation of care in the community.

CONCLUSION

Numbers of older people continue to rise, both in the United Kingdom and worldwide. This increasing number, of whom the great majority of both sufferers from mental illnesses and carers are women, require services for mental health. The model for future care is of multidisciplinary services – working predominantly in the community. These should be needs-based and involve partnership between different medical disciplines, paramedical personnel, social services, voluntary services and the private sector. Suggested models of good practice should be evaluated and implemented if found to be effective. This process has only just begun in old-age psychiatry, but the rapid changes in knowledge and therapeutic potential make a dynamic, flexible and responsive service a necessity.

CROSS-REFERENCES WITHIN THIS BOOK

Chapter 8   Women as carers of the severely mentally ill
Chapter 10   Women with drug and alcohol problems
Chapter 14   Women and primary care

REFERENCES AND FURTHER READING

Blanchard, M., Wattereus, A. and Mann, A.H. (1995) 'The effect of primary care nursing intervention upon older people screened as depressed', *International Journal of Geriatric Psychiatry* 10: 289–298.

Cullen, M., Blizzard, B., Livingston, G. and Mann, A. (1994) 'The Gospel Oak Project 1987–1990: provision and use of community services', *Health Trends* 25: 142–145.

Department of Health and Social Services Inspectorate (1992) *Confronting elder abuse*, London: HMSO.

Hinchliffe, A., Hyman, I., Blizzard, B. and Livingston, G. (1995) 'Behavioural complications of dementia – can they be treated?', *International Journal of Geriatric Psychiatry* 10: 839–47.

Jacoby, R. and Oppenheimer, C. (eds) (1991) *Psychiatry in the elderly*, Oxford: Oxford University Press.

Jorm, A.F., Korten, A.E. and Henderson, A.S. (1987) 'The prevalence of dementia: a quantitive integration of the literature', *Acta Psychiatrica Scandinavica* 76: 465–479.

Levin, E., Sinclair, I. and Gorbach, P. (1989) *Family services and confusion in old age*, Newcastle upon Tyne: Athenaeum Press.

Livingston, G. and Hinchliffe, A. (1993) 'The epidemiology of psychiatric disorders in the elderly', in M. Orrell and C. Katona (eds), *International Review of Psychiatry* 5: 317–326, Carfax Publishing Company.

Livingston, G., Thomas, A., Graham, N., Blizzard, B. and Mann, A. (1990) 'The Gospel Oak Project: the use of health and social services by the dependent elderly in the community', *Health Trends* 22: 70–73.

Murray, J. (1995) *Prevention of anxiety and depression in vulnerable groups: a review of the theoretical epidemiological and applied research literature*, London: Gaskell.

Nettan, A. (1994) *Unit cost of community care 1994*, University of Kent: Personal Social Services Research Unit.

OPCS (Office of population census and surveys) (1987) *Population projections 1985–2025*, London: HMSO.

Orrell, M. and Katona, C. (eds) (1994) *International Review of Psychiatry. Psychiatry of the elderly II Ageing: developments in research and service provision*, Carfax Publishing Company.

Victor, C.R. and Vetter, N.J. (1986) 'Poverty, disability and the use of service by the elderly', *Social Services and Medicine* 22: 1087–1091.

Chapter 6

Planning services for black women

Khalida Ismail

INTRODUCTION

Mental health services for women of different ethnic origins have been a long-standing area of weakness in the NHS. Britain is one of the most ethnically diverse nations in the world, but has neglected the health needs of its ethnic minorities. Yet in the new era of community care, the imperative to meet these demands is great. The success of Britain's mental health service of the 1990s and beyond will be judged by its ability to meet the diverse needs of its various ethnic constituents. The increasing knowledge of the relationship between mental illness and culture, and of the impact of racism on patients' care, has to be borne in mind by service planners. The introduction of citizens' charters, not in themselves legally binding, emphasises patient satisfaction, and the NHS and Community Care Act 1990 has created the necessary opportunities to develop individually tailored and culturally appropriate packages of care.

This chapter will address the needs of black women in several stages. The concept of race and ethnicity is integral to considering for whom services are being planned, and this is discussed first. The problems encountered in trying to identify needs for services among women of different ethnic origins are then explored. The contribution of ethnic-related factors to patterns of mental illness and to pathways into care is also described. Some general principles for service planning for black women are then outlined, both at organisational and at patient–therapist levels. Finally, this chapter makes a plea for new approaches to addressing racism within the health service. In particular, a move towards a more psychodynamic understanding of race and ethnicity will be suggested.

WHO IS A BLACK WOMAN?

What does being a 'black woman' mean? It encompasses a variety of political, social, racial and ethnic meanings, and is such a heterogeneous concept that there is no clearly correct definition. Attempts to define it commonly lead to confusion and misunderstandings. This chapter takes the liberty of not defining it, but a general understanding of race and ethnicity, and of their relationship with social class and migration, is essential to service planners and providers.

Race is a method of distinguishing people by comparing their physical characteristics. Although it is useful as a political and social term, it no longer has validity as a biological marker for allocating people into 'genetic groups'. There is more genetic variation within races than between them. Ethnicity is a more useful basis for distinguishing different groups of people, and is not synonymous with race. Ethnicity is a sociological concept, which utilises many different variables. Senior and Bhopal (1994) described a practical model of an ethnic group as having one or more of the following characteristics: sharing social origins or backgrounds; sharing a distinctive culture which is essentially maintained with successive generations and leads to a sense of identity; and sharing a language or religious tradition. Nevertheless, even ethnic groups are limited by imprecisions due to fluidity both over time and over geographical boundaries.

Socioeconomic status has profound effects on lifestyles, values and self-identity. These may not be appreciated in a clinical setting because professionals may hold preconceived beliefs that certain ethnic groups are always poor and behave as such, disregarding the impact social mobility and education have on behaviour.

Migration can also affect an individual's perception of her own ethnicity. Many first-generation families are in a state of cultural lag, where they hold on to their own culture, yet live side by side with the host culture. Successive generations may not adhere to their parents' culture so firmly, participating in cultural exchanges more freely, for instance, 'mixed marriages' which can blur the original ethnic boundaries.

The Commission of Racial Equality advocates self-assessment of ethnicity. In 1995 the NHS introduced an ethnic monitoring database which requires compulsory collection of self-reported ethnicity data for every patient passing through the NHS. This will provide valuable data for future service planners. However, the subjective reporting will not be validated against an objective assessment of patients' ethnicity, and there are no plans for collecting information on the views of patients from different ethnic groups about the services they have received. This database uses the Office of Population Censuses and Surveys criteria for ethnic origin. There are many important sources of difference, such as religion, education and class, which these criteria do not acknowledge, so that the usefulness of the groups into which patients are divided will be limited by not taking these variables into account.

This chapter uses the terms women, black women and women of specific ethnic origins synonymously. However, the experiences of women from different ethnic groups are very diverse, so that not all the issues discussed in this chapter are relevant to all women. If one particular ethnic group is being discussed, this will be indicated. It is also assumed that the reader is aware that the experiences and needs of women in general, as described throughout this book, are as relevant to black as to white women.

PROBLEMS IN ASSESSING NEEDS

Epidemiological data on the patterns of mental illness among women from different ethnic backgrounds are very limited. Yet such information is vital to resource allocation and planning for specific services. Many studies are limited in their applicability by size, definitions of race and ethnicity, and unknown validity and reliability of measurements across cultures.

A second difficulty is that Western psychiatry has not generally been interested in mental disorders in other ethnic groups. Western interests are limited to the high prevalence of schizophrenia among Afro-Caribbean men (Littlewood and Lipsedge, 1988), or to disorders where the psychopathology is a spillage of traditionally Western illnesses into specific ethnic groups, such as eating disorders among young Asian women.

A further problem in the field work of collecting ethnic-specific data is that of training researchers to learn the language and develop an understanding of the culture. Sometimes, researchers of the same ethnic group are appointed. However, this may then displace the need for other team members to develop the necessary skills.

The universal stigma of mental illness is a further obstacle to collecting data. In most societies, mental illnesses are associated with social penalties, especially for women. Mentally ill Asian women may be sent 'back home' or treated as outcasts of their community, often living literally on the physical edges of their family home. Other ill women may never be given the opportunity to marry, and are at risk of physical and sexual abuse. The social dividends of denying a mental illness are clearly high. Women are further abused by often being 'forced' to marry men with mental disorders, especially those with mental impairments, with parents paying large sums of money for a wife. Some societies may only acknowledge mental illness in its most extreme forms and deny or minimise more common conditions, such as mild depression and neurotic disorders.

The growing body of literature on the relationship between culture and mental illness emphasises that an understanding of the former is essential to the diagnosis of the latter. The presence of many psychiatric symptoms cannot be established without a knowledge of the patient's cultural background. This is especially relevant for women from developing countries, such as India. It is often argued that they cannot intellectually express emotional problems, and therefore frequently somatise and are hysterical. However, a recent WHO collaborative study has shown that the frequency of somatic symptoms in depression is similar throughout the world (Gater *et al.*, 1991), so this widely held belief may be inaccurate.

The WHO study suggests that culture affects illness behaviour rather than the illness itself. This is relevant to those women who are so disenfranchised from self-determination that they rarely visit their GP. If they do, they may be accompanied by a family member to interpret or chaperone. Such women may find themselves too embarrassed to discuss their problems and instead present those symptoms that are associated with the least stigma.

ETHNIC FACTORS RELATED TO MENTAL ILLNESS

There are a number of specific ethnic or transcultural factors that are related to mental illness in women. These include integration and transgenerational problems, wars, specific physical diseases including HIV, language, marital difficulties and racism.

The social and political dialogue between the sexes varies very widely between societies, and is often more rigidly defined than in the West. Women's social roles within their own ethnic groups have a strong influence on the nature and degree of their integration into Western society. The process of acculturation is therefore very different for women and for men. It is impossible to judge successful integration objectively because the experience is so subjective. Given that any objective assessment of integration is limited, useful approximate checklists include the adoption of Western dietary habits and dress code, acquisition of Western goods and learning the host language. Women, especially those from lower socioeconomic levels, are more likely to be left behind in the integration process. For many women, English is not their first language, or they had not learnt it before settling in Britain. Despite intensive home-based English lessons in the 1960s and 1970s, acquisition of the language has been slow, and has recently been impeded by lack of funding. This further disenfranchises these women from the English-speaking world and exacerbates communication problems. It is also important to remember that under stress, people regress to their native language and lose their acquired language. Poor integration can lead to social isolation which, in itself, is associated with depression.

There are also specific transgenerational problems for women. Adolescence is a major transition point in all cultures. Particularly in the Asian community, daughters are in the most unfortunate position of making, or having made for them, life decisions earlier than their Western counterparts. Two major transition points causing great conflict are marriage and career. Sexual relationships before marriage or with partners of different ethnic groups exist precariously. Pressures to end such relationships can precipitate family crisis and mental health problems. The opportunities for crisis intervention by mental health professionals are limited by the family's wishes to prevent 'outsiders' from getting involved.

There seems to be a growing incidence of young Asian girls with eating disorders. Mumford *et al.* (1991) found the prevalence of bulimia nervosa among South Asian girls, mainly Pakistani and second generation, was higher than among their Caucasian peers; 3.4 per cent and 0.6 per cent respectively. These high rates seemed to be occurring among the 'traditional' rather than the 'Westernised' group of Asian girls. The authors argued that the more traditional girls experienced more intensely the conflict between the two cultures, yet seemed to be, paradoxically, expressing this by adopting 'Western' ways of reacting to personal conflicts. The study also hypothesised that these girls came from more rigid families, which is held to be an aetiological factor in eating disorders among Western girls. This study has been criticised for over-interpreting the results when the validity and reliability of the measurements have not been established across ethnic groups. There is also an increasing prevalence of suicide and parasuicide among young Asian girls, which is a reversal of the normal pattern of Asian men committing suicide in their native countries (Soni-Raleigh and Balarajan, 1992).

Women from war-torn areas of the world arrive in the West with multiple traumatic experiences and mental health problems. In the ten years up to 1992, Britain accepted approximately 64,000 applications. Women may be experiencing multiple bereavements, anxiety and guilt about those whom they have left behind, and loss of their home and livelihood, as well as physical ill health. The recent Yugoslavian conflict has brought to attention the sexual violation of women in wartime as a military weapon of social destruction of the enemy. The status of refugee and fear of deportation may contribute to mental health problems. Recent UK legislation and immigration policy have made it much more difficult for refugees to be granted asylum, so that many now spend long periods in deportation centres. If the collective and individual experiences of trauma are not understood within their own cultural framework, Western psychiatric models may be limited in their applicability (Summerfield, 1993). Mental health problems may not be immediately detected when an individual is in transit or has recently arrived in a new country. There are other priorities, such as housing, finance, legal status, physical illnesses and injuries. Many refugees are settled close to one another and local mental health services may find themselves managing a small but significant group of people with multiple mental health problems.

Certain physical diseases which have specific effects on women, either as sufferers or as carers of sufferers, are more common in people of Afro-Caribbean, Mediterranean, and Asian origins. The most common of these conditions is sickle-cell disease, an inherited blood disorder. There are an estimated 5,000 people in Britain suffering from this condition, mostly living in large cities. Sickle-cell disease in women increases the risks of stillbirths, spontaneous abortions, miscarriages and poor foetal growth. All these complications are themselves associated with psychiatric morbidity. Women may have psychosexual problems and depression associated with chronic pain. There has been very little psychiatric input, apart from counselling services organised by the medical services and the voluntary organisations (Midence and Elander, 1994).

Mental illnesses may go undetected in women with other chronic medical conditions. Poor communication skills and language difficulties may impede diagnosis, and the professional has to be observant for non-verbal cues, such as tearfulness and depressed affect. There is also a lack of information on the needs of black people with terminal illnesses. The psychiatric problems of HIV infection in women, especially of African origin, are largely unknown. There are now very effective and supportive services for people with AIDS, but these are culturally geared to meet the needs of the white male gay community.

Marital conflicts are managed differently in different ethnic settings. In many cultures, inquiring about a woman's marriage and sexual problems can be misinterpreted as socially inappropriate and damage a therapeutic relationship. Yet such questions may be very important, for example when a woman presents with depression or unexplained injuries. They should be asked with sensitivity, in private and in confidence. Some women may not discuss marital problems for many reasons. They may not know of the various agencies that could help them, such as law centres, refuges and support groups. They may fear rejection by their community, that they will be physically reprimanded, that their in-laws will abduct the children, or that white professionals will not understand their culture.

Domestic violence is a particular problem. No statistics are available as to whether women of certain ethnic groups are more likely to be exposed to domestic violence than others. There is also a lack of information about how women of different ethnic backgrounds cope with and survive domestic violence. Those women who are most isolated, regardless of ethnicity, are more likely to be undetected and more vulnerable to developing mental illnesses, especially depression.

Racism has a serious impact on the mental health of black people but, again, gender issues are less frequently discussed. Overt racism is usually associated with violence, and women are particularly vulnerable to physical and sexual assaults. In areas with high levels of racism, such as Tower Hamlets in East London, Bangladeshi women have become practically housebound.

Institutionalised racism is more difficult to detect and resolve. Black people's experiences of health services have consistently been shown to be unsatisfactory. Problems have included difficulties with access to services, inadequate communication, and poor interpreting facilities and psychological support. Patients' families are especially neglected. Afro-Caribbeans are more likely than white people to be detained under the Mental Health Act, they are more often diagnosed as suffering from a psychotic illness than from any other mental illness, and they are more likely to be given high doses of medication. The experience of racism makes black people suspicious of mental health services, so that many deny their mental health problems and avoid services until they end up presenting in crisis.

Substance misuse among black women is another mental health problem that has been poorly researched. A pilot study by DAWN (1988) of 500 black women in Greater London suggested that there may be a significant alcohol misuse (see Appendix for address of DAWN). Black women were less likely to self-refer for help, because they perceived the services as predominately white and male oriented, and unable/unwilling to offer help. A popular misconception is that Asian women do not drink. This is based loosely on social information rather than research. Black communities have also, unfairly, been given a reputation for illegal drug taking. The pilot study suggested that the majority of black women did not take drugs, and of those that did, cannabis was the most common drug taken, with other drugs such as heroin seen as white drugs.

PATHWAYS INTO CARE

There are marked international variations in the pathways to mental health care (Gater *et al.*, 1991). One would expect this diversity of routes to health care to be reflected in the illness behaviour of the ethnic groups settled in Britain.

The first stage of illness behaviour is for the patient to experience symptoms. She then asks for the opinion of her family and friends. The illness then has to be legitimised, usually by a doctor, before the patient adopts the sick role. For women of different ethnic origins, legitimisation does not necessarily require a medical doctor, but can include pathways via spiritual healers, the voluntary agencies and the forensic route.

Primary care

As for the general population, primary care is the main route to care for black women in Britain. Despite this, GPs, even those of the same ethnic background as the patient, are less likely to refer black patients to specialist psychiatric services (Bhui *et al.*, 1993).

Mental health services

Young black people are more likely to present in crisis, by-passing primary care. It may be that they find twenty-four-hour emergency services more accessible than primary care.

Spiritual healers

Most societies, including the West, have their own versions of 'healers'. There is almost no information on the sociodemographics of healers, witch-doctors and shamans in this country. They are usually known by hearsay and there is no directory! Although they may serve a useful social role, they can delay treatment and potentially aggravate a mental illness (Gater *et al.*, 1991). Young women are particularly vulnerable to abuse by 'healers' as their families tend to have a very controlling influence. The recent case of a young Middle Eastern woman who was beaten to death during a violent exorcism demonstrates this risk and the need to know about it.

Voluntary sector

The voluntary sector has all but taken over provision of a broad-based mental health service for specific ethnic groups. It provides an excellent service of support, advocacy, counselling and social work. Particular strengths of these services tend to be the provision of keyworkers of the same ethnic group, use of clients' native languages, and the provision of culturally appropriate environments, activities and food.

Forensic services

The ratio of black women to white women in forensic psychiatric services and in prisons is much higher than the ratio between the two groups in the general population. Black people are more likely to be compulsorily detained under the Mental Health Act and brought to hospital by the police.

Finally, there will always be a group of women with mental health problems who never present to any services, because the stigma of illness is so high. This group is an important one to target in trying to create more accessible services.

PLANNING SERVICES

The current era of community care is an exciting time for setting up new, well-designed and ethnic-appropriate services for women. It offers opportunities for the NHS to set up partnerships of care with the voluntary sector. However, the relationship between the two sectors has historically been poor. The agenda of the voluntary sector has been client-based, destructuring the concept of mental illness, and focusing less on diagnosis and more on psychosocial support. It argues that the NHS has failed ethnic groups. The voluntary-sector model works well with women with milder mental illnesses, and is particularly effective in offering social support. However, more severe mental illnesses may go undetected. This contrasts with the NHS which focuses on diagnosis and pharmacological treatments and considers that the voluntary sector disregards its scientific methods of care. NHS professionals rarely visit or provide clinical sessions for voluntary organisations. This conflict has often not worked in the best interest of patients. Now, with decreased resources for both institutions, development of community care and increasing pressure to meet the needs of black people, it is imperative that there be a better working relationship between the two.

In a partnership, the voluntary sector could represent itself more effectively within the NHS, with a more regular presence in day centres, outpatients and wards. They could also benefit from NHS training programmes and participation in research and service planning. In return, they could provide a wide variety of services to statutory mental health services at all stages of care. The voluntary sector is likely to want to retain its independence, especially in the area of advocacy. The balance of sharing care, clinical responsibility and confidentiality of patient information is potentially a sensitive and problematic issue.

Community care is particularly suited to those women who have acculturated little and may be unable to adapt to the traditional Western psychiatric hospital. It is also easier for the family to provide further support. Notwithstanding, remaining within the home may perpetuate the illness, especially if the home environment has some causal bearing. For instance, marital or in-law difficulties, or racism in the local community, have to be excluded in the assessment before deciding on community rather than in-patient care.

Planning services for black women can be considered at two levels: the organisational, which looks at the structure of the whole service, and the individual, which reviews the professional–patient relationship.

Some districts may already have a portfolio of services for local ethnic populations. However, they may not have specifically addressed the needs of women patients from different ethnic backgrounds. The services may have been organised haphazardly, exempting the more isolated and less vocal groups, and repeating the work of a voluntary organisation of which they may not be aware. For these reasons, there is an imperative for all districts to set up working groups in close liaison with the voluntary sector, in order to bring the issues of mental health care for black women into the public arena.

Changing services at the organisational level

Working groups considering local service provision for black women should review and plan for the following areas: describing and quantifying needs; planning services on the basis of these; and training of professionals. This process can be separated into stages.

The first stage is to establish the size of the local ethnic population. The demographics, although not totally accurate, can be obtained from the Office of Population Censuses and Surveys and stratified into age, socio-economic class and ethnicity. A more difficult task is to quantify the mental health load, as so little is known of the prevalence of mental illnesses in different ethnic groups. Funds may be needed for research to establish prevalence. Perhaps a useful rule of thumb is to assume that the prevalence of a category of mental illness in a specified ethnic group is at least the same as the national average, unless known otherwise. All services should have enough flexibility to be capable of adapting to varying demands over time.

The second stage is to assess which services are currently available and to whom. Particular attention should be given to the relative involvement of voluntary and statutory sectors. Types of services currently available in the voluntary sector include:

- counselling and psychotherapy for women of specific ethnic background, e.g. Shanti/Nafsiyat (see Appendix for addresses);
- advocacy;
- self-help groups;
- support groups;
- social work support;
- assertiveness training;
- befriender service;
- day care/day centres;
- housing.

Statutory services may include outreach, interpreting and information and community-based mental health centres.

The working group should also enquire about local religious organisations. They may already have a service set up and, if not, may be interested in jointly doing so, especially in the area of befriending and counselling.

It is good practice to consider patient representation in planning. This is particularly important for those groups of women where accessibility, awkwardness with men, privacy and stigma are sensitive issues.

The third stage is organising or reorganising the service. This has to be an integrated and collaborative process. There are two important questions to consider: whether services should be segregated by ethnicity and whether by gender.

One important question in planning services for black women is whether they are better served by establishing specific, segregated services or by improving awareness of their needs within mainstream community services. Integrating services for black women into the generic community services encourages the whole profession to participate actively in providing multi-cultured care and in maintaining a high profile for ethnic issues. Also, as professionals would then be trained uniformly in maintaining standards, this allows for easier transfer of care between units. This is particularly important as mental health services are constantly in a state of change, with high turnover of staff, structural reorganisations and fluctuating resource limitations. Integration prevents services for specific ethnic groups from being marginalised. It also may have advantages for black workers, who do not become segregated from the rest of the service. However, there are disadvantages to integrated services, especially when training has been inadequate. Patients may be unhappy and uncomfortable in non-segregated facilities, and may not comply with treatment. The provision of some spaces for particular ethnic groups within the generic service thus seems appropriate – the most marginalised and least acculturated may find facilities such as separate groups or day centres particularly helpful.

Sex-segregated environments also need to be discussed when planning services for black women. Resources will be a major limiting factor for in-patient and day care services. Day centre environments and obviously the voluntary sector may not find this a particular problem. Ultimately, patients' choice should be maximised where possible, but the key issue is sensitivity to a woman's wish for privacy, for instance separating patients' rooms into single-sex corridors or dormitories, or providing a women-only lounge area.

Organising new and current services will require a summary of met and unmet needs. Needs that are easily neglected are those of more isolated ethnic groups such as the Chinese and the Vietnamese communities, and those of the black elderly population. It is essential to create a local catchment area directory of all statutory and voluntary services. Unfortunately, there is no national directory of voluntary mental health organisations. Organisations such as the King's Fund and Good Practices in Mental Health (see Appendix for addresses), have databases of nominated services and are useful starting points in collecting information. However, the databases are not complete, and though some services have been categorised as for black people and/or mental health, this may not be gender specific. The local directory should be circulated throughout the catchment, and should be advertised and readily available.

Interpreting services are essential. Interpreters should be professionally trained people, whose role is clearly defined. These services are only effective if they are easily accessible at short notice, that is, within twenty-four hours. It is unethical to rely on family members for interpretation, as they are biased and may have a poor command of English themselves; professionals would be at risk of breaching patient confidentiality and of neglecting the family's own psychological needs.

The physical environment should aim to welcome black women. Information leaflets and notices in different languages are easy to provide. The decor should be sensitive to multi-ethnic patient populations, and menus should also reflect the ethnic mix.

A core part of the management plan is family involvement, as this is usually an area that is neglected. Early appointments should be made with family members. Policies of patient confidentiality need more reinforcing, as it is easier to release medical information without consent when the patient herself cannot effectively communicate.

The fourth stage is to organise education and training for professionals. The specifics of the programme need to be negotiated locally, but essential components are regularity of sessions, obligations to attend, feedback, adaptability and users' views. Training programmes based on political correctness have face validity in reforming attitudes, but understanding other cultures and racism does not prevent an individual from manifesting institutionalised or unconscious racism (Kareem and Littlewood, 1992). Many professionals do not ask themselves or the patient what it is like to be black, Asian or Chinese, etc. There is a pressing need to develop focused psychodynamic models for addressing unconscious 'racist organisations'. Such models would be individual-focused, exploring with each professional, regardless of his/her own ethnicity, their own understanding and experience of racism and of being racist themselves. The aim of this novel approach is to be empathic, rather than being superficially politically correct or policing racist thoughts. This type of focused therapy should be seen as part of the supervision of a patient's care, either by a senior trained member of the team or by the local psychotherapy unit. Developing such programmes for a whole mental health service is an exciting and challenging opportunity to improve the patient–professional relationship.

Changing services at the individual level

Under community care, each patient receives a tailor-made package, and the keyworker is an essential figure. However, he/she does not have to be of the same race or sex as the patient. It is more important that within the team there is an ethnic mix across the professional hierarchy, and that the professional has received appropriate training.

The keyworker is expected to develop a care plan that tunes into the patient's ethnic needs, especially providing an interpreter if indicated. At this point, the directory mentioned above is a useful reference point, reducing the workload of a busy community psychiatric nurse or social worker.

A frequent problem is that black patients are not offered counselling or psychotherapy readily, even when there is a clear need for it (Campling, 1989). Most mental illnesses need a minimum of psychotherapeutic support, and for people of different ethnic groups this is probably even more important because of racism and of their alienation from mainstream Western culture. For instance, family work for Expressed Emotion in schizophrenia has been shown to benefit all ethnic groups, yet black patients are less likely to be offered it. As part of any individual care plan the type of psychotherapy should be indicated, offered and delivered. This is an ideal opportunity to liaise with the voluntary sector, which has already set in motion many centres that offer some form of psychotherapy. Organisations such as Nafsiyat have pioneered the development of intercultural therapy (Kareem and Littlewood, 1992) and the work of Shanti is described later in the book (see Chapter 16).

There is little practical knowledge of ethnic and sex differences in the effects of psychotropic medication. Mental health teams should always consider the psychotherapeutic alternatives to medication.

CONCLUSION

Considering how to plan services for black women highlights the lack of good research and information about their needs. Black women are a very diverse group, for whom no one definition will suffice. There are specific factors that link ethnicity and gender and which can predispose women to different mental health problems. Several principles have been suggested to meet the varying needs of these groups of women. These include liaison with the voluntary sector, which has been responsible for the majority of service provision, and developing psychodynamic strategies for dealing with racism. There is a need to develop specific services for black women, but it is more important that mainstream services have uniformly high standards of care for all ethnic groups. The opportunities for new developments in this field are enormous and, if taken, will help to bring forward a new era of multi-cultured health care.

ACKNOWLEDGEMENT

I would like to acknowledge the help of Sajida Ismail of Salford Law Centre.

CROSS-REFERENCES WITHIN THIS BOOK

REFERENCES

Bhui, K., Strathdee, G. and Sufraz, R. (1993) 'Asian inpatients in a district psychiatric unit: an examination of presenting features and routes into care', *International Journal of Social Psychiatry* 39: 208–220.

Campling, P. (1989) 'Race, culture, and psychotherapy', *Psychiatric Bulletin* 13: 550–551.

Department of Health (1992) 'Services for people from black and ethnic minority groups: issues of race and culture', in *Review of health and social services for mentally disordered offenders and others requiring similar services*, London: HMSO.

Drugs, Alcohol, Women, Nationally (DAWN) (1988) *Black women and dependency*, London: DAWN.

Gater, R., de Almeida e Sousa, B., Barrientos, G., Caraveo, J. *et al.* (1991) 'The pathways to psychiatric care: a cross-cultural study', *Psychological Medicine* 21: 761–774.

Kareem, J. and Littlewood, R. (eds) (1992) *Intercultural therapy: themes, interpretations and practice*, Oxford: Blackwell Scientific Publications.

Littlewood, R. and Lipsedge, M. (1988) 'Psychiatric illnesses among British Afro-Caribbeans', *British Medical Journal* 296: 950–951.

Midence, K. and Elander, J. (1994) *Sickle cell disease: a psychosocial approach*, Oxford: Radcliffe Medical Press Ltd.

Mumford, D.B., Whitehouse, A.M. and Platts, M. (1991) 'Socio-cultural correlates of eating disorders among Asian schoolgirls in Bradford', *British Journal of Psychiatry* 158: 222–228.

Senior, P.A. and Bhopal, R. (1994) 'Ethnicity as a variable in epidemiological research', *British Medical Journal* 309: 327–330.

Soni-Raleigh, V. and Balarajan, R. (1992) 'Suicide and self burning among Indians and West Indians in England and Wales', *British Journal of Psychiatry* 161: 365–368.

Summerfield, D. (1993) *Addressing human responses to war and atrocity: major themes for health workers*, Medical Foundation for the Victims of Torture, Ref DS/102.

Chapter 7

Women, lesbians and community care

Rachel E. Perkins

Over the last two decades women and lesbians whose mental health problems are transient or less disabling have received considerable attention, both from feminists and from mental health professionals. This has not been the case for those whose disabilities are more profound: these women, these lesbians, all too often remain invisible – lost among the legions of 'chronic patients'. The purpose of this chapter is to consider the needs of women and, in particular, of lesbians who are experiencing serious ongoing mental health problems.

The chapter has two main focuses: first, matters of general importance in service provision for women and lesbians experiencing serious ongoing mental health problems are discussed. The philosophies of community care and normalisation guiding current service provision are examined, and ways in which these approaches can be as oppressive as institutional incarceration are described. The second part of the chapter is specifically devoted to the experiences of lesbians who use mental health services, and to the forms which anti-lesbianism takes within these services. In each section, views expressed by some seriously socially disabled women and lesbians are considered, and specific suggestions are made about ways of improving services.

Although it may appear linguistically cumbersome, the phrases 'women and lesbians' or 'lesbians and women' are used throughout, in the interests of conceptual precision and political accuracy. Some writing assumes that the term 'women' covers both heterosexual women and lesbians. This is problematic in two major ways. First, as Wittig (1981) shows, the category 'woman' is socially constructed rather than natural and eternal: society defines what women are, and it does so in terms of certain economic, physical and personal obligations to men. In refusing to be heterosexual, lesbians escape inclusion in this definition. Second, writing about 'women' as a single overall category is often based on the liberal heterosexual assumption that lesbian refers merely to choice of sexual partner, and that otherwise lesbians are exactly the same as any other women. This renders lesbians invisible by denying the fact that they experience a different culture, different communities, and different stresses. It resembles the racist view that someone of

African Caribbean or Asian origin is just the same as a white person except for the colour of their skin. Thus, where women are written about as a unitary category it is often the experiences of women who are young, white, heterosexual and middle class that are in reality being discussed: the points of view, experiences and difficulties of a wide range of other groups are disregarded. Because of these difficulties with the use of 'women' as a general category, lesbians and women are distinguished throughout this chapter.

SOCIAL DISABILITY

The cognitive and emotional difficulties experienced by women who have serious mental health problems often lead to profound distress, an inability to cope with the demands of everyday life, and behaviour that others consider unusual and unacceptable. These problems have attracted diagnoses such as 'schizophrenia' and 'manic depressive illness': debate continues as to whether such labels should be abandoned as inappropriate and oppressive. Whatever the rights and wrongs of this debate, the problems experienced by these women and lesbians are very real. A way in which it is helpful to think about these difficulties is in terms of *social disability*. Serious emotional and cognitive problems make it difficult for lesbians and women to negotiate the able-minded social world unaided, just as serious physical and sensory limitations cause problems in negotiating the able-bodied physical world without aids, assistance and adaptation of that world to ensure access (Perkins and Dilks, 1992; Kitzinger and Perkins, 1993; Perkins and Kitzinger, 1993).

Social disability cannot, of course, be defined in a vacuum: a person can only be disabled in relation to a context. The social world in which women and lesbians have to function is one in which sexist and heterosexist social organisation prevails: women are urged to see their identity in terms of their success as wives, mothers and sexual companions, and social institutions and dominant ideologies maintain women's subordinate positions and limited power.

It is impossible to tell how much social disability among women and lesbians is a consequence of this oppression. Human systems such as sight, hearing and mobility are vulnerable to disability: there is no reason why this should not also apply to cognition and emotion. However, the disabilities of women and lesbians with serious ongoing mental health problems are clearly exacerbated by the stresses of oppression, such as male violence, sexual abuse, poverty, exclusion because of lesbian identity, and the strains of living in a world defined by men (Kitzinger and Perkins, 1993; Perkins and Kitzinger, 1993).

PHILOSOPHIES OF CARE

Hospitals and residential care

Traditionally, socially disabled women and lesbians have been excluded from society via hospitalisation. This rendered those who deviated from prescribed norms powerless until they conformed. The degradation of women and lesbians incarcerated in institutions has been well documented (for example, Chesler, 1972). The purpose of this chapter is not to dwell on these abuses. However, some observations are warranted about practices in hospital and residential care in this era of community care.

Unlike the old institutions, most residential facilities are now mixed. Mixed facilities are often defended as 'natural', and there is some truth in this. It is indeed 'natural' for women and lesbians to be harassed by men, and the harassment experienced in mixed facilities is unusually great. Few women and lesbians share houses with strange men not of their choosing, and have to run the gauntlet of harassment on the way to the toilet in the morning, at meals, or when trying to sit quietly in the sitting room. Even the limited and unsatisfactory respite from the oppressive expectations of men which the old single-sex facilities provided has been lost.

Other practices in residential facilities reinforce sexist and heterosexist imperatives. Johnstone (1989) has shown how looking and behaving in a 'feminine' manner is often seen as an index of recovery. There are numerous 'women's groups' in which make-up, hair, dress, dieting and varnishing one's nails are key agenda items. Women are exhorted to 'take a pride in their appearance', and 'normality' still frequently means doing one's hair, dressing up and wearing make-up.

Community care and deinstitutionalisation

We now live in an era of 'deinstitutionalisation', 'community care' and 'normalisation'. Most women and lesbians who experience serious long-term mental health problems live outside hospital. These developments have had various adverse effects on socially disabled women and lesbians.

The run-down of large hospital populations has resulted in the invention of the 'revolving door' patient. Women and lesbians are often discharged from hospital with little or no support, and are then particularly vulnerable to male violence and sexual exploitation (Test and Berlin, 1981). Homelessness has increased, but most provision is for men, despite suggestions that severe mental health problems are more widespread among homeless women. Neglect, abuse and denial are as destructive in the community as they were in the institution.

More effective community services can avoid some of this neglect, but the philosophies underlying such services still present problems for lesbians and women. Community care aims to maintain women in 'normal' social roles in the communities in which they live. But whose normality is this? Normality is not a neutral, value-free concept: it is defined by men in the service of men. Success in ordinary social roles refers to the extent to which a disabled woman or lesbian can fulfil the expectations of men.

Community care encourages marginalised women and lesbians to believe that their only hope of acceptance lies in conforming with roles and expectations defined by men. Bachrach (1985) has shown that community care programmes for women are based on male views of 'normal' women as passive, emotional, childlike and definitely heterosexual. Dependent roles and domestic pursuits are encouraged. Work is seen as less important for women (Goering et al., 1988; Perkins and Rowland, 1990), and they are deemed less capable than men. Lower expectations reinforce helplessness.

The term 'normalisation' is prominent in many policy documents. The concept originates in learning disabilities, and its condemnation of sickness models has given it a liberal campaigning flavour. However, it is deeply problematic in relation to women and lesbians.

The prime exponent of normalisation, Wolfensberger (1970), has described it as a 'deceptively simple' principle. It involves enabling the 'deviant person to function in ways considered to be within the acceptable norms of his [sic] society'. In subsequent writings these ideas have been modified a little. The gender-specific pronouns are gone, and 'socially normative' is replaced with 'socially valued' (Wolfensberger, 1983). This does not change the basic premise that the disabled person should be maintained in 'normal' or 'valued' roles as defined within a sexist, heterosexist, not to mention racist, ageist and ableist society.

Community care and normalisation approaches can be oppressive and dangerous for socially disabled women and lesbians. If they are to be adequately served by care in the community, the main aim should not be to fit them into an inherently oppressive world, whose pressures will necessarily exacerbate their problems. A shift in focus is needed towards ideas of access: changing the community to accommodate disabled individuals, rather than changing the individual. We need to consider the aids, adaptations and assistance which women and lesbians need in order to use their skills, to realise their ambitions and to live the lives they want in the communities they choose (Perkins and Dilks, 1992; Kitzinger and Perkins, 1993; Perkins and Kitzinger, 1993). For this to be achieved, the wishes of women and lesbians with serious mental health problems must be paramount.

DEVELOPING GOOD PRACTICE: LISTENING TO SOCIALLY DISABLED WOMEN AND LESBIANS

Planning and refining appropriate services cannot be based on a particular, fixed blueprint. A continuous cycle is needed of considering how current practice fails; seeking, hearing and understanding the views both of those who use services and those who find them so unacceptable or inaccessible that they do not; and then changing services.

All too often the voices of women and lesbians are not *heard*. As one woman in the discussions described below said, 'men shout and get lots of attention'. Even where their voices are heard, it is easy for them not to be *understood*. This may arise from failing to understand and acknowledge the woman or lesbian's cognitive and emotional problems, or else from not understanding the context of their lives: their cultures and communities, the pressures these exert and the opportunities they offer.

It is always easy to find reasons *not* to act upon the views of those who use community services: they are 'mad'; they don't know what is best for them like the professionals do; they are unrealistic; the group chosen is unrepresentative. There will always be competition between different interest groups for expertise in how to provide community services, with relatives, professionals, pressure groups and policy makers all claiming to know best. Yet, if services are really to meet the needs of those on the receiving end of them, these women and lesbians must be considered experts in what they need.

Discussions involving 24 women and lesbians were organised at a London rehabilitation and continuing community care service, in order to look at the needs they identified. All had serious ongoing mental health problems. They included those of African Caribbean, Asian and white European descent and their ages ranged from twenties to sixties. I will identify the main themes which emerged, and, on the basis of these and of the problems in philosophies of community care described above, I will suggest how services might be improved for socially disabled women and lesbians. Some considerations for good practice which apply particularly for lesbians are considered in the next section.

Women-only space and choice of women staff

Most wanted some women-only spaces. Those in hospitals and community sheltered living situations said such things as:

> We should have all men's and all women's wards – men's and women's houses as well.

Several also wanted women-only space in community facilities. One, who had for years been a member of a women's group, said:

> People outside try to be sympathetic for a while but if your problems go on they just don't want to know. I don't know how I'd manage without this group – we can talk about our problems, but we also have a laugh. It's these women who keep me going.

The wish for female staff to be available was also strongly expressed:

> I want a keyworker who I can relate to. I want a choice of a woman.

> We should not be expected to have baths with male staff. It's just wrong. All wrong.

> I want a woman doctor.

Thus an adequate range of services must include women-only facilities of all types, including groups, day facilities, supported accommodation and in-patient facilities, as well as the option of having a woman worker.

Safety

Safety was one of the areas generating most anger:

> I'm not safe out there. I'm not safe in here. Where are you safe?

> We need protection. Protection from being attacked. And protection from always being nagged for cigarettes, lights and sex. The men threaten to hit you if you don't give them what they want.

Minimising the dangers of harassment, sexual abuse and violence must be a priority. As well as women-only facilities, appropriate measures include providing personal alarms, and help and support in reporting any abuse to the police. Harassment and violence should always be taken seriously, and a woman should be available for the victim to talk to. There should be a clear policy on action to be taken in the event of harassment or abuse.

Supporting social networks

Various comments were made about access to friends, partners, and children, particularly in hospitals and other residential settings:

> They don't seem to approve of me having friends in.

> I can't get a moment to myself with my husband.

Several had concerns about visits from their children, reliance on estranged husbands, and childcare:

> There should be a room where kids can visit in private. My son came to visit me in hospital – he was five years old and I had to see him in the day room. He was so scared of all the people he ran away.

> We were supposed to be sharing custody of our children. But because I was in hospital at the time he didn't bother to tell me they were going on holiday. He didn't consult me about the school they went to. He didn't tell me anything.

Maintaining contact with friends and family may be difficult, particularly if the woman or lesbian's problems have been disturbing to them, or if she is removed from them through protracted periods in hospitals or sheltered living situations. Professionals need actively to help women and lesbians keep in touch with their social networks. This will involve making available welcoming visiting arrangements, childcare and help with parenting. Advocacy in childcare proceedings may also be needed, as well as residential and day facilities that can accommodate mothers with their children.

Choice

Many talked about the importance of choice:

> Being able to choose what I do, where I go, without being told and to get help to do the things I want to do. That's what's important.

Providing a choice means letting women and lesbians decide what sort of treatments they want, ensuring access to services twenty-four hours a day, providing both domiciliary and non-domiciliary services, and facilitating engagement in non-segregated work, social activities and accommodation within relevant communities.

Two common practices deny real choice. First, people should not be helped and supported *only* if they make what professionals see as the 'right' choice. Second, one form of help should not be contingent upon another: for example, accepting medication should not be a condition of obtaining sheltered housing or having a support worker call for a chat.

Access to someone who listens

There was great concern about having access to someone to talk to, and about the quality of these contacts when available. Many complained that they were often disbelieved:

> Not believing that I really feel, see or hear things that trouble me – that's what really makes me lonely. Staff say things like 'it's in your imagination', 'of course no-one is talking in your head and at your ears', 'it's just not happening'. Well all I can say is 'yes it is happening, more's the pity' and 'yes it is difficult', but they don't understand.

There was general agreement about the importance of developing a relationship with someone who understood:

> It's having someone who listens, who understands. It's listening and being concerned. My world's different from yours, but we get close. We talk well. You really listen, you really want to know. We've got a relationship.

You share something of yourself with me, almost no-one else does. They think I'm mad and don't listen, or tell me to 'pull myself together'.

Recognising diverse communities and aspirations

The aspirations of the women and lesbians spanned the normal range: many talked about jobs they wanted, wishing to improve their education, wanting a nice house, money, friends, children or holidays, or to be able to go to pubs and clubs they once knew. They also spoke of difficulties in doing these things: lack of money, having no-one to go with, feeling too tired because of medication, not knowing how to get started, and often feeling 'odd' or 'different' and not knowing how to explain mental health problems:

> Last time I went to a pub with a friend this man started chatting me up at the bar and bought me a drink. Eventually, he asked me where I lived and I said I was in hospital because I'd been a bit depressed lately. He went off saying he was going to the toilet, but he never came back.

This range of aspirations needs to be understood, and services should assist in achieving them, rather than deeming them 'unrealistic' (see some of the 'strengths' approaches advocated, for example, by Rapp and Chamberlain (1985)).

Community support services must also recognise that women with serious mental health problems are a diverse group. The different cultures and communities they come from must be explicitly understood: lesbian cultures and communities as well as those of race and class. The different ways in which cognitive and emotional difficulties are understood and can be minimised in these different settings must be explored. Supports must be provided to ensure access to relationships, activities and facilities within these communities.

Longevity of problems

Community services must understand that disabilities related to serious mental health problems may go on for a very long time: time-limited help of any kind denies this reality and therefore the help that such women and lesbians need. Demanding 'throughput' or 'movement' is destructive for those who fail to achieve the targets set ('if your problems go on they just don't want to know').

Asylum

The concept of asylum continues to be important in a world in which normality is defined by men in the interests of men: socially disabled women and lesbians need respite from these expectations. Partial asylum, perhaps in the form of a women's group or someone to listen, is sometimes enough. At other times a more total form of asylum may be necessary, not in the form of a psychiatric hospital, but what Judi Chamberlin (1977) has called 'true asylums':

> Places to which people can retreat to deal with the pain of their existence ... These asylums would not simply be more humane mental hospitals, they would be true alternatives to the present mental hospital system – voluntary, small, responsive to their own communities and their own residents.

WITH RESPECT TO LESBIANS

The concerns discussed so far are of general importance for lesbians and women who have severe and long-term mental health problems. However, certain needs and certain problems in obtaining appropriate help apply particularly to lesbians, and the philosophies of community care and normalisation may have especially pernicious effects for them. Even more than for heterosexual women, the social disabilities lesbians experience will be exacerbated by the social world in which they live: they are excluded, abused and pathologised simply because of their lesbian identities, and experience the doubly oppressive effects of both sexist and heterosexist assumptions and prescriptions.

These difficulties are compounded by the anti-lesbianism that is rife within mental health services. This can be quite subtle and has various forms. Four broad types can be discerned (Falco, 1991).

First, many mental health professionals still believe that lesbians are by definition unhealthy, immature, or acting out. In the recent past, lesbianism was considered inherently pathological: in many respects this is still with us. Enough lesbians have experienced therapists who have endeavoured to 'cure' their lesbianism to make them singularly suspicious of mental health services. Two of the UK's leading psychoanalytic training institutions will, to this day, not train lesbian and gay male therapists, and some continue to use lesbianism as an index of disturbance. When psychologists were given hypothetical case histories and asked to rate subjects for severity of problems, likelihood of recovery, and so forth, people were judged as more severely disturbed when labelled 'gay' (Kitzinger, 1990). Although less frequent than in former times, some professionals still use the position of power that they have over clients in an explicitly anti-lesbian manner, by trying to assist the lesbian to resolve the supposed difficulties that lead to her lesbianism.

Second, there is the 'don't worry, you're not a lesbian' response – the professional says that a client need not be concerned, she is not a lesbian because she has had relationships with men in the past, or has never had sex with a man (so how could she possibly know), or only thinks that she is a lesbian because she has had bad experiences with men, or because she was sexually abused as a child, or because she is still young and all young women have 'crushes' on other women. . . This assumes that heterosexuality is by definition the preferred option: the woman is thus prevented from exploring her lesbian identity and what this might mean. By 'reassuring' a client that she is not really lesbian, the mental health professional purports to know the client better than she knows herself and abuses professional power in an anti-lesbian way.

A third variant of anti-lesbianism is the 'inadequate' response: the professional avoids the client's lesbianism, thus silencing her about her lesbianism and ignoring the specific stresses and dynamics of her world. There is rarely any consideration that some service recipients may be lesbians: even purportedly feminist texts (e.g. Mowbray *et al.*, 1985) do not mention lesbians' needs and focus on primarily heterosexual women's concerns about (heterosexual) sex education, birth control and motherhood. Professionals very often fail to ascertain whether their client is lesbian and make it impossible for her to say that she is. This is particularly true if the client does not meet the professional's notions about what 'a lesbian' looks like. If a woman is in her twenties or thirties, white, with cropped hair and wearing a boiler suit, it might occur to the professional to ask if she is lesbian. If she is in her sixties, Asian and wearing a sari, the professional is unlikely to entertain this possibility.

Most assessment interviews assume heterosexuality by enquiring about marital status, husbands, boyfriends. Given the anti-lesbianism in society, clients are unlikely to volunteer to talk about their lesbianism if the professional assumes they are heterosexual. This form of inadequate response is also common in service planning, where little attempt is made to make facilities accessible and welcoming to lesbians. In clinical research, stating the race and gender of subjects is usual, but information about whether they are heterosexual is rare: 'ten women' is assumed to mean 'ten heterosexual women'.

The final form of anti-lesbianism is the 'liberal' response: the professional or service treats the lesbian as if she were heterosexual – as if her lesbianism were irrelevant to her life except in relation to what she does in bed. Lesbianism is not simply something that one does in bed: it profoundly affects the whole of life. A lesbian's problems can only be understood in the context of the lesbian culture and experience in which they occur:

> The therapist may think 'An eating disorder is an eating disorder; I should treat it the same whether the client is heterosexual or lesbian.' This is simply not the case. The lesbian lives in a different world . . . she experiences stresses that are unique to her as a lesbian . . . These will affect her entire life functioning. (Falco, 1991)

Professionals also often fail to understand the stresses of living in an anti-lesbian world. Liberal professionals argue that it is healthy to be open about one's lesbianism: possible costs like being disowned by one's family, beaten up or losing one's job are not considered.

Thus anti-lesbianism in a number of forms prevents the provision of appropriate community services. In considering the environments provided for lesbians with severe ongoing mental health problems, one should note that lesbians working in the health service do not feel safe: most lesbian psychologists, psychiatrists, nurses and other community workers think it expedient to be 'closeted' because they fear their careers will suffer. If lesbian professionals cannot be visible, the outlook is poor for lesbian service users who are already marginalised by serious social disabilities.

In our discussions, lesbians described how services assumed that everyone was heterosexual and how the importance of their lesbianism was not recognised:

> At the day centre they were always trying to pair me up with men – I'm really not interested in men, you know, I like women, but at [the day centre] it's always about men. I left.

> When I finally got to tell her [the doctor] I was a lesbian she just said 'It doesn't matter' – well it matters to me, but I couldn't say anything after that.

TOWARDS APPROPRIATE SERVICES FOR LESBIANS

In relation to lesbians, services have a very long way to go. Lesbian clients experience all the same difficulties as anyone else, but may also have problems specific to lesbianism: decisions about being a lesbian, coming out, anti-lesbianism, custody of children, and so forth. Whatever the problems the lesbian client presents, her lesbianism is important in understanding how these might be resolved, and in designing and evaluating services that meet her needs. There are numerous ways of changing practice, many of which apply both for lesbians with transient, less disabling problems and for those who are seriously disabled.

Examining assumptions of heterosexuality

All mental health professionals should review their practice to eliminate heterosexual assumptions, and should specifically give everyone permission to say that they are a lesbian. Partners should thus be referred to as 'he or she' rather than the neutral 'they'. Professionals should ask not only about spouse and family, but about all important relationships with both men and women: whether or not these relationships are defined by the woman as 'lesbian', they remain important. It is difficult for any lesbian to disabuse someone of the wrong assumption that she is heterosexual: how to come out – when it is safe, what might be the consequences – is probably the most frequently discussed topic within lesbian culture and numerous books have been written about experiences of so doing (e.g. Penelope and Wolfe, 1989). If coming out is difficult for any lesbian, then it must be doubly difficult for someone who has social disabilities and also experiences the stigma attached to these. As well as allowing clients to say that they are lesbian, the importance of this to them needs to be recognised, and their beliefs about it must be understood. The impact of their lesbianism on all areas of their lives should be explored.

Relationships with colleagues should also be considered: one should avoid making anti-lesbian jokes and should not assume that all colleagues are heterosexual. Equal opportunities policies should refer explicitly to lesbians. Teaching needs to include specific components on working with lesbian clients: the assumption that all trainees are heterosexual also needs to be avoided.

Understanding lesbian communities and culture

I have never known a community service to provide someone with information about facilities, events and activities in the lesbian community, let alone assistance to avail themselves of these. Professionals should acquaint themselves with lesbian culture and community in general, and with local facilities, activities, groups and venues within their own areas. They should understand the diversity of lesbian culture and the different beliefs and values within it: someone who calls herself a 'political lesbian', for instance, is very different from one who identifies as a 'gay woman'. Some lesbians consider lesbianism to be a choice they have made, whilst others believe they were born this way; some lesbians identify closely with gay men, some do not; some lesbians are feminists, others are not; some lesbians have never labelled themselves lesbian at all, but all their important relationships (whether sexual or not) are with women. Care should be taken to avoid lumping together lesbians and gay men: the culture, life and experiences of lesbians and gay men are quite different.

Professionals' views of lesbians are often very narrow and homogeneous: if someone turns up wearing a badge saying 'I am a lesbian', she may just be recognised as such – otherwise, mental health practitioners and facilities almost universally assume that all of their users are heterosexual. Lesbians may be of any age, race, culture, class; may be, or have been, married; may have, or have had, sex with men; may or may not have, or want to have, children; may or may not be able-bodied.

Mental health workers need to understand the importance of 'coming out' and of 'coming out' stories: for a lesbian, her lesbian becoming – her coming out story – is at least as important as the routine history of childhood, family, schooling that clinicians typically collect.

Acknowledging anti-lesbianism

As well as informing themselves about lesbian culture, professionals must understand the extent of anti-lesbianism within society. If they fail to appreciate this, they may regard the lesbian's fears as somehow pathological. Decisions about whether and with whom to be open about one's lesbianism can be deeply problematic because of anti-lesbianism. Professionals must understand not only the benefits of visibility and openness, but also the real costs in terms of rejection, violence, job loss or poorer career prospects. Many lesbians also fear the consequences of having their lesbianism recorded in their medical casenotes.

Professionals should also appreciate the understandable suspicion with which many lesbians regard the mental health services, which, at least until recently, regarded their lesbianism as inherently pathological. Active acceptance, acknowledgement and welcoming of lesbian clients will be necessary if such fears are to be dissipated.

Making services appropriate for lesbians

Overall service planning, as well as individual interventions, needs to take lesbian users into account. Mental health facilities need to make specific attempts to be welcoming to lesbian users, for example by providing posters and leaflets. They need to ensure that lesbians are not harassed and excluded by other service users.

Ideas of normalisation are particularly perilous for lesbians users, and professionals need to examine closely whether the roles and ways of functioning towards which they encourage service recipients are really appropriate for lesbians. If community care is intended to provide support in 'normal' social roles in the communities where a person lives, what about programmes for socially disabled lesbians within lesbian communities? Professionals need to take the social networks, the ties with partners, children and friends of lesbians as seriously as those of heterosexual women, and must provide explicit help in maintaining their social networks.

As in heterosexual communities, workers should provide support to ensure that lesbian clients can gain access to these facilities and activities within their communities, and should liaise with such agencies to facilitate this access. Lonely and isolated lesbians often need therapy less than they need contacts with other lesbians. Clinicians may do most good for clients by acting as a source of information about resources in the local lesbian community and helping them to access these.

CONCLUSION

For women and lesbians experiencing severe ongoing mental health problems, care in the community has now largely replaced institutional incarceration. However, community care also has problematic and oppressive aspects. Community facilities and treatment programmes aim to increase lesbians' and women's ability to conform with 'normal' social roles. However, in a sexist and heterosexist world, normality is defined by men for men. For lesbians, the oppressiveness of many programmes is increased by the anti-lesbianism that pervades the mental health services. This may take the form of overt dismissal of lesbianism as pathological, but there are also subtler forms, such as ignoring the possibility that some service users are lesbian, or not acknowledging that the communities and cultures of lesbians are any different from those of heterosexual women. Various ways of starting to improve practice in community mental health services have been proposed in this chapter, and some major principles for such improvements have been identified. The views of recipients of mental health services need to be heard, understood and acted upon, and professionals and service planners need to understand and take into account the diversity of aspirations, experiences, cultures and communities of these women and lesbians. With respect to lesbians, all mental health professionals and service planners need to examine their practice closely, to work to eliminate the many current manifestations of anti-lesbianism and to base their practice on a knowledge of lesbian cultures and communities. If these principles can be implemented, forms of practice may develop which, rather than trying to alter individuals to fit into particular social roles not of their own choosing, are based on the idea of rendering communities accessible to socially disabled lesbians and women.

CROSS-REFERENCES WITHIN THIS BOOK

Chapter 15   The user's perspective: our experiences and our recommendations
Chapter 17   Campaigning for change

REFERENCES

Bachrach, L.L. (1985) 'Chronically mentally ill women: emergence and legitimation of programme issues', *Hospital and Community Psychiatry* 36: 1063–1069.
Chamberlin, J. (1977) *On our own*, London: MIND Publications (1988 edition).
Chesler, P. (1972) *Women and madness*, New York: Avon Books.
Falco, K.L. (1991) *Psychotherapy with lesbian clients: theory into practice*, New York: Brunner/Mazel.
Goering, P., Cochrane, J., Potasnik, H., Wyslenski, D. and Lancee, W. (1988) 'Women and work: after psychiatric hospitalisation', in L.L. Bachrach and C.C. Nadelson (eds), *Treating chronically mentally ill women*, Washington DC: American Psychiatric Press.
Johnstone, L. (1989) *Users and abusers of psychiatry: a critical look at traditional psychiatric practice*, London: Routledge.
Kitzinger, C. (1990) 'Heterosexism in psychology', *The Psychologist* (September): 391–392.

Kitzinger, C. and Perkins, R. (1993) *Changing our minds: lesbian feminism and psychology*, London: Onlywomen Press.

Mowbray, C.T., Lanir, S. and Hulce, M. (eds) (1985) *Women and mental health*, New York: Harrington Park Press.

Penelope, J. and Wolfe, S.J. (1989) *The original coming out stories*, revised edition, Freedom CA: Crossing Press.

Perkins, R.E. and Dilks, S. (1992) 'Worlds apart: working with severely socially disabled people', *Journal of Mental Health* 1: 3–17.

Perkins, R.E. and Kitzinger, C. (1993) 'Madness, social disability and access', *Lesbian Ethics*, 5 (1) : 96–107.

Perkins, R.E. and Rowland, L. (1990) 'Sex differences in service usage in long-term psychiatric care: are women adequately served?', *British Journal of Psychiatry* 158 (suppl. 10): 75–79.

Rapp, C.A. and Chamberlain, R. (1985) 'Case management services to the chronically mentally ill', *Social Work* 30 (5): 417–422.

Test, M.A. and Berlin, S.B. (1981) 'Issues of concern to chronically mentally ill women', *Professional Psychology* 12: 136–145.

Wittig, M. (1981) 'One is not born a woman', reprinted in M. Wittig (1992) *The straight mind*, London: Harvester Wheatsheaf.

Wolfensberger, W. (1970) 'The principle of normalisation and its implications to psychiatric services', *American Journal of Psychiatry*, 127: 291–297.

Wolfensberger, W. (1983) 'Social role valorisation: a proposed new term for the principle of normalisation', *Mental Retardation* 21: 234–239.

Chapter 8

Women as carers of the severely mentally ill

EDITORS' INTRODUCTION

An aspect of the development of community care policy which has particular importance for women is the increasing reliance on informal carers, who are very often women, for many components of community care for the mentally ill. It has been suggested that an important disadvantage of community psychiatry may be the extensive and often unmeasured demands made on these unpaid carers. In this chapter, this question is examined from two complementary perspectives. In the first part of the chapter, Gillian Parker outlines developments in mental health policy and the ways in which expectations about informal care and the position of informal carers have altered. She also discusses the implications for people with mental health problems of being reliant on informal care. In the second section, Marcia Scazufca and Elizabeth Kuipers describe the characteristics of women carers of the seriously mentally ill, and the psychological and social effects of providing care. Finally, they outline some clinical strategies for alleviating the burden on carers.

Carers and the development of community mental health policy

Gillian Parker

The families and friends of people with mental health problems hold a curious position in current social policy, being seen by some practitioners, at least, as part of the 'problem' (i.e. as being in some way responsible for their relative's condition), while policy makers increasingly regard them as the *solution* to the 'problem' of providing care in the community. In this chapter, I review the recent history of community care policy for people with mental health problems and examine the role of families and friends (carers) within this.

COMMUNITY CARE POLICY

Current policy for people with mental health problems cannot be understood fully without some knowledge of its history, particularly the growth of institutional care. The major development of institutions in Britain took place from the 1840s. At the end of the eighteenth century, there were perhaps 2,000 inmates in licensed madhouses and asylums and a further 3,000 in workhouses; by the end of the nineteenth century there were 100,000 inmates in public asylums alone, and perhaps another 25,000 to 30,000 people classed as mentally infirm in Poor Law institutions or institutions other than asylums. Growth continued and by the 1950s there were almost 148,000 people in mental hospitals.

The development of the 'welfare state' at the end of World War II had little impact on services for people with mental health problems. Neither local authorities nor the health service were required to provide community-based facilities, and there was no commitment to reducing levels of institutional care. The only real shift brought about by the post-war changes was the transfer of asylums into the health service.

Voluntary-sector campaigning led to the establishment of a Royal Commission on Mental Illness and Mental Deficiency. The 1957 Report of the Commission recommended a shift from hospital towards community-based care and a *duty* for local authorities to provide community services. Unfortunately, this duty was not implemented in the subsequent legislation (the 1959 Mental Health Act).

Research into the quality of accommodation and treatment provided in institutional settings and a series of public outcries about conditions in long-stay hospitals (see Brown, 1980) further strengthened arguments against institutional care and influenced the direction of policy for people with mental health problems in the 1960s.

Long-term goals in the 1962 Hospital Plan for England and Wales included a reduction in hospital beds for mental illness by almost a half, with services increasingly provided through short-stay units in district general hospitals. The plan was complementary to the expected development of services for 'prevention and care in the community' with a consequent adjustment of bed ratios.

The equivalent ten-year plan for health and welfare services, subtitled 'the development of community care', followed in 1963. Many service developments were outlined under accommodation, domiciliary support, training and occupation, rehabilitation and recreation. However, this vision never materialised, although the (very) gradual run-down of mental illness hospitals did begin. While there were some increases in the levels of community-based services, none of the targets set for the provision of domiciliary services was achieved and there was no large-scale transfer of resources from institutional to community care (Walker, 1982).

The impetus to community-based care since 1957 has been based on the assumption that it is better for people to live outside large-scale, segregated institutions and that this accords with their wishes and those of their families and friends. From the mid-1970s onwards, however, as Britain was experiencing economic change as a result of the oil crisis, a new imperative entered the policy debate: that of cost. The 1975 White Paper on mental illness highlighted the slow development of services in the community and argued for an accelerated shift of resources from hospital care. The Paper also recognised, perhaps for the first time in a policy document of this sort, the role of families. However, this appeared to have as much to do with economic anxieties as it did with concern for family members. The Paper recognised the demands on families and stressed the need to support them. However, it also argued that statutory services could not provide the whole answer; the 'community' – family, relatives and the public at large – also had its role to play.

Despite its relatively long history, the general public probably associates community care policy with the 1989 White Paper, 'Caring for People' and the subsequent 1990 National Health Service and Community Care Act. The 1989 White Paper made specific recommendations for the main components of locally based services for people with mental health problems. These were that they should be primarily community-based, but with adequate provision for assessment and treatment on a short-term, in-patient basis, including provision for 'asylum' for those requiring longer term care; and that there should be sufficient *residential* places in the community, along with a range of day and respite services, and co-ordination between health and social services.

The House of Commons Social Services Committee (1990) responded to 'Caring for People' by examining services for people with a mental illness. It commented on the slow development of community-based services while the number of hospital beds was falling. It also pointed out that the bulk of expenditure was still on in-patient services. The Committee welcomed the planned introduction of a specific grant for mental illness, as outlined in the White Paper. However, it pointed out that if, as suggested, the grant was restricted to people who had contact with specialist psychiatric services, 'the much larger group of people with a mental illness' who did not use such services would be 'unlikely to fare well in the competition for scarce local authority resources' (para. 56). The impact that this would have on relatives and friends was also highlighted.

Since this report, the NHS and Community Care Act has gradually been implemented. Its impact for people with mental health problems remains to be evaluated fully. There has been much public concern about the care of people who are potentially a danger to themselves or to others, and arguments continue about whether community care policy is in some sense responsible for certain well-publicised incidents. There is a danger that this attention, and the policy reaction to it, will delay yet again improvements to services for the much greater numbers of people with mental health problems who are no danger to anyone and whose needs (and those of their families and friends who support them) can be met successfully in the community.

COMMUNITY CARE AND FAMILIES

In addition to the economic considerations that entered policy in the 1970s, the 1980s saw a new emphasis on the roles and responsibilities of the 'community'. This can be traced back to the 1981 White Paper 'Growing Older', which acknowledged the 'immense contribution' of families, friends and neighbours but declared that, 'Care *in* the community must increasingly mean care *by* the community' (para. 1.9). Public authorities simply would 'not command the resources to deal with it alone' (para. 1.11).

This change was driven not just by concern about resources; it signalled an ideological shift about the balance of state and individual responsibility which has now been applied to all groups. The emphasis has changed from statutory provision (seen as expensive) to informal or voluntary provision (seen as inexpensive or even free) as a means of implementing community care. The 'first task of publicly provided services' has thus become 'to support and where possible strengthen' informal networks (Griffiths, 1988, para. 3.2).

For the families of people with mental health problems, this is a curious change. While 'carers' are increasingly referred to in Department of Health documents, this description is infrequently applied to the families and friends of those with mental health problems.

There is a relative lack of research on carers of people with mental health problems compared to other carers, and when research has been carried out its orientation has been different from that on other carers (Perring *et al.*, 1990).

First, the tradition of research in mental health has been to concentrate on the individual concerned, looking to families usually only for evidence of 'causality' or, at least, some link with onset, prognosis and progress. As a result, professionals, particularly those from the health service, can be equivocal about their relationship to families (Twigg and Atkin, 1994).

This is related to a second factor, the nature of the mental health problem. Most searching for 'causes' in families has been in relation to psychoses, particularly schizophrenia. Despite this, it seems that with psychotic illnesses professionals are more likely to take relatives into account and to apply the model of caring derived from other client groups. With neuroses, the issues are less clear cut; the social circumstances of the patient, including family and marital relationships, are often bound up with the condition, so that the appropriateness of using the term 'carer' becomes questionable (Twigg and Atkin, 1994). Further, the nature of the relationship between 'carer' and patient is not independent of the condition. Thus the carers of people with schizophrenia are likely to be parents, while those of people with, say, depression are more likely to be spouses. This influences how the situation is perceived by both carers and service providers. Consequently, those caring for people with neurotic conditions may not be seen (or see themselves) as carers at all; they thus fail to gain access to intervention or support in their own right. By contrast, the parents (usually) of people with schizophrenia may be seen and see themselves as carers, but this may actually bring them into conflict with practitioners whose objectives for their offspring may be at odds with their own (Twigg and Atkin, 1994).

This situation would not be particularly important if supporting a person with a mental health problem had no impact on those doing it. What little research there is which addresses this issue directly suggests that this is far from the case.

THE IMPACT OF CARING FOR PEOPLE WITH MENTAL HEALTH PROBLEMS

The tasks that informal carers carry out can be summarised as personal care, physical care, practical help and 'other' help, such as keeping an eye on someone or taking them out. For those who live with people with mental health problems, caring tends to involve fewer of the 'hands on' elements but rather being responsible for and sharing their life with someone else (Twigg and Atkin, 1994).

The existing literature on the impact of caring for people with mental health problems will be summarised only briefly here: it has been reviewed by Perring *et al.* (1990), and is discussed further by Marcia Scazufca and Elizabeth Kuipers in the next section. Practical aspects of caring for this group may include helping with financial problems and with domestic chores. Carers may also have to cope with difficult or unusual behaviour both within the home and outside. Mediating between the mentally ill person and a largely unsympathetic or uncomprehending outside world is one particularly stressful task that carers take on. They also often take on new roles and responsibilities within the family, particularly if they are looking after a spouse.

Social lives often suffer, with long-term consequences for general social support. Evidence about effects on employment is equivocal, with some studies reporting considerable impact while others report little. However, when carers *are* in paid work, performance may be reduced, either through strain and worry or through having to take time off. The financial effects of caring seem more clearly demonstrated, with over a third of households reporting adverse effects, although the degree of impact will vary with household composition.

The effect of caring on physical health is complicated by the inter-relationships between age, sex and ill health (Parker, 1990). Physical ill health has been identified in some studies of those caring for people with mental health problems, but as Perring *et al.* (1990) point out, 'many people diagnosed as mentally ill are cared for by their parents', thus possibly confounding the effects of age and caring.

As in the general literature on caring, there is more reliable evidence that caring for a person with mental health problems is associated with poor psychological status in the carer. The problems of cause and effect, however, are more problematic here; while it is unlikely that a carer's psychological state will have precipitated *physical* impairment in the person being cared for, such causal relationships cannot be entirely ruled out where impaired mental health is involved.

THE VARIETY OF CARING EXPERIENCES

Although carers are now more visible to professionals and policy makers than previously, there is a tendency to perceive them as an undifferentiated group, with similar experiences, problems and concerns. Most carers find their lives restricted because of their responsibilities. However, the ways in which these are experienced vary considerably, depending on the relationship to the person being cared for, the carer's age, gender, family, social and economic circumstances, and, to a degree, the nature of the condition of the person they assist.

Much research on informal care in the UK has been committed to exposing the 'double equation' of community care (Finch and Groves, 1980). That is, that care in the community means care by the family, care by the family means care by women and that, therefore, care in the community means care by women. However, carers of people with mental health problems (other than dementia) have been relatively neglected within this body of research. As a result, as we see in the next section of this chapter, it is difficult to tease out the differential impact that caring for people with mental health problems might have on women.

As with other groups, women are more likely than men to be caring, but this will be influenced by age of onset. For people with schizophrenia, for example, where onset may be in young adulthood, parents often take on caring responsibilities and the bulk of these tends to fall to mothers rather than fathers. For people with neuroses the picture is less clear; if onset is after marriage, partners are likely to become 'carers' with a more equal distribution of responsibility between men and women. With dementia, who becomes a carer will be influenced both by the marital status of the person who needs care and by their living circumstances. Thus, partners tend to be the main carers of people with dementia until death or ill health of the carer intervenes. Offspring – most often daughters – become involved where the person with dementia is already widowed or where they share a household.

These patterns should influence the type of support that might be offered to carers, but also the proper balance between meeting the needs of the carer and those of the person being cared for. This latter issue takes us into the heart of a debate that has major implications in the field of mental health.

The acknowledged reliance on informal carers as the main deliverers of community care policy has changed perceptions about those 'on the receiving end' in ways that may not be helpful in the longer term. Younger disabled adults and people with mental health problems argue that while they may need assistance in their daily living, they do not need 'care'. Further, when they do need assistance, they do not wish to be forced to rely on their families, friends and neighbours. Yet the new community care arrangements open up the possibility of *informal* carers becoming a much more *formalised* part of the 'care packages' put together to support disabled and older people (Parker, 1991).

From a position where they were all-but-ignored in community care policy, carers have almost taken centre stage (Parker, 1994). This does not necessarily mean that they are receiving any more support than they might have done in the past, but it does mean that issues about whose needs should have preference in planning and delivering services have been exposed in a way that they were not previously.

Research on caring has tended to concentrate on the experiences of the 'givers' of care rather than the 'receivers'. Evidence about stresses that might result from being on the 'receiving' end of informal care is thus difficult to come by. Indeed, the *possibility* that relying on one's family and friends to provide domestic or personal care may create stress is disguised by the assumption that community is good, home is better, and 'mother' (or at least family) is best.

Anxieties about the inadequacies of care and imbalances of power that can occur in institutional settings may have blinded us to similar issues that can arise in the private household. Disabled people have said this themselves for some time. Brisenden, for example, argued that where there are no options other than dependence on a relative or partner, then this can be

> the most exploitative of all forms of so-called care delivered in our society today for it exploits both the carer and the person receiving care. It ruins relationships between people and results in thwarted life opportunities on both sides of the caring equation.
>
> (Brisenden, 1989, cited by Morris, 1991: 164)

Care-receiving can cause imbalance in relationships by altering the existing patterns of reciprocity, thus making the older or disabled person even more vulnerable (Morris, 1991). Women, who experience such imbalances as part of their lives in any circumstances, can thus be *further* disadvantaged when needing 'care' from others.

These issues may be even more difficult in the mental health field where interpretations of what is in the best interests of the person with mental health problems are highly contested. Recent debate about long-stay provision between those who represent people with mental health problems and those who represent their families highlights this tension.

Women's beliefs about their 'deservingness' of support, whether they are people with mental health problems or carers may also be important. This has an impact in two ways. First, women with mental health problems may feel guilty about receiving support from their families, particularly their husbands, because this reverses the conventional direction of give and take. Consequently, they may agree to service interventions which they dislike – for example, respite care away from their homes – because they feel they *should* give their families a break (Parker, 1993). Second, women who are carers may be reluctant to accept support from formal sources because, again, this transgresses 'normal' areas of responsibility. Women feel themselves responsible for the well-being of their families and accepting service support may be perceived as failure. This is particularly the case where the support that is on offer is a 'substitute' for usual female domestic labour, such as cooking or cleaning. What women caring for men, particularly their husbands, may want is a substitute for *his* usual domestic labour (decorating, household repairs, car maintenance) rather than their own.

In contrast, men with mental health problems may see women in their families, particularly wives, as the most appropriate sources of support and therefore resist any attempt to enrol support from formal sources. At the same time, men who are carers may be more likely to claim a 'right' to support and thus make demands on services more than do women (Parker, 1993).

The issues of gender and caring/disability thus interact in complex ways that make it difficult to argue that *all* carers or *all* disabled people are disadvantaged. What does seem likely is that, regardless of whether they are carers or people with mental health problems, women are less likely to assert their needs.

CONCLUSIONS

The changed balance between public and private responsibility for community care changes the role of the state from one where it supports disabled and older people through the provision of services directly to them, to one where it encourages informal sources of assistance to substitute for the formal. This has resulted in a higher profile for (and greater expectations of) informal carers. However, this is not without its dangers. The implications for mental health of the increased expectations are substantial. The stress experienced by carers, as a result of providing informal care, may be matched by that of those obliged to be the 'recipients' of their activity.

As Croft (1986: 34) has pointed out, there is a danger that current community care policies will increase 'divisions and conflicts of interest between [carers and disabled people] instead of encouraging alliances and solidarity'. Energy which could be put into challenging the effects of community care policies might, instead, be diverted into a conflict between disabled people and carers.

The new community care arrangements and the policy documents which preceded them emphasise a system which is needs-led rather than service-led – where identified needs determine the shape of service provision, rather than the other way around. If this truly became the guiding principle behind the changes, much of the potential tension between people with mental health problems and carers could be resolved. However, given the context within which the new arrangements have been introduced, with restricted resources and a reliance on informal networks to deliver the majority of 'community care', it is difficult to see how this principle can be applied to all. There is a danger, therefore, that an even greater wedge will be driven between people with mental health problems and their families and friends.

Well-balanced support for people with mental health problems and those who support them on an informal basis must recognise rights on both sides. To do this poses a considerable challenge to professionals and service providers.

REFERENCES

Brown, J. (1980) 'The Normansfield Inquiry', in M. Brown and S. Baldwin (eds), *The yearbook of social policy 1978*, London: Routledge and Kegan Paul.

Croft, S. (1986) 'Women, caring and the recasting of need – a feminist reappraisal', *Critical Social Policy* 6 (1):23–39.

Department of Health and Social Security (DHSS) (1975) *Better services for the mentally ill*, Cmnd 6233, London: HMSO.

—— (1981) *Growing older*, Cmnd 8173, London: HMSO.

—— (1989) *Caring for people: community care in the next decade and beyond*, Cm 849, London: HMSO.

Finch, J. and Groves, D. (1980) 'Community care and the family: a case for equal opportunities?', *Journal of Social Policy* 9 (4): 487–514.

Griffiths, R. (1988) *An agenda for action on community care*, London: HMSO.

House of Commons Social Services Committee (1990) *Community care: services for people with a mental handicap and people with a mental illness*, London: HMSO.

Ministry of Health (1957) *Report of the Royal Commission on Mental Illness and Mental Deficiency*, Cmnd 169, London: HMSO.

—— (1962) *A hospital plan for England and Wales*, Cmnd 1604, London: HMSO.

—— (1963) *Health and welfare: the development of community care*, Cmnd 1973, London: HMSO.

Morris, J. (1991) *Pride against prejudice: transforming attitudes to disability*, London: The Women's Press.

Parker, G. (1990) *With due care and attention: a review of research on informal care*, 2nd edition, London: Family Policy Studies Centre.

—— (1991) 'Whose care? Whose costs? Whose benefit? A critical review of research on case management and informal care', *Ageing and Society* 10: 459–467.

—— (1993) *With this body: caring and disability in marriage*, Buckingham: Open University Press.

—— (1994) *Where next for research on carers?*, Leicester: University of Leicester, Nuffield Community Care Studies Unit.

Perring, C., Twigg, J. and Atkin, K. (1990) *Families caring for people diagnosed as mentally ill: the literature re-examined*, London: HMSO.

Twigg, J. and Atkin, K. (1994) *Carers perceived: policy and practice in informal care*, Buckingham: Open University Press.

Walker, A. (1982) 'The meaning and social division of community care', in A. Walker (ed.), *Community care: the family, the state and social policy*, Oxford: Basil Blackwell and Martin Robertson.

The impact on women of caring for the mentally ill

Marcia Scazufca and Elizabeth Kuipers

As Gillian Parker describes in the section above, the responsibility of caring for the severely mentally ill has been gradually shifting since the 1950s to the community. The families of patients discharged to the community have become their major caregivers, and sometimes their only resource. Many people with severe mental illnesses are single, so that blood relatives are central to their care in the community. Mothers, sisters and daughters most often function as the carers of mentally ill patients at home. For this reason, Thurer (1993) considered deinstitutionalisation a women's issue. However, there has been no focus on women's experiences and views as carers, and there is remarkably little information on any particular difficulties they may experience or needs they may have.

In this section, we review existing studies on carers, including our own, and outline the findings of these studies about women's role in providing informal care and about gender differences in the experience of caring. We then discuss gaps in current understanding of women's experiences of caring for the mentally ill, and how these might begin to be filled. Finally, we discuss ways in which service planners and providers may better take into account the needs of carers.

Caring tasks may be divided into three main categories: the practical tasks performed by carers, coping with difficult behaviour, and new roles and responsibilities carers assume (Perring *et al.*, 1990). The impact of the patient's behaviour upon his/her family, household and significant others has been called the 'burden of care' by mental health professionals.

The effect that people suffering from mental illnesses and their relatives have on each other's lives has been the impetus behind many studies. In the early 1950s studies were set up to determine the feasibility of discharging patients into the community; later, they were aimed at refining the concept of caregiving, its content and its underlying structure. More recently, their objective has been to measure burden as an outcome variable in programme evaluations.

BACKGROUND: EARLY STUDIES ON 'BURDEN OF CARE'

Early investigators found that most families of schizophrenic patients discharged from London hospitals in 1959 did not complain about patients coming home (Wing *et al.*, 1964). They concluded that the policy of early discharge of patients in the absence of effective community services 'was based to a large degree on relatives' willingness to attempt the role of nurse and to put up with considerable discomfort and distress'. Grad and Sainsbury (1968) emphasised the serious hardship suffered by families before they first sought help, and the importance of supplementing clinical care in the community with adequate social support to the family.

In these early studies, the nature of stresses on carers began to be identified. Hoenig and Hamilton (1965) distinguished 'objective burden', in the form of disruptions to household life, from 'subjective burden' consisting of personal and emotional feelings of burden. In a four-year follow-up study, they found that both objective and subjective burden increased as the patient's duration of illness became longer. Creer and Wing (1975) described two types of behaviour commonly identified by families as difficult to cope with. The first group were behaviours associated with social withdrawal (little interaction, slowness, lack of conversation, few leisure interests, and self-neglect), whilst the second group were disturbed and socially embarrassing behaviours (restlessness, odd ideas such as delusions and hallucinations, and talking and laughing to themselves).

These studies did not generally discuss whether women were particularly likely to be the main caregivers, or whether the experience and burden of caring were affected by the carer's gender and relationship with the patient. However, in one study, the mother or wife of the patient was almost always the person interviewed by researchers (Wing *et al.*, 1964), whilst in another, mothers considered themselves virtually the patient's only social contact (Creer and Wing, 1975).

MORE RECENT STUDIES

Some more recent studies have investigated particular groups, such as elderly carers or carers of demented patients, or have studied particular situations, comparing, for example, effects on relatives of living and not living with patients.

In middle age, people with schizophrenia may be dependent on elderly carers, often female. Stevens (1972) reported that 20 of a group of 29 'middle-aged' schizophrenic patients were dependent on mothers, sometimes widowed. Disadvantages reported for this situation include lack of communication, financial problems and worry about what would happen to the patient after their relative's death. However, advantages have also been reported, including prevention of social isolation through the company and support received from the patient, and help in household tasks, which becomes more necessary with ageing.

Depressed patients are much more likely to be living with a partner than are patients with schizophrenia. Wives of depressed patients tend to be more affected than husbands, especially if they have to become the chief earner. They also have fewer social contacts. Many wives feel stressed when they have to take over roles that are traditionally male (Fadden *et al.*, 1987).

Approximately 70 per cent to 80 per cent of patients suffering from Alzheimer's disease are cared for by women (Morris *et al.*, 1991). In a review of studies concerning gender differences in carers of dementia sufferers, Morris *et al.* (1991) found that strain is higher in women carers. Services such as home help, meals on wheels, rehabilitation/assessment and long-term care, are often disproportionately received by male carers.

Carers of people suffering from a mental illness have to cope with behaviour not usually present in other situations. Some of the coping strategies depend on the sex of the carer. Among carers of demented patients, women generally feel less confident in coping with the role of carer, may have a more intimate relationship with their demented relative, and take longer than men to distance themselves emotionally from the patient (Morris *et al.*, 1991). In a study by Namyslowska (1986) of families with a schizophrenic spouse, wives were more informed about their partner's illness than were husbands (diagnosis, name of medication, side effect of medication), and more often initiated looking for additional information, whilst husbands were more inclined to deny their partners' illness. Goldstein and Kreisman (1988) suggested that differences in gender influence how people enter or remain in treatment. Sons may be sent to hospital more often than daughters.

Carpentier *et al.* (1992) compared burden of care, psychological distress, and needs for services of the families of young patients with schizophrenia living with the patient, and families where the patient was living in other accommodation. The great majority of key relatives interviewed were women. They found that living apart from the patient is not associated with lower levels of burden of care and emotional distress, and indeed relatives who did not live with patients reported a greater need for services. This study thus suggests that it is important to take seriously the needs of carers who live apart from patients as well as those in the same household. Overall, the psychological distress in carers was higher than that found in a survey of Quebec's general population. Single women appeared particularly affected: they expressed greater needs for services and a feeling of greater burden than women carers living with their husbands.

FAMILY ENVIRONMENT AND BURDEN OF CARE

The literature outlined above focuses on the emotional and practical effects on carers of their situation. Another major concern in recent literature has been the effects on the mentally ill of the emotional atmosphere of their homes. 'Expressed Emotion' (EE), has been found to be a robust predictor of relapse in schizophrenia (Vaughn and Leff, 1976). EE may be rated from the 'Camberwell Family Interview': relatives are categorised as high or low on EE, depending on the number of critical comments they make, and the levels of emotional involvement and hostility they show during the interview.

Most studies on EE involve parents of patients with schizophrenia and spouses of depressed patients. Parents were more frequently mothers, and they could be living with spouses, other adults or alone with their offspring (Brown *et al.*, 1962; Vaughn and Leff, 1976). Although most relatives in EE studies have been women, none of the papers included in extensive reviews (Kuipers and Bebbington, 1988; Kavanagh, 1992) were set up specifically to investigate gender differences in carers' EE and in the characteristics and experiences associated with 'high EE'.

One of the consequences of the value of the EE measure for predicting relapse has been the proliferation of studies of psychosocial intervention with families where one member suffered from schizophrenia. These interventions were aimed at strengthening the coping capacities of families and patients and modifying the stressful climate of the family. The aim was also to reduce the likelihood of relapse, improve the patient's level of functioning and the quality of life for all family members (Lam, 1991). These interventions have not been aimed specifically at women carers, nor do they always take into account the particular social pressures that may affect their responses to the caring task. For example, women may have to care for more than one family member, and may also be working: the contribution made by role overload to women carers' emotional states may need to be considered in planning interventions.

OUR STUDY

In 1992 and 1993, we surveyed 67 relatives of 50 patients suffering from schizophrenia to investigate the relationship between burden of care and expressed emotion (EE). Our results provide an up-to-date description of the characteristics of a group of informal carers, and allow us to look for gender differences in the impact of care. Our interview included assessment of EE, objective and subjective burden, and relatives' perception of patients' symptoms and social functioning. We also assessed relatives' emotional distress.

Relatives who were living with patients, or were in contact with them at least once per week were included. When more than one relative of the same patient was interviewed, the carer who spent most time with the patient and felt most responsible for him/her was considered the primary carer. Of the 67 relatives identified, 46 were women, of whom 34 were mothers and 10 were sisters. Women were more likely to be considered primary caregivers: 83 per cent of the women interviewed were identified as the primary caregiver, compared with 57 per cent of the men, a statistically significant difference. Mothers were also primary caregivers more often than fathers. Among women primary carers, 21 (56 per cent) were in regular employment outside the home, compared with 5 (41 per cent) of the men who were primary caregivers.

Mothers were much more frequently living without partners than were fathers (71 per cent and 17 per cent, respectively). Among the relatives who were living with the patients, there were 18 mothers without partners, but no fathers without partners. Of the 50 relatives considered primary carers, 27 women were living with the patient, of whom 9 were living alone with the patient. Seven of the male primary carers lived with the patient, of whom only one was living alone with the patient, and he was the husband.

The areas of objective burden where particularly high proportions of primary carers felt affected were relationship with the patient, household affairs and social life. Outside employment and finances were less affected. Over 80 per cent reported some subjective burden in at least one of these areas. There were no differences between male and female carers in the total burden of care, in their perceptions of patients' social functioning, or in their reports of emotional distress. There were no significant gender differences in the emotional climate in the household: 58 per cent of the men and 61 per cent of the women were assessed as high EE.

The population we studied consisted of relatives of patients admitted to a psychiatric hospital in a deprived inner-city area in South London. In our study, the majority of primary carers were women, mainly mothers. Mothers seem to take responsibility for their offspring 'for life' more often than fathers. However, the burden of having someone suffering from schizophrenia at home or in a close relationship seems to be the same regardless of the sex of the carer.

Most of the women carers lived with the patient and also worked outside home, indicating that they were accumulating the roles of providing an income for the household and caring for the patient. The caring role was demonstrated not to be an easy one, since most women primary carers experienced a lot of strain. Their lives were affected mainly in the relationship they had with the patient, in the management of the household and in their social lives.

IMPLICATION FOR SERVICE PROVISION

The results of our study confirm those found in earlier papers, but the focus on women carers makes it easier to consider their needs separately. Most informal carers are still women, but they are not a homogeneous group. It is likely to be important to investigate the needs for care and support of particular sub-groups among the women who are informal carers, such as single mothers, elderly women carers, and women who occupy multiple roles, such as informal caring and work. This sort of information may provide a basis for planning a more comprehensive network of community services that fulfils the needs of these diverse groups of women carers.

The single-women parents, wives and siblings who so often have to cope alone with the external and internal demands inevitably made by the caring role may well need specifically targeted services to reduce the burden of care. The common picture of a mother caring alone for a son with schizophrenia is well known to mental health professionals. Sharing the caring experiences within a group of 'single carers' may create a more supportive environment in which they can express their worries and the problems caused by having to care alone for an ill relative.

Relatives' groups have been shown to be effective in offering some of this help and can be cost-effective in terms of staff time. They also offer increased social networks and an opportunity to discuss the negative emotional issues that caring can easily inspire (Kuipers *et al.*, 1989). Setting up a relatives' group requires staff commitment, a convenient venue with kitchen facilities, and offers of transport to maximise the numbers of relatives who might attend. Even so, not all relatives will be willing or able to come to a group and it will always be necessary to provide alternatives such as home visits to enable some relatives to receive support. The ideal core number of relatives for a viable group is between ten and fifteen people. If problems are long term then monthly meetings allow for some change to occur between sessions, and are frequent enough to offer support without being too demanding. Group leaders should aim to be facilitative and constructive, using the group's likely reserves of humour, social skill and successful coping strategies. Initially the group will focus on practical and immediate concerns, but as trust is established between members and as the similarity of problems becomes apparent, then the group will begin to deal with the wide range of emotional issues that need support. These include guilt, grief, anger, anxiety, fear and vulnerability.

The specific use of respite care for psychiatric clients and their carers is not established yet and still depends on local and voluntary initiatives. It is still not always seen as justified to offer a hospital bed or its equivalent for social rather than crisis care, and this requirement is now more likely to be funded by social services rather than health. However, the need for respite care is well documented (MacCarthy *et al.*, 1989), and if used in a planned way by services, would be likely to both reduce crises and prevent problems from escalating. If offered more readily, particularly for relatives who care alone for patients, and do not have any option other than staying with them for most of their time, then this would be likely to be perceived as direct and practical support from services. If offered in a planned way, for instance one weekend in every month, this will reduce costs, because even one emergency admission is likely to last more than a few days. The offer may not even be taken up, but its existence is an acknowledgement by services that respite is a legitimate request (Kuipers, 1993). This need is consistently underestimated by services (MacCarthy *et al.*, 1989), but might be particularly useful if targeted on single-women carers (either parents or spouses) whose own networks are likely to be reduced and whose freedom to socialise is often impaired by the caring role.

The provision of facilities such as respite care and relatives' groups may go some way towards alleviating the burden on informal carers. However, one further question that has not been discussed in this context is the changing role of women in society and the likelihood that caring for a family member will not continue to be the main role. Already in the most recent survey the majority of women carers were also in employment and thus having to balance the demands of at least two roles. While women may in future still feel pressure to be carers, this is likely to be at the cost either of other social roles or of problems with their own mental health. Most carers already have raised levels of anxiety and depression compared to the general population (Fadden *et al.*, 1987; MacCarthy *et al.*, 1989). Thus the strain of caring is already apparent and appears detrimental (Noh and Turner, 1987). In a disorder such as schizophrenia where care may well be lifelong, such dedication and sacrifice cannot be relied upon. It then becomes imperative for services to be more sensitive to these issues. Relatives need to be offered support and practical help in their own right and at an early stage, if such care is to continue. Otherwise there is a real risk of exploiting and exhausting the many female carers who currently offer such care in the community.

(See Appendix for address of the Carers National Association.)

ACKNOWLEDGEMENT

Marcia Scazufca is sponsored by the 'CNPq-Brasilia, Brazil'.

CROSS-REFERENCES WITHIN THIS BOOK

Chapter 5   Planning community mental health services for older women
Chapter 14   Women and primary care

REFERENCES

Brown, G.W., Monck, E.M., Carstairs, G.M. and Wing, J.K. (1962) 'Influence of family life on the course of schizophrenic illness', *British Journal of Preventive and Social Medicine* 16: 55–68.

Carpentier, N., Lesage, A., Goulet, J., Lalonde, P. and Renaud, M. (1992) 'Burden of care of families not living with young schizophrenic relatives', *Hospital and Community Psychiatry* 43: 38–43.

Creer, C. and Wing, J.K. (1975) 'Living with a schizophrenic patient', *British Journal of Hospital Medicine* 14: 73–82.

Fadden, G., Bebbington, P. and Kuipers, L. (1987) 'Caring and its burdens: a study of the spouses of depressed patients', *British Journal of Psychiatry* 151: 660–667.

Goldstein, J.M. and Kreisman, D. (1988) 'Gender, family and schizophrenia', *Psychological Medicine* 18: 861–872.

Grad, J. and Sainsbury, P. (1968) 'The effects that patients have on their families in a community care and a control psychiatric service – a two year follow-up', *British Journal of Psychiatry* 114: 265–278.

Hoenig, J. and Hamilton, M.W. (1965) 'Extramural care of psychiatric patients', *The Lancet* 19 June: 1322–1325.

Kavanagh, D.J. (1992) 'Recent developments in Expressed Emotion and schizophrenia', *British Journal of Psychiatry* 160: 601–620.

Kuipers, L. (1993) 'Family burden in schizophrenia: implications for services', *Social Psychiatry and Psychiatric Epidemiology* 28: 207–210.

Kuipers, L. and Bebbington, P. (1988) 'Expressed emotion research in schizophrenia: theoretical and clinical implications', *Psychological Medicine* 18: 893–909.

Kuipers, L., MacCarthy, B., Hurry, J. *et al.* (1989) 'Counselling the relatives of the long-term adult mentally ill. (ii) A low cost supportive model', *British Journal of Psychiatry* 154: 775–782.

Lam, D.H. (1991) 'Psychosocial family intervention in schizophrenia: a review of empirical studies', *Psychological Medicine* 21: 423–441.

MacCarthy, B., Lesage, A., Brewin, C.R., Brugha, T.S., Mangen, S. and Wing, J.K. (1989) 'Needs for care among the relatives of long-term users of day care', *Psychological Medicine* 19: 725–736.

Morris, R.G., Woods, R.T., Davies, K.S. and Morris, L.W. (1991) 'Gender differences in carers of dementia sufferers', *British Journal of Psychiatry* 158: 69–74.

Namyslowska, I. (1986) 'Social and emotional adaptation of the families of schizophrenic patients', *Family Systems Medicine* 4: 398–407.

Noh, S. and Turner, R.J. (1987) 'Living with psychiatric patients: implications for the mental health of family members', *Social Sciences and Medicine* 25: 263–272.

Perring, C., Twigg, J. and Atkin, K. (1990) *Families caring for people diagnosed as mentally ill: the literature re-examined*, London: HMSO.

Stevens, B.C. (1972) 'Dependence of schizophrenic patients on elderly relatives', *Psychological Medicine* 2: 17–32.

Thompson, E.H. and Doll, W. (1982) 'The burden of families coping with the mentally ill: an invisible crisis', *Family Relations* 35: 379–389.

Thurer, S.L. (1983) 'Deinstitutionalization and women: where the buck stops', *Hospital and Community Psychiatry* 34: 1162–1163.

Vaughn, C.E. and Leff, J.P. (1976) 'The influence of family and social factors on the course of psychiatric illness', *British Journal of Psychiatry* 129: 125–137.

Wing, J.K., Monck, E.M., Brown, G.W. and Carstairs, G.M. (1964) 'Morbidity in the community of schizophrenic patients discharged from London mental hospitals in 1959', *British Journal of Psychiatry* 110: 10–21.

Chapter 9

Homeless women

Jane Cook and Jane Marshall

INTRODUCTION

It is estimated that there are approximately two million homeless people in Great Britain. This includes people living in hostels, bed and breakfast accommodation, squats, in prison and those staying with friends: the 'hidden homeless' (Siddall, 1994). Approximately 10 to 25 per cent of the homeless population is made up of women. This chapter addresses aspects concerning both the homeless women themselves and the legislative climate in community care provision, which may hamper the development of appropriate services for this group of women. Case histories and models of current good practice will then be used to exemplify how services might be better planned for homeless women in the future.

The problem of homelessness in the United Kingdom and the United States has become more visible in the past decade due to many factors. These include the lack of easily available and affordable accommodation, loss of job and redundancy, financial problems, break-up of relationships and racial harassment. In addition, the homeless population is now younger and comprises more women and individuals from ethnic minorities. The number of homeless households, many headed by a woman, is also increasing, particularly in urban centres. Siddall (1994) estimates that 10,000 are sleeping rough in Britain, of whom 3,000 are in London.

Homelessness in women is hard to define because of women's specific relation to the home and to their role in the family. Women may be better at avoiding homelessness than men and are more likely to conceal it by staying with friends or remaining in unsuitable relationships. Watson and Austerberry (1986) describe a 'home to homelessness' continuum in relation to homeless women. This ranges from staying in unsatisfactory settings, specific accommodation for the homeless (hostels, bed and breakfast hotels, shelters), through to squats, prisons and the streets. They found that younger, employed women were more likely to stay with friends or to remain in unstable relationships when they lost accommodation, whereas older, married women with no qualifications were more likely to enter direct-access hostel accommodation when they became homeless. In the United Kingdom, homeless families are often housed in temporary bed and breakfast hotel accommodation, usually at some distance from their previous residence. This effectively cuts them off from any community support that they might previously have had.

CHARACTERISTICS OF HOMELESS WOMEN

Few studies have specifically addressed the problems and needs of homeless women. In those that have been carried out, accessible samples, such as women living in hostels, shelters or psychiatric hospitals have been used. These studies indicate that homeless women are younger and more socially stable than homeless men and that they are more likely to have stayed on at school, to have a history of employment and to have married, had children and maintained contact with their families (Drake et al., 1982; Scott, 1991; Marshall and Reed, 1992). In British studies the women have largely been white, but a recent study, based in London, reported that a significant proportion of women with families in bed and breakfast accommodation were of Indo-Pakistani origin (Paterson and Roderick, 1990). Since the early 1970s, American studies have revealed high numbers of black homeless women.

Homeless women are less likely to have been in prisons and institutions than homeless men. Although the prevalence of self-reported mental illness among homeless women has been as low as 8 per cent (Drake et al., 1982), most studies suggest that homeless women have higher levels of major mental illness than homeless men. Four recent studies of homeless women in London hostels reported rates for schizophrenia ranging from 19 per cent to 64 per cent. This wide variation in rates can be explained by the different age range of the women in the samples, with older women being more likely to suffer from a schizophrenic illness (Marshall, 1994).

Homeless women have a lower prevalence of alcohol and drug misuse compared with homeless men. Breakey et al. (1989) screened 298 homeless men and 230 homeless women in the missions, shelters and jails of Baltimore and found that 69 per cent of the men and 38 per cent of the women were definite or probable alcoholics. Marshall and Reid (1992) reported that 25 (36 per cent) of a sample of 70 homeless women were drinking heavily and that 7 (10 per cent) admitted to a current or serious drug problem.

Physical illness is common in both homeless men and women and the problems are similar. However, Breakey et al. (1989) reported that two-thirds of the Baltimore sample of homeless women had gynaecological problems and that 32 per cent of the women had some kind of arthritis, compared with 26 per cent of the men. Anaemia was also more common in the homeless women, occurring in 35 per cent of the sample, compared with 18 per cent of homeless men.

WHY DO WOMEN BECOME HOMELESS?

While it is hard to generalise, women seem more likely than men to become homeless for social reasons, such as family break-up, marital and parental disputes (Drake *et al.*, 1982). Social factors are intimately bound to economic factors such as the lack of affordable housing, due to a decrease in the supply over the past thirty years, and poverty. Younger homeless women often have a history of family break-up and of being in care. Homelessness is not due to just one of these factors. Often a combination of factors occurring at a critical period precipitates homelessness or causes a further slide down the pathway. Psychological factors are also important. There is evidence that women with psychiatric illness and substance misuse are likely to end up in hostels because they are unable to cope on their own, or to secure their own housing (Watson and Austerberry, 1986). In the United States, deinstitutionalisation, together with the lack of provision of shelters for homeless women, appear to have been factors (Bachrach, 1984).

HOMELESSNESS AND MENTAL ILLNESS

The relationship between homelessness and mental illness is a complex one and mental illness is only one of many interacting factors leading to and perpetuating homelessness. Cohen and Thompson (1992) challenge the assumption that the fundamental problem of the homeless mentally ill is their mental illness. Homeless people who are not 'mentally ill' are likely to have many mental health problems and the 'mentally ill' homeless may have non-psychiatric problems arising from the sociopolitical elements affecting all homeless people. Their model views homelessness as the core element of the broader socioeconomic-political context, which in turn becomes intertwined with personal biography and illness.

SERVICES AND HOMELESS WOMEN

The homeless mentally ill in general do not access psychiatric and substance-misuse services, despite needing them (Padgett *et al.*, 1990). Women are even less likely to do so than men. Breakey *et al.* (1989) reported that only 30 per cent of 230 homeless women were able to name a usual source of health care, compared with 47 per cent of 298 homeless men. Factors related to service utilisation are poorly understood and little research has been carried out in this area. Higher rates of hospitalisation have been reported among homeless women (Robertson, 1986).This may be due to the fact that homeless women are more likely to be admitted to hospital, whereas homeless men in the same situation may be taken to prison (Herzberg, 1987).

In general, services have failed to recognise the broad range of needs of homeless women and have ignored the fact that even overtly psychotic women may have adapted to life in hostels and/or the streets and do not always need acute in-patient care. In addition, many projects for the homeless are dominated by homeless men. Homeless women, often with a history of physical or sexual abuse, find this difficult. Services are not client-centred and homeless women have no choice in service provision.Thus, few services have been designed specifically to meet the needs of homeless women.

Harris and Bachrach (1990) describe an assertive clinical case-management programme for homeless women based in Washington DC, USA. In the first three years, 25 homeless mentally-ill women aged between 24 and 66 years were referred. This group was extremely disabled, with histories of multiple in-patient admissions; 16 had a diagnosis of schizophrenia and 13 a history of alcohol or other substance misuse. Homelessness had been a recurrent theme in their lives and they had frequently moved in and out of the homeless population, many showing great geographic mobility. Despite these problems, it was possible to engage them in an assertive, clinical case-management programme and there was a significant reduction in their use of psychiatric in-patient facilities. However, they continued to be residentially mobile. This mobility was thought to be a restlessness rather than a rootlessness and the authors suggested that the freedom to move about among residential settings was instrumental in helping the women to leave the streets and to become involved in a treatment programme.

The degree of disability of homeless individuals, their personal strengths and social support networks must be recognised in planning any services (Breakey et al., 1989). However, factors such as the lack of funding for community care, both in the voluntary and statutory sectors, and the complexities of housing legislation and the Community Care Act further complicate the issue. In our opinion, recent government legislation has complicated the problem of homelessness and may directly contribute to it. In the following, we shall outline these policies and discuss their implications for the homeless.

LEGISLATION AND ITS IMPACT ON THE HOMELESS

Housing

The Housing Act (England) 1985 placed a duty on local authorities to secure accommodation for certain homeless people who are deemed not to be intentionally homeless and whose needs meet priority criteria or who are seen to be vulnerable. In addition, homeless people have to prove a connection to the local authority to which they apply, and this can be difficult if the homeless person has been mobile or if a local authority is divided up into neighbourhoods. Furthermore, local authorities have no guidelines as to the definition of 'vulnerability', so this may vary from one authority to another and clients who are vulnerable may 'fall through the net'. With the general underinvestment in housing there is a shortage of special-needs funding for housing associations and a lack of appropriate housing for people with multiple problems. Short-term government initiatives are also a problem, because they do not provide for continuity of care.What is needed is long-term funding and commitment to housing.

The Criminal Justice Act

For many homeless people the only housing option for them is to squat. Squatters are criminalised under clauses 56 and 57 of the Criminal Justice Act. An initiative is needed that will ensure that empty properties are repaired and made fit for habitation, rather than money being wasted on criminalising the homeless.

Good practice guidelines and their implementation

1 Investment in funding should be encouraged to increase housing stock and, in particular, appropriate housing for specific groups of homeless women, e.g. women with mental health problems. More funding should be made available for housing associations.
2 A central body within government should deal with all aspects of homelessness funding.
3 Someone presenting as homeless in a particular local authority should be the responsibility of that local authority. More money should be available from government for local authorities to provide permanent housing and this should be related to the number of homeless people in that local authority.
4 The word 'vulnerable' needs to be clarified; housing workers should have training with respect to the application of the term and should use a vulnerability 'checklist' (HHELP Team, 1993).

The Community Care Act (1994)

The Community Care Act came into being on 1 April 1994 with the broad aim of helping people to live as independently as possible, either in their own homes or in residential or nursing homes. The general principles of the Act are as follows:

1 Assessment of need: this should be needs-led rather than service-led.
2 Co-ordinated assessments involving housing, health, statutory and voluntary agencies with the local authority as the lead agency.
3 Local authority to provide funding for purchasing care.
4 Discharge planning on or before admission to hospital.

5 Provision of care, co-ordinated through a care manager.
6 Emphasis on home care, day care and respite care.
7 Access to nursing/residential homes based on assessment of need.

Despite well-meaning principles, the Community Care Act fails to deliver community care to homeless people because they have multiple needs and, as is illustrated below, integration of the services they need is often not possible:

Good practice guidelines and their implementation

1 Choice should be provided for the client.
2 Government to respond to the need for increased funding.
3 Structures that are not yet in place, such as joint contracts between various agencies enabling joint assessments, need to be encouraged.
4 Staff working with homeless people should be trained to carry out assessments.
5 Policies for adequate discharge planning from hospital and prison are required.
6 Clarification of who is responsible for final decisions. Advocates and a complaints procedure must be available.

SERVICES FOR HOMELESS WOMEN – WHAT IS REQUIRED?

Concern about the quality of care should be an integral part of the planning and development of services for homeless women. Maxwell (1984) suggests the following six dimensions of health care quality which can be used as a starting point in setting up services for homeless women.

Dimensions of health care quality

Accessibility

To be readily and immediately accessible, any service for the homeless should be situated where homeless people are to be found and should offer flexible opening times. Workers should be prepared to do outreach-work assessments on the street. Homeless individuals trying to survive have other basic priorities such as food, shelter and money, and are unlikely to comply with the rigidity of hospital out-patient appointments.

Questions to be addressed include: the location of homeless women with mental health problems; existing local services for homeless people and those with mental health problems and number of women using them; opening hours of these services; clients' views of the facilities and their accessibility as well as suggestions for alternatives; are the facilities well advertised and well signposted, and in relevant languages?

Relevance to need

The relevance of a service can be assessed by using evaluation forms, in groups, or by individual interviews with homeless women and workers with whom they are in contact. This can include hostel workers, nurses in accident and emergency departments and workers in housing departments. Clients should be involved in service planning to ensure the appropriateness of services.

Questions to be addressed include: establishing the number and location of homeless women in the area; evaluation of needs as perceived by both users and workers; access to studies about homelessness and homeless women, either nationally or locally, which may be useful when setting up the service.

Effectiveness

Services are likely to be more effective if they are needs-led, i.e. planned in partnership with the client.

Equity

Homeless women with mental health problems often feel stigmatised where available services are usually male orientated and dominated. Women from black and other ethnic communities and lesbians can be made to feel excluded. Homeless women should have the option of women-only facilities and the right to a woman keyworker if they wish.

Questions to be addressed include: the availability of separate services for women; a charter stating clients' rights, an equal opportunity statement and a complaints procedure should all be displayed at the facility. Advocates and interpreters, along with women workers, should be available for clients.

Acceptability

Women should be involved in the planning of services so that they are relevant and acceptable. Regular evaluation involving service users should ensure that gaps in service provision are recognised and met. Women not using services should also be consulted.

Questions to be addressed include: are the services provided welcoming? Are the workers friendly and helpful? In addition, women require privacy and space and to be treated with dignity.

Efficiency

Any service will be efficient if it is well planned with client involvement and is relevant to need. This should be regularly appraised. Homeless women with mental health problems are often reluctant to engage with services. Likewise it can often take a long time before they show any change or improvement.

Questions to be addressed include: assessment of efficiency by regular review. It should be clarified how this will be measured: the number of women clients seen in a given time? Or a measure of the improvement in their mental health, or of the meeting of their needs? Are clients able to assess their own needs?

Flexibility is another dimension of health care that should be considered when setting up services for homeless women. Drop-in centres are often more helpful to homeless women who are fatigued from lack of sleep or the struggle of living rough, as well as preferring the informal approach of a no-appointment system.

Services for homeless women – checklist

- use the client as the resource/specialist
- client-led – go at client's pace
- choice of worker/housing
- each client should have a named keyworker
- multidisciplinary approach
- care plans and case reviews
- planned discharges
- work with client from point of contact through to resettlement
- the service should not be abusive
- the service should empower the client
- BE INNOVATIVE, BE ADVENTUROUS!

SETTING UP SERVICES FOR HOMELESS WOMEN – PROBLEMS AND EXAMPLES OF GOOD PRACTICE

This section begins with three case histories which exemplify the variety and severity of problems experienced by homeless women users. Consideration of these is essential in planning relevant services.

Case histories

Jenny is 18 years old and is street homeless. She was born in Wales and was taken into care when she was 5 years old because of sexual abuse. She ran away when she was 13 and has been street homeless since. She does not receive benefits and prostitutes and begs to get money. She attends a drop-in centre for young homeless people intermittently. She has a history of chronic alcohol, illicit drug and solvent misuse. She is depressed and is prone to episodes of deliberate self-harm. She has repeated kidney infections and suffers with incontinence. She is malnourished. What are her basic needs? What is the priority need? How can her needs be met?

Jane is 29 years old. She left home at the age of 16 due to a breakdown in her relationship with her father. She has mild learning difficulties and few daily living skills. She has a history of chronic heroin abuse and is HIV and Hepatitis B positive. She has been street homeless for six months following discharge from a psychiatric hospital with no follow-up care. During this time she has prostituted to pay for heroin.

Debbie is 26 years old and lives in a night shelter. Her parents divorced when she was young and she was brought up by her father. In her teens she spent three years in an adolescent psychiatric unit. From there she was placed in independent accommodation but was unable to cope. She has a history of learning difficulties, has been abusing solvents since she was 14 years old and is experiencing auditory hallucinations. She also has a history of violence.

In the following sections we discuss the problems encountered in the various settings where homeless women may be found, and provide examples of good practice in setting up services for these women.

STREETS/SQUATS

Problems	*Good practice*
Isolation – women not in touch with good services.	Women outreach workers on the street build relationships with individual clients.
Traumatised by a past experience – may be suspicious/distrustful.	Continuity of care and commitment essential. Building a relationship may take a long time, even years. Long-term funding for projects is vital.
Multiple needs.	Multidisciplinary team required to meet these needs. Different agencies should work together. No homeless woman should be discharged from hospital onto the streets. Joint planning through Care Programme Approach.

Model of good practice

The East London Homeless Health Primary Care Team (HHELP) began as a three-year project in 1986, to look at the health needs of homeless people (see Appendix for address). It is now an outreach, multi-agency, multidisciplinary team of health, social, housing and administrative workers, offering primary health care, social care and housing advisory services to single homeless people in the City and East London area. The mental health outreach workers were part of the Homeless Mentally Ill Initiative (HMII) which was a three-year research project funded by the Department of Health. They worked with three groups of clients:

1 clients with a mental health problem who had never been in touch with services;
2 clients with long-term mental health problems who had been in a psychiatric hospital;
3 clients with frequent/acute psychiatric admissions.

The mental health workers are involved with clients from point of contact through to resettlement. Much of the work with clients is a joint effort with statutory and voluntary agencies, co-ordinated by the keyworker system and the use of care plans. The HHELP team is now part of the local statutory services with the prime function of accessing mainstream services for single homeless people.

The team works in day centres, hostels, squats and on the street. Street work is carried out throughout the year using a set routine and at set times. A high-quality service has been developed and joint work between voluntary and statutory agencies is carried out. A GP and consultant psychiatrist are available to carry out street assessments. The work has been innovative and some clients with severe mental health problems who had been street homeless for long periods of time (12–30 years) have been resettled. The HHELP team were able to identify that many services for homeless people were dominated by men and, therefore, developed a service sensitive to women's needs by:

• women having a choice to work with a woman worker;
• setting up groups for women to provide a safe environment;
• highlighting the needs of women to agencies.

Unfortunately, some of the momentum of the HMII project has been lost with its integration into the statutory services, because the purchasing and providing mechanism has meant that the team has been restructured and certain jobs regraded. In some cases this has led to a change in keyworkers working with the street homeless. A change of worker is always difficult for homeless individuals, especially if a lot of time and effort was required to build a relationship of trust with them.

The following is an example of where flexible care in the community produced a good result for the client.

Case history

Eleanor is in her 60s. In the past she worked on a women's magazine, but became street homeless after being made redundant seven years ago. She was sleeping in an alleyway with her dog and had contact with local shopkeepers and a nun who gave her tea. She was suffering with swollen ankles, leg ulcers and was experiencing auditory hallucinations. Her physical and mental condition was deteriorating but she refused hospital admission because of her dog. When arrangements were made for her dog to go into kennels, and with the nun as her keyworker, she agreed to be admitted to hospital.

DAY CENTRES

Problems	*Good practice*
Male dominated.	Day centres should either be for women only, or women should have their own space with their own entrance. Failing that, there should be a women-only session at some stage during the day. Women workers and a multidisciplinary team should be available, e.g. housing workers, social workers, etc.
Staff staying for short periods only, due to short-term funding.	Long-term funding for day centres ought to be a priority.
Day centres too small and often over-crowded.	Day centres should be of a sufficiently high standard and be housed in buildings that are purpose-built, with a wide range of facilities. This implies improved funding.

Model of good practice

St Botolph's Day Centre (see Appendix for address) is of a high standard. There is a variety of activities during the day and a drop-in centre in the evening. A wide range of workers, both men and women, is available, an equal-opportunity statement, a women's group and a women's room.

The following is a successful example of working with a client at a day centre to make a more accurate assessment of her needs.

Case history

Sandra is aged 50. She spent her childhood in Essex before moving to London. She became street homeless twelve years ago following the death of her child in a house fire. She has lived alone in a doorway for the past five years. She uses several day centres for her basic needs and has a good relationship with the workers. She suffers with chronic urinary-tract infections and has swollen ankles. Workers also observed that she was experiencing auditory hallucinations. When her mental state deteriorated the day-centre workers intervened and organised her admission to a psychiatric hospital under Section. After a period in hospital she moved into a small group home where she is doing well.

Hostels

Problems	*Good practice*
Institutionalisation	Treat people as individuals and recognise their rights.
	Residents should have their own space and possessions and a group with a say in how the hostel is run.
	Provide high levels of staff/client contact and reduce the time that clients are unoccupied.
	Each resident should have a care plan which they have helped to draw up.
Low staff morale	Staff require good training, adequate support and to be involved in decision-making.

Model of good practice

The Mental Health Unit at Hopetown Hostel is a 13-bedded unit for homeless women with mental health problems (see Appendix for address). The aim of the unit is 'to help residents function more adaptively' (Salvation Army, 1991). Each resident has her own room and has chosen the wallpaper. She has a keyworker and a care plan which she has helped to draw up. Regular case reviews involve outside agencies. Standards are set using a charter drawn up by the residents. There is a resident's group and a training flat in preparation for some residents to move on to more independent living. Staff also receive training.

PRISONS

A proportion of homeless women find themselves in the 'revolving door' situation between prison, psychiatric hospital and homelessness. Prisons are clearly not a therapeutic environment for homeless women with mental health problems. The following case raises questions as to the appropriateness of prison, as opposed to the mental health services, for some women.

Case history

Mandy was physically, emotionally and sexually abused as a child. She had no formal education and first came into contact with the psychiatric services when she was 11. She left home when she was 14 years old and lived on the street and in bed and breakfast hotels. Mental health problems included depression, self-harm and intravenous heroin use. From the age of 16 she was in and out of prison, mainly on charges of theft to finance her drug abuse. She became dependent on the prison system because she felt contained in prison and could not cope on her own in bed and breakfast accommodation. She died in prison at the age of 28.

Problems	*Good practice*
Homeless women with mental health problems enter the criminal justice system.	Training for police re: available options.Court diversion schemes should be linked into multidisciplinary teams and able to carry out needs assessments, with resources to provide care. Bail hostels should have psychiatric support.
No planned release from prison.	Multidisciplinary resettlement teams in prisons/secure units.
Inappropriate housing.	Funding for appropriate housing schemes to be developed and adequately staffed.

Model of good practice

WISH (Women in Special Hospitals and Secure Units) is a registered charity working on behalf of women in or released from Special Hospitals, Regional Secure Units and prison psychiatric units (see Appendix for address).

The aims of WISH are to:

1 Review and reform psychiatric provision for women at risk of secure containment by raising awareness and initiating research.
2 Be accessible to women who are at risk of secure psychiatric containment and work to prevent inappropriate admissions.
3 Inform, advise and give voice to women in secure psychiatric containment and reduce their isolation.
4 Work with staff to improve the daily life of women in secure psychiatric containment.
5 Empower and support women on discharge from secure psychiatric containment.
6 Promote provision of appropriate resources and facilities within the community.
7 Promote equality of opportunity and respond to the individual needs of women in and discharged from secure psychiatric containment.

REFUGEES

Many homeless women are refugees with traumatic experiences, who are displaced and unsure of their legal status in Britain and who suffer the additional burden of racism. These factors in turn have an effect on their mental health and problems range from simple anxiety to serious psychiatric problems. Homeless refugees do not appear in the homelessness statistics because many are 'hidden homeless', or are mobile and thus do not appear on local population statistics. Health services for refugees are often inaccessible, inappropriate and inadequate. Racist, cultural and language barriers need to be overcome and the service should be adequately funded at a national level.

Model of good practice

Nafsiyat – intercultural therapy centre (see Appendix for address) – offers specialised therapeutic help to people from ethnic and cultural minority groups, who have often found it difficult to obtain appropriate treatment from the generic mental health services. Nafsiyat was set up to provide a specialist psychotherapy service taking into account the cultural and racial component in mental illness.

CONCLUSION

Homeless women are a heterogeneous group, largely younger and more socially stable than homeless men. Proportionately more have major mental illness than men. Homeless women are restless rather than rootless and can engage with appropriate services. We have outlined the basic principles for setting up services for homeless women and described problems in a range of areas that need to be addressed. The building of trust is an essential element in setting up a service. Women will use services in which they feel safe and considered. In the future, therefore, homeless women must be involved in setting up and evaluating services.

CROSS-REFERENCES WITHIN THIS BOOK

REFERENCES

Bachrach, L.L. (1984) 'Deinstitutionalization and women', *American Psychologist* 10: 1171–1177.
Breakey, W.R., Fischer, P.J., Kramer, M. *et al.* (1989) 'Health and mental health problems of homeless men and women in Baltimore', *Journal of the American Medical Association* 262: 1352–1357.
Cohen, C.I. and Thompson, K.S. (1992) 'Homeless mentally ill or mentally ill homeless', *American Journal of Psychiatry* 146: 816–823.
Drake, M., O'Brien, M. and Biebuyck, T. (1982) *Single and homeless*, Department of the Environment Report, London: HMSO.
Harris, M. and Bachrach, L.L. (1990) 'Perspectives on homeless women', *Hospital and Community Psychiatry* 41: 253–254.
Herzberg, J. (1987) 'No fixed abode: a comparison of men and women admitted to an East London psychiatric hospital', *British Journal of Psychiatry* 150: 621–627.
HHELP Team (1993) 'Vulnerability check-list', London: HHELP.
Marshall, E.J. (1994) 'Homelessness and schizophrenia', *Schizophrenia Monitor* 4: 1–4.
Marshall, E.J. and Reed, J.L. (1992) 'Psychiatric morbidity in homeless women', *British Journal of Psychiatry* 160: 761–768.
Maxwell, R.J. (1984) 'Quality assessment in health', *British Medical Journal* 288: 1470–1472.
Padgett, D., Struening, E.L. and Andrews, H. (1990) 'Factors affecting the use of medical, mental health, alcohol and drug treatment services by homeless adults', *Medical Care* 28: 805–821.
Paterson, C.M. and Roderick, P. (1990) 'Obstetric outcome in homeless women', *British Medical Journal* 301: 263–266.
Robertson, M.J. (1986) 'Mental disorder among homeless persons in the United States of America: an overview of recent empirical literature', *Administration in Mental Health* 14: 14–26.
Salvation Army (1991) 'Needs assessment in Hopetown Hostel', London: Salvation Army.
Scott, J. (1991) 'Resettlement unit or asylum?' Paper presented at the Royal College of Psychiatrists, Brighton, 3 July 1991.

Selzer, M.L., Vinokur, A. and Van Rooijen, L. (1975) 'A self-administered Short Michigan Alcohol Screening Test (SMAST)', *Journal of Studies on Alcohol* 36: 117–126.

Siddall, R. (1994) 'Homelessness – in another world', *Community Care* (30 April, suppl.): 15–16.

Watson, S. and Austerberry, H. (1986) *Housing and homelessness: a feminist perspective*, London: Routledge & Kegan Paul.

Chapter 10

Women with drug and alcohol problems

Sophie Davison and Jane Marshall

INTRODUCTION

Interest in gender differences in drug and alcohol problems has been increasing in recent years. Despite this, the development of a thorough understanding of women's problems has been slow and many of the prevention and treatment needs of alcohol- and drug-dependent women have not been met (Blume, 1992). In this chapter we outline the extent and nature of alcohol and of drug problems in women, before moving on to a discussion of the important issues in providing and planning services to meet the particular needs of this group.

EPIDEMIOLOGY OF ALCOHOL PROBLEMS IN WOMEN

Surveys of drinking behaviour in the general population have generally found that women have lower rates of consumption and alcohol-related problems than men. The exact prevalence of alcohol problems in women in Britain remains unclear. According to the Office of Population Censuses and Surveys estimates, 1 per cent (250,000) of all women in Britain are drinking at a potentially dangerous level of more than 35 units a week (Goddard and Ikin, 1988) and a further 2 million women (8 per cent) are drinking above the 'safe limit' of 14 units a week (National Association of Health Authorities, 1989).

The five-site Epidemiological Catchment Area study (ECA), a community study in the United States, found a lifetime prevalence of alcohol abuse and dependence in women between 4.2 per cent and 4.8 per cent (Robins *et al.*, 1984). The overall one-month prevalence rate for women was 0.9 per cent with the highest rate in the 18–24-year-old group (2.4 per cent) (Regier *et al.*, 1988).

In Britain there has been an increase in alcohol consumption and alcohol problems in women (Goddard and Ikin, 1988). This increase has mainly been among unemployed and unmarried women under 25 (Breeze, 1985). Younger cohorts of women seem to be showing higher rates of heavy, frequent drinking than the generations who preceded them.

CHARACTERISTICS OF WOMEN WITH ALCOHOL PROBLEMS

Women with alcohol problems are a heterogeneous population. They are vulnerable to developing alcohol-related problems at various ages. There has been an increase in alcohol consumption among adolescent girls in recent years. Many are drinking not only regularly but also heavily (Litman, 1986). A survey in the United States found that the highest rates of alcohol-related problems and of alcohol-dependence symptoms occurred in women aged 21 to 34 years. The highest proportion of heavy drinkers was among women aged 35 to 49 years (Wilsnack *et al.*, 1986). Elderly women may also be at risk.

Transition points in life may also be associated with vulnerability to alcohol problems. For example, problems may develop during pregnancy, in the postnatal period, following the breakdown of a marriage or a relationship, following bereavement (especially loss of a partner or child), or during physical illness.

Marital status and work are also important. In Wilsnack *et al.*'s (1986) survey, married women had fewest problems overall, while those cohabiting in common-law marriages had the most. The characteristics of the women with the highest consumption varied considerably with age. In the 21 to 34-year-old group, those who had never married, were single, unemployed and childless had the most problems. In the 35 to 49 age group, women described as 'lost role' (divorced or separated, children not at home and not employed) had the most problems (Wilsnack *et al.*, 1986). In the oldest group (age 50 to 64), those with the most alcohol problems were those who did not have a clearly defined role of their own and tended to live vicariously through partners and children. Professional women may respond to the stresses of competing in a male-dominated world by drinking excessively. Multiple roles, for example where women have to cope both with children and with a full-time job, may also create vulnerability to alcohol problems.

Women over 30 are more likely to report alcohol abuse alone, whilst younger women with alcohol problems also report using cannabis, cocaine, other stimulants and hallucinogens (Harrison and Bellile, 1987). Both age groups use tranquillisers. This difference appears to be the result of increasing availability of drugs, rather than of women giving up drug use as they get older.

In the United States, the prevalence of alcohol problems appears higher in black women than in white women (Amaro *et al.*, 1987). Black women are more likely to start drinking at an early age, drink more heavily and drink with groups of friends. It remains unclear what ethnic and cultural differences there may be in the drinking patterns of women in Great Britain, and this needs clarifying.

DIFFERENCES BETWEEN MEN AND WOMEN WITH DRINKING PROBLEMS

There are several ways in which women with drinking problems appear to differ from men. Women start drinking and develop alcohol-related problems at a later age than men. However, they present for treatment at approximately the same age. This implies that their problems develop more rapidly.

There is evidence that women are more likely than their male counterparts to have unstable families of origin and to have suffered physical and sexual abuse. They are also more likely to date the onset of their drinking problem to a stressful life event, and to say they started misusing alcohol to forget family problems, especially alcohol problems in a partner, and to increase their social confidence (Copeland and Hall, 1992). They report lower self-esteem and are more likely to describe drinking when they feel powerless and inadequate.

Women show greater levels of marital instability and are more likely than men to be divorced or living with partners who also have alcohol-related problems when they enter treatment. They are also more likely to have child-care responsibilities and to experience opposition from friends and family to treatment (Institute of Medicine, 1990). Women's drinking patterns are much more influenced by those of their partners than are those of men (Wilsnack et al., 1986).

THE PSYCHOLOGICAL STATUS OF WOMEN WITH ALCOHOL PROBLEMS

Some studies suggest that women with alcohol problems are more likely than men to have histories of suicide attempts and previous psychiatric treatment, to suffer from primary mood disorders and to report symptoms such as anxiety and depression (Blume, 1992). They are also more likely to present with histories of other substance misuse, particularly tranquillisers, sedatives and amphetamines, in addition to their alcohol problem. Both men and women have high rates of associated psychiatric disturbance and it is unclear whether women overall have more than their male counterparts. They do, however, show a different pattern of psychiatric disorder, with higher rates of anxiety disorder, psychosexual dysfunction and bulimia (Ross et al., 1988).

PHYSICAL COMPLICATIONS AMONG WOMEN WITH ALCOHOL PROBLEMS

Women metabolise alcohol differently from men. Women who drink excessively are therefore more likely to develop physical complications such as liver disease and alcohol-related brain damage than men. These problems occur after a shorter drinking history and at lower levels of alcohol intake (Dunne, 1988).

The effects of heavy drinking on women's sexuality and reproduction are complex and not completely understood. Chronic, heavy drinking may be associated with inhibition of ovulation, infertility and a wide variety of gynaecological and obstetric problems (Blume, 1992). Many alcoholic women report that they feel more aroused when using alcohol, and fear their sexual responsiveness will decrease if they abstain. Despite this subjective feeling, it is clear that women's physical responses are adversely affected by alcohol and that sexual desire, capacity and responsiveness improve after periods of abstinence.

Women who drink during pregnancy are at risk of having a baby with the foetal alcohol syndrome, which has an estimated incidence of between 1 and 3 cases per 1,000 live births (Blume, 1992), making it one of the three most frequent causes of birth defects associated with mental retardation.

Women who are alcohol dependent have a greatly shortened life expectancy. A Swedish study (Lindberg and Agren, 1988) of alcoholics who had received treatment showed that alcohol abuse increased rates of premature death substantially more for women than for men (death rate increased by a factor of five for women, compared with three for men). The causes of these premature deaths were alcohol intoxication, cirrhosis of the liver, suicide and other violent deaths, as well as breast cancer.

EPIDEMIOLOGY OF DRUG PROBLEMS AMONG WOMEN

Women who misuse psychoactive drugs have a similar range of difficulties to women with alcohol problems, and many may be abusing both. In addition, women who misuse illicit drugs face the stigma of engaging in an illegal activity, whilst those who misuse prescription drugs may suffer because their problem is not recognised.

There is little precise information about the extent of drug misuse among women. In the UK, figures are obtained from the Home Office Addicts Index and the regional drug misuse databases. These numbers reflect only drug users who have presented to services and, in the case of the index, who are using notifiable drugs such as opiates and cocaine. A substantial proportion of drug misusers have never presented to services. The Advisory Council on Drug Misuse estimated that there were between 90,000 and 150,000 regular opiate users in the UK in 1986 (HMSO, 1988). Around 25 per cent of drug misusers presenting to treatment services are women. If this accurately reflects the population, there were between 22,500 and 37,500 female opiate users in the UK in 1986. Regional databases show that in the six months ending March 1993, 4,525 women presented for treatment for the first time or after a break (Department of Health, 1994).

In the US, the ECA community study found a lifetime prevalence of drug abuse or dependence of 3.8 to 5.1 per cent in women (Robins *et al.*, 1984), with the highest one-month prevalence rate in the 18 to 24-year-old group. There was a male to female ratio of 2:1 in the one-month prevalence of drug dependence or abuse (Regier *et al.*, 1988).

More is known about opiate-dependent women, as they are the group most represented in current services. Accurate figures are not available for primary stimulant users, the vast majority of whom are not known to services (Klee, 1993). Amphetamine remains second only to cannabis in its popularity and the use of cocaine, especially crack cocaine, continues to increase in the UK. It is thought that these drugs are particularly attractive to women because of the associated mood elevation, weight reduction and increase in self-confidence and energy. Thus women may make up a greater proportion of stimulant users than opiate users (Klee, 1993).

Women are prescribed more anxiolytic drugs, such as benzodiazepines, than men, but the extent of misuse remains unclear. In the past two decades drug use by adolescents, both female and male, has increased dramatically (Trad, 1993). The extent of misuse by adolescent girls is unclear but it may increase further as the norms of social behaviour of males and females converge.

This chapter concentrates on the misuse of psychoactive drugs. However, it should not be forgotten that women also misuse non-psychoactive drugs such as laxatives for weight control, non-steroidal analgesics and tobacco with potentially harmful consequences.

SOCIODEMOGRAPHIC CHARACTERISTICS OF WOMEN DRUG MISUSERS

Women presenting for treatment have higher rates of unemployment, fewer financial resources and qualifications, and fewer job skills than their male counterparts. Community studies in the UK have found consistently that more female drug misusers have a regular sexual partner, and a far greater proportion have a drug-using partner than do male drug users (Gossop *et al.*, 1994). Women are more likely to be financially and practically dependent on a partner for obtaining their supply of drugs. More women have children (Gossop *et al.*, 1994) and more are single parents with sole responsibility for childcare. Women are less likely than men to be involved in criminal activities related to their drug habits. However, more women are involved in prostitution (7 per cent of those attending a community drug team (Gossop *et al.*, 1994)). Even though fewer women go to prison than men, 36 per cent of a sample attending a community drug team had been to prison (Gossop *et al.*, 1994).

ANTECEDENTS AND FACTORS PERPETUATING DRUG USE IN WOMEN

Though similar numbers of men and women give experimenting and peer pressure as the reason for first drug use, far more women give relief from personal distress, psychosocial stressors, increasing their social confidence and a drug-using partner as the reason for drug use (Hser *et al.*, 1987; Suffet and Brotman, 1976). More women than men are initiated to drug use by a sexual partner (Hser *et al.*, 1987). Women who have been sexually abused as children are more likely to abuse drugs (Rohsenhow *et al.*, 1988).

THE PSYCHOLOGICAL STATUS OF WOMEN WITH DRUG PROBLEMS

A number of studies have shown that women drug misusers have higher rates than their male counterparts of psychological distress, low self-esteem and psychiatric disorders, in particular anxiety disorders, depression, post-traumatic stress disorder, psychosexual difficulties and eating disorders (Blume, 1992; Ross *et al.*, 1988). This may reflect differences in the preval-ence of psychiatric disorders in the rest of the population, but is nonetheless important in considering the treatment needs of women drug misusers.

WOMEN WITH DRUG PROBLEMS – A HETEROGENEOUS GROUP

Though most women who misuse drugs are of childbearing age, the needs of women of all ages should be considered. Diagnosis of drug abuse in adolescence can be difficult and requires an understanding of the norms of adolescent behaviour. It may present as repeated injuries, excessive weight change, truancy, decline in school performance and odd behaviour (Trad, 1993).

Older women are a neglected group who are vulnerable to drug misuse through loneliness, loss of role, physical illness and financial hardship. They have the highest rates of prescription of psychotropic medication in response to distress and life crises. Misuse of prescription drugs often goes unnoticed. Older women are frequently prescribed a large number of different drugs and are more vulnerable to drug–drug and drug–alcohol interactions. They may present with confusion, falls, memory impairment, depression and anxiety (Szwabo, 1993). It is not known whether illicit drug use by older women will increase as the generation that started to abuse drugs in the 1960s gets older.

Little has been written about the needs of ethnic-minority women in relation to drug abuse. Studies in the US suggest that certain ethnic groups have particular problems, with African Americans facing problems of isolation and deprivation.

COMPLICATIONS OF DRUG MISUSE IN WOMEN

Many of the social, psychological and physical complications of drug misuse are common to men and women. However, some are specific to women or affect them in different ways.

PHYSICAL COMPLICATIONS OF DRUG MISUSE IN WOMEN

HIV, hepatitis B and C

Many women who inject drugs are doubly at risk of contracting HIV, hepatitis B and hepatitis C, through sexual intercourse and through sharing needles. Many female intravenous amphetamine and heroin users have regular sexual partners, around 90 per cent of whom also inject (Klee, 1993). Many of these women share their injecting equipment with their partner and engage in high rates of unprotected sex. Many do not perceive these behaviours as posing a high risk. Male to female sexual transmission occurs more easily than the reverse. If a woman is dependent on a partner for drugs, this may create a power imbalance which makes it difficult for her to negotiate safe sex and injecting, especially as doing so may imply a lack of trust. The particularly high risk of HIV faced by women injectors is illustrated by the fact that 54 per cent of HIV-positive intravenous-drug users in Glasgow are female, even though women account for a much smaller proportion of the overall injectors. Female drug users engaging in prostitution are a particularly high-risk group.

Women injecting amphetamines and cocaine may be at particular risk due to the increase in sexual behaviour associated with these drugs (Klee, 1993).

Pregnancy and childbirth

Women misusing drugs are at high risk of obstetric complications for general reasons such as poor nutrition, poor antenatal clinic attendance, poor physical health, adverse life events and violence, as well as for drug-specific reasons. Opiate-dependent mothers are at increased risk of premature deliveries, intrauterine-growth retardation and neonatal deaths. Babies may also be born with opiate-withdrawal symptoms. There is an increasing awareness that cocaine adversely affects the foetus, causing high rates of preterm delivery, low birth weight and infants with signs of psychomotor impairment.

As many female intravenous-drug users are having unprotected sexual intercourse and many believe themselves infertile due to interference of opiates with menstrual function, there is a risk of unwanted pregnancies. There is also a 25 to 40 per cent risk of transmission of HIV from an infected mother to her unborn child.

Drug overdose

Men and women have similar overall rates of drug overdose and hospitalisation. Studies of sedative and opiate overdoses in drug misusers have shown that women report more intentional overdoses whereas men report more accidental overdoses. Though both are life-threatening, this may have implications for management.

SOCIAL COMPLICATIONS OF DRUG MISUSE IN WOMEN

Many drug-dependent women have children and have sole responsibility for their care. Drug dependence *per se* does not automatically make a woman unable to care for a child, but such responsibility can be a severe additional stressor. It can also have damaging effects on the child, including physical and emotional neglect. Children of drug-abusing mothers have more educational and emotional difficulties. Maternal substance abuse is a potent risk factor for subsequent substance abuse in her offspring. There is a real risk of family breakdown. Hospital admission and prison sentences place a particular burden on women as they are less likely than their male counterparts to have their children cared for by a co-parent or family member, leading to loss of contact and discharge to a splintered family.

PLANNING AND PROVIDING SERVICES FOR WOMEN WITH DRUG AND ALCOHOL PROBLEMS

Barriers to seeking help

In recent years there has been an increase in women presenting to alcohol treatment services. There is, however, evidence that women still under-use alcohol treatment services (Litman, 1986; Blume, 1992). For example, national prevalence rates for alcohol problems and dependence in the United States indicate that the male : female ratio is approximately 2 : 1 in the community, whereas the ratio is 4 : 1 in treatment settings (Institute of Medicine, 1990). There is also debate as to whether women are under-represented in current services for drug users. Whether or not this is the case, there are many women who do not present to drug or alcohol services, and among those who do present there are many whose special needs are not fully met. Community studies suggest that women not known to services are a functionally impaired group, whose failure to seek help is not due to a lack of need for help.

General social attitudes towards drug- and alcohol-misusing women remain moralistic. They are perceived to have deserted their feminine role and are held in lower esteem than their male counterparts (Copeland and Hall, 1992).

Failure to seek help may result from some of the barriers faced by women drug users (Reed, 1985). The barriers more likely to be experienced by women than by their male counterparts include:

- Many women do not see addiction as their primary problem (Thom, 1986).
- Women are more likely to see associated health and psychosocial problems as their primary problem (Thom, 1986; Blume, 1992).
- Basic needs may be more urgent in the short term, e.g. housing, safety from violence, money, clothing and food.
- Alcohol- or drug-using partners. Partners may discourage or prevent help-seeking, or the severity of their problem may lead women to see their own problems as not severe enough to be taken seriously (Thom, 1986).
- Fear of stigma and social disapproval (Thom, 1986).
- A good relationship with the GP can be as much of a barrier as a bad one because of fear of disapproval (Thom, 1986).
- Negative professional attitudes.
- Opposition from friends and family (Beckman and Amaro, 1986).
- Women pay a higher social cost, such as problems with family, children and money, than men do on entering treatment (Beckman and Amaro, 1986).
- Lack of resources to arrange childcare.
- Fear of removal of children.

Barriers to detection

A further barrier to receiving help is lack of detection by others. Many women, fearing social disapproval, may conceal their alcohol or drug use (Blume, 1992). Women also use fewer illegal drugs and engage in less overt rule-breaking behaviour than men. Their addiction therefore either goes unrecognised or is not taken seriously (Reed, 1987). Women may in fact be presenting to their GP, A&E departments, crisis centres, women's refuges (Reed, 1987) with a host of physical, psychological and social problems, but their drug or alcohol misuse goes unidentified because they do not complain of an addiction problem and it is not routinely inquired about.

Barriers to engaging in and remaining in treatment

Once identified, women face further barriers to engaging in treatment. Addicted women are often regarded as more sick, more difficult to help and less motivated. This may be due to a misunderstanding of the extreme anxiety, low self-esteem, hopelessness, depression and feelings of loss of control which interfere with treatment (Reed, 1987). Confrontational techniques used in treatment with men may actually be harmful to women by compounding these factors.

Where women have been the victims of sexual abuse, they may feel unsafe or may be harassed in a treatment environment where they are outnumbered. Lack of provision of appropriate help for their needs may lead them to feel the service is of no use.

Barriers to achieving and maintaining abstinence

Barriers to achieving and maintaining abstinence include all the above. A partner's continuing drug or alcohol use is a poor prognostic factor. Lack of psychological and financial resources to achieve some degree of independence make it extremely difficult to remain abstinent. Unresolved issues, such as past sexual abuse or untreated depression, will impede recovery.

Current services in the UK

Current services for alcohol and drug users include primary care (GPs and practice nurses), in-patient care (general, specialist and private), out-patient care, community-based teams, voluntary agencies and self-help organisations. They offer a range of treatments, from detoxification to ongoing support.

General practitioners are at the forefront of the medical response and are probably the people with whom the majority of women with drug and alcohol problems have most contact.

In the 1980s, multidisciplinary community drug teams and community alcohol teams were set up in a number of regions to try to bridge the gap between primary and specialist care. It was originally intended that they work in collaboration with general practitioners and other agencies, in a consultative and educational capacity. However, they have become increasingly involved in direct delivery of care as collaboration from colleagues has been inconsistent. These teams provide outreach work, with advice, information and counselling, out-patient detoxification, and a referral mechanism for in-patient detoxification if necessary. The facilities vary widely. The majority of patients refer themselves to community teams, even though many have recently visited their general practitioners.

About two-thirds of patients seen by community drug teams are primarily dependent on opiates, with a small number primarily dependent on benzodiazepines, amphetamines and cocaine. It is unclear how far this reflects the drugs women are actually misusing in the community.

Community drug and alcohol teams are well placed to meet the needs of women, as they are easily accessible and have a philosophy of co-operation with other community agencies. The lack of shared care with general practitioners suggests, however, that a considerable proportion of women who need help are not receiving it because they are not identified and referred on. Better liaison between general practitioners and community drug teams would help to remedy this.

In recent years, with the advent of HIV, the emphasis in drug treatment has moved towards harm minimisation. As part of this movement, a number of needle exchanges have been set up where drug users can obtain clean injecting equipment. Some provide a range of other drug-related services in the hope that they will engage users who do not usually present to services. Women are particularly poor users of needle exchanges, largely because of the stigma associated with identifying themselves as intravenous-drug users.

MODELS OF GOOD PRACTICE

Dawe *et al.* (1992) describe a liaison service for pregnant opiate addicts which successfully addresses their needs. A keyworker, usually from the community drug team, co-ordinates all involved caregivers. This facilitates inter-agency collaboration, which is a key feature in meeting all the women's medical, social, psychiatric and paediatric needs. Good liaison with antenatal clinics leads to better attendance and better neonatal outcome. The inter-agency liaison includes a multidisciplinary pre-delivery case conference to share information and highlight problems.

RECOMMENDATIONS FOR FUTURE SERVICE PLANNING

Prevention of drug and alcohol problems in women

There are two main components to prevention:

1   Address antecedents of drug and alcohol misuse:
    - effective treatment of women's psychiatric problems
    - services for survivors of sexual abuse
    - treatment of parental substance misuse.
2   Education of high-risk groups:
    - adolescents
    - partners of drug- and alcohol-dependent men
    - survivors of incest
    - children of alcohol and drug misusers
    - women in transition.

Improving detection and identification of women with drug and alcohol problems

Improved detection will facilitate early intervention. This can be approached in two ways:

1 Educate those living and working with women with drug and alcohol problems and their families:
   - family
   - teachers
   - health visitors.
2 Improve screening by agencies involved with these women:
   - general practitioners
   - crisis agencies
   - women's refuges and shelters
   - accident and emergency departments
   - antenatal clinics.

Professionals working with children are well placed to detect parental substance abuse as mothers may find it easier to seek help for their children than for themselves. After childbirth all women have contact with a health visitor, who comes to know the woman in her home and social context. Childbirth is a time of transition and therefore risk. The relationship with a health visitor is an excellent opportunity for both prevention and screening.

Reducing the barriers to seeking help

Barriers to seeking help can be reduced by planning services which:

- are perceived by women with drug and alcohol problems as relevant to their needs;
- are seen by women as safe and free of harassment;
- provide women with education in recognising their drug and/or alcohol problem;
- provide support in overcoming stigma;
- provide assistance with childcare arrangements.

Childcare facilities should be planned to allow women to attend meetings and appointments in private and without disruption.

Comprehensive assessment

Providing a service that concentrates exclusively on the alcohol consumption or drug-taking is unlikely to be effective.

Women alcohol and drug misusers need a thorough assessment including:

- alcohol consumption
- drug-taking
- family history of drug and alcohol problems
- family and social problems

- relationship problems
- education and work skills
- financial and legal problems
- psychiatric problems
- history of physical and sexual abuse
- physical problems
- psychosexual problems.

Once this is completed there should be a mechanism for *prioritising needs*, as basic ones such as food, housing, money, or safety may need to be addressed urgently before tackling the drug or alcohol misuse.

Core services

A number of core services need to be available in addition to the traditional ones (Reed, 1985). These include some services which should be available for all women, and some additional ones for women with drug- or alcohol-misusing partners and women with children.

Services for all women drug misusers

(a) Skills training
   - to increase assertiveness
   - to increase self-esteem
   - to improve coping strategies with stress and anxiety.
(b) Assistance with social problems
   - housing
   - finance
   - domestic violence.
(c) Assistance with legal problems
   - criminal
   - childcare
   - divorce.
(d) Vocational training
   - job skills
   - education.
(e) Treatment of associated mental health problems
   - psychiatric disorders
   - sequelae of sexual abuse.
(f) Help forming new social ties with women who do not use drugs and alcohol
   - women's organisations
   - self-help groups
   - social service agencies.

(g) Physical healthcare
- during pregnancy
- for non-pregnant women.

(h) Contraceptive advice
- to allow informed decisions about pregnancy
- to protect from infection.

(i) Support and education for family and friends.

2 Services for women with alcohol or drug misusing partners

(a) Couple work.

(b) Skills training and support to improve negotiating skills for
- safe sex
- safe injecting practices.

(c) Help gaining financial and psychological independence to leave partner
- if partner continues to use
- undermines woman's efforts
- or is violent.

3 Services for women with children

(a) Babysitting.

(b) Child and family psychiatry services
- family assessment and support
- family therapy
- treatment of children's mental health problems.

(c) Parenting classes
- to enable effective care for children
- to reduce stress of caring for children.

(d) Support through childcare procedures.

(e) Liaison with voluntary agencies and self-help organisations (e.g. NEWPIN).

Treating families is time-consuming and requires specialist skills. Many women are frightened that their children will be removed and may be motivated to learn to care for them adequately. If the child has to be taken into care, all professionals involved should explain clearly to the woman what they are doing at all stages.

Inter-agency co-operation

Few treatment agencies will be able to address all needs. *Close inter-agency co-operation* is required. Drug and alcohol misusers have low attendance rates when referred to other services, and many other agencies may have prejudices and be resistant to helping them. The co-ordinating role of a sympathetic *keyworker* is central to engaging alcohol- or drug-misusing women and to educating other agencies.

Style and context compatible with women's needs

Services should be sensitive to women's different orientations, cultural and ethnic backgrounds. Interventions should be *targeted at the specific drug- and alcohol-taking patterns and behaviour of women*. For example, with reference to harm minimisation, women are more likely to share needles with a partner, whereas men are more likely to share socially. Services should be *easily accessible* and strategies used must be *based on a thorough understanding of the different peer groups, the social pressures and developmental tasks* they face, and of the coping strategies they use.

Interventions should be provided in a style that is compatible with women's needs. A supportive confidence- and skill-building approach may be more effective than the traditional confrontational approaches, particularly in engaging women who may feel guilty and out of control.

Women seeking help should be safe and free from harassment: all services need specific sexual-harassment policies. There should be enough female staff at all levels of service planning and provision to provide role models for women drug misusers and the option of a female worker, as well as to ensure that the organisation takes women's needs into account.

It remains unclear and controversial whether women need women-only services. Women-only facilities may recruit women who might not otherwise have sought treatment, especially those with a history of sexual abuse or with dependent children (Copeland and Hall, 1992). However, some areas may not have the financial resources to provide women-only services. If women are treated separately this may marginalise them further, allowing traditional services to avoid the issue altogether.

There are, however, some issues that it may be easier to discuss in all-women groups, such as sexual abuse, sexuality and possibly parenting. It is not sufficient simply to add a couple of women's groups on to a programme. A service must thoroughly review its basic assumptions, practice and culture and help staff at all levels to explore their own gender socialisation and how it affects their working lives. Providing women-sensitive services has considerable resource implications in terms of staff training and facilities. Service planning should also involve extensive consultation with service users.

Little is known about treatment outcome in women with drug and alcohol problems (Litman, 1986), so it is not yet clear which services are most effective. In order to inform the discussion and continue to develop more gender-sensitive services, systematic evaluation is required of any service that aims to meet women's needs appropriately.

CONCLUSION

Women with alcohol and drug problems are a disadvantaged group whose needs are not fully met by current services. They are a heterogeneous group with multiple social, psychological and physical problems. They are less likely than their male counterparts to see addiction as their main problem and are more likely to want help for associated health and psychosocial problems. Women with addiction problems face considerable social stigma and are still under-represented in formal treatment settings. A greater understanding of their experiences and needs is essential to overcoming the barriers to treatment that exist and to providing a service that is perceived as safe, accessible and appropriate and that addresses these multiple difficulties.

CROSS-REFERENCES WITHIN THIS BOOK

Chapter 4   Girls in distress: an unconsidered issue
Chapter 6   Planning services for black women
Chapter 9   Homeless women
Chapter 11   The impact of childhood sexual abuse
Chapter 12   Women and violence

REFERENCES

Amaro, H., Beckman, L.J. and Mays, V.E. (1987) 'A comparison of black and white women entering alcoholism treatment', *Journal of Studies on Alcohol* 48: 220–228.

Beckman, L.J. and Amaro, H. (1986) 'Personal and social difficulties faced by women and men entering alcoholism treatment', *Journal of Studies on Alcohol* 47: 135–145.

Blume, S.B. (1992) 'Alcohol and other drug problems in women', in: J.H. Lowinson, P. Ruiz, R.B. Millman (eds), *Substance abuse, a comprehensive textbook* (2nd edition), Baltimore: Williams & Wilkins.

Breeze, E. (1985) *Women and drinking*, London: HMSO.

Copeland, J. and Hall, W. (1992) 'A comparison of women seeking drug and alcohol treatment in a specialist women's and two traditional mixed-sex treatment services', *British Journal of Addiction* 87: 1293–1302.

Dawe, S., Gerada, C. and Strang, J. (1992) 'Establishment of a liaison service for pregnant opiate-dependent women', *British Journal of Addiction* 87: 867–871.

Department of Health (1994) 'Drug misuse statistics', *Statistical Bulletin* 3: 2–21.

Dunne, F. (1988) 'Are women more easily damaged by alcohol than men?' *British Journal of Addiction* 83: 1135–1136.

Goddard, E. and Ikin, C. (1988) *Drinking in England and Wales in 1987*, London: HMSO.

Gossop, M., Griffiths, P. and Strang, J. (1994) 'Sex differences in patterns of drug taking behaviour', *British Journal of Psychiatry* 164: 101–104.

Harrison, P.A. and Belille, C.A. (1987) 'Women in treatment. Beyond the stereotype', *Journal of Studies on Alcohol* 48: 574–578.

HMSO (1988) *AIDS and drug misuse. Part I: Report of the Advisory Council on the Misuse of Drugs*, London: HMSO.

Hser, Y.-I., Anglin, M.D. and Booth, M.W. (1987) 'Sex differences in addict careers. 3: addiction', *American Journal of Drug and Alcohol Abuse* 13: 231–251.

Institute of Medicine (1990) 'Populations defined by structural characteristics', in *Broadening the base of treatment for alcohol problems. Report of a study by a committee of the Institute of Medicine*, Washington, DC: National Academy Press.

Klee, H. (1993) 'HIV risks for women drug injectors: heroin and amphetamine users compared', *Addiction* 88: 1055–1062.

Lindberg, S. and Agren, G. (1988) 'Mortality among male and female hospitalised alcoholics in Stockholm 1962–1983', *British Journal of Addiction* 83: 1193–1200.

Litman, G.K. (1986) 'Women and alcohol problems: finding the next questions', *British Journal of Addiction* 81: 601–603.

National Association of Health Authorities (1989) *Briefing: alcohol and National Drinkwise Day*, Birmingham: NAHA.

Reed, B.G. (1985) 'Drug misuse and dependency in women: the meaning and implications of being considered a special population or minority group', *International Journal of the Addictions* 20: 13–62.

Reed, B.G. (1987) 'Developing women-sensitive drug dependence treatment services: why so difficult?', *Journal of Psychoactive Drugs* 19: 151–164.

Regier, D.A., Boyd, J.H., Burke, J.D., Rae, D.S., Myers, J.K., Kramer, M., Robins, L.N., George, L.K., Karno, M. and Locke, B.Z. (1988) 'One month prevalence of mental disorders in the United States. Based on five epidemiological catchment area sites', *Archives of General Psychiatry* 45: 977–986.

Robins, L.N., Helzer, J.E., Weissman, M.M., Orvaschel, H., Gruenberg, E., Burke, J.D. and Regier, D.A. (1984) 'Lifetime prevalence of specific psychiatric disorders in three sites', *Archives of General Psychiatry* 41: 949–958.

Rohsenhow, D.J., Corbett, R. and Devine, D. (1988) 'Molested as children: a hidden contribution to substance abuse?', *Journal of Substance Abuse Treatment* 5: 13–18.

Ross, H.E., Glaser, F.B. and Stiasny, S. (1988) 'Sex differences in the prevalence of psychiatric disorders in patients with alcohol and drug problems', *British Journal of Addiction* 83:1179–1192.

Suffet, F. and Brotman, R. (1976) 'Female drug use: some observations', *International Journal of the Addictions* 11:19–33.

Szwabo, P.A. (1993) 'Substance abuse in older women', *Clinics in Geriatric Medicine* 9: 197–208.

Thom, B. (1986) 'Sex differences in help-seeking for alcohol problems. 1: the barriers to help-seeking', *British Journal of Addiction* 81: 777–788.

Trad, P. V. (1993) 'Substance abuse in adolescent mothers: strategies for diagnosis, treatment and prevention', *Journal of Substance Abuse Treatment* 10: 421–431.

Wilsnack, S.C., Wilsnack, R.W. and Klassen, A.D. (1986) 'Epidemiological research on women's drinking, 1978–1984', in *Women and alcohol: health related issues*, National Institute on Alcohol Abuse and Alcoholism Research Monograph no. 16. Washington, DC: US Government Printing Office, 1–68.

Chapter 11

The impact of childhood sexual abuse

Emma Staples and Christopher Dare

INTRODUCTION

Clinical practice with children, adolescents and adults makes it clear that sexual abuse of children is common. Many surveys have confirmed this and have shown that girls are much more frequently abused than boys (up to three times), that the offenders are disproportionately male and that it is an international problem (Finkelhor, 1994). The seriousness of the consequences of such abuse is considerable, although it is difficult to disentangle the effects of rejection, deprivation and emotional and physical abuse that often accompany childhood sexual abuse (Mullen *et al.*, 1993, 1994). Despite the frequency with which sexual abuse is revealed in contemporary clinical practice, until twenty years ago, sexual abuse within families was regarded as rather uncommon. It is remarkable that awareness about the phenomenon has only come about in recent years, because there can be no doubt that sexual abuse of girls and women has existed for ever. This failure of twentieth-century psychiatry to appreciate the extent of childhood sexual abuse and its psychological consequences until the 1960s requires explanation. The obvious nature of the effects, and their implication for the mental health and personal relationships of women, makes even more striking and, in an important sense, incomprehensible, the long silence and denial of childhood sexual abuse. In this, there are parallels in the way society has failed to meet the needs of women who have suffered rape or domestic violence, being misled by denial and false assumptions.

There is good reason to attempt a theoretical understanding for the social pretence that sexual abuse was not happening. Likewise, trying to understand why mental health professionals have proposed alternative explanations for women's statements about their suffering is useful. In the light of what we now know, such explanation appears to lie between the unlikely and the preposterous. It seems to us that the reasons behind previous denial and alternative explanation are still at work and hinder the creation of a social context in which the sexual abuse of children can be stopped and the victims helped.

WAYS IN WHICH THE ABUSED MAY BE FAILED BY SOCIETY AND PROFESSIONALS

This lamentable difficulty has occurred in a variety of ways. First, there seems to be a 'barricade' against accurate acceptance of the facts about childhood sexual abuse, both in general and in response to the individual. Second, there have been painful failures in social and professional responses to childhood sexual abuse and further abuse, rather than effective help, may ensue from the discovery of childhood trauma. Despite the good intentions, professionalism and theoretical knowledge of workers, means of assessment and methods of treatment for both children and adults can stray into this repetition of abuse: questioning and evaluation of the abuse may be carried out in an insensitive, intrusive way further hurting the victim and failing to help them. Third, the actuality of the abuse can be ignored or can become the sole and obsessive focus. An abused person can be seen as though the sexual abuse (particularly if it was especially horrific) is the *only* relevant fact about the patient. Alternatively, the mental health worker can avoid the topic, or enquire in such a manner as to prevent revelation of the actual history. Our own studies, conducted in a psychiatric hospital, have highlighted the continuing failure to elicit or to acknowledge a history of childhood sexual abuse in women in this setting. Specific investigation has revealed many female patients who have been extensively abused, and for whom this continues to have an impact: yet those involved in their care are unaware of these traumatic experiences. Finally, subsequent procedures can become abusive: legal systems, in principle designed to protect the victim, can end up traumatising her by the investigatory and adversarial process; childcare arrangements that *should* alleviate the suffering and provide a health-inducing environment can all too often turn out to be careless, inadequate and actually abusive (by staff or other clients of the service).

Mental health professionals cannot assume that they are exempt from the influences of the psychological, cultural and social processes that exist. This chapter examines the background to these states of affairs and attempts to suggest explanations. It goes on to address the ramifications for women's mental health and for provision of services to survivors of sexual abuse, with particular emphasis on some of the psychodynamic processes involved.

UNDERSTANDING THE SILENCE

Attitudes to women

The current state of concern about childhood sexual abuse and its effects on women has evolved in parallel with twentieth-century feminism. The recent development of greater acceptance of the facts of childhood sexual abuse, the setting up of legislation for child protection that acknowledges its existence, and professional interest in the clinical phenomena, owes much to the increased awareness of gender politics and the imbalance of power between women and men. Attitudes to women within masculine-dominated professions have denied the effect of male institutions on women as Showalter has shown (1987). In her account of the history of mental health beliefs and women, Showalter conjures up a vivid picture of a perception of women as both vulnerable and dangerously sexual. She demonstrates the mythology (presumably largely created by men) whereby the psychological disturbances of women were attributed on the one hand to a supposed immaturity of women, that is, being unable to stand the rigours of the real, that is male, world, as though women were children. On the other hand, they were seen as dangerously, wantonly sexual. Psychological illness in the nineteenth century was regularly attributed to women and regularly seen as a reason why men should take control of women. The portrayal of women in psychological distress in nineteenth-century literature is a vivid example of this. Lady Deadlock in Charles Dickens' *Bleak House* is a characteristic figure: fierce and passionate, out of control, irresponsible and self-destructive, destroyed by her inability to contain her own emotions.

Sigmund Freud

It is not unexpected that services for women, being provided within a male, medical view of psychiatric illness, have not been tuned to the needs of women traumatised by men. For much of this century, the scale of sexual traumatisation of women in and out of childhood has been consistently played down. One way to explore this is to reconsider the important influence of Sigmund Freud on twentieth-century medical psychology.

Freud evokes a view of women as both immature and potentially uncontrolled in their passion, which contributes to his well-known ambivalent attributions about women. At times, he describes women and men as being prevented from having a full relationship by the failure of women's sexuality to be acknowledged (Freud, 1930). At other times, he suggests that female sexuality is intrinsically under the control of men so that, in his view, women have the potential for polymorphous perverse sexual expressions as demanded by their (male) lovers (Freud, 1905, 1923).

One hundred years ago Freud declared that he had discovered the cause of the 'psychoneuroses' to be sexual. He used this term to cover most psychological disturbances, including paranoid states and other psychotic illnesses (Freud, 1900). He came to believe that there were two forms of neuroses, both of which had a sexual origin. First were the 'actual neuroses', regarded by Freud (1912) as the result of abnormal sexual practices such as excessive masturbation, coitus interruptus or prolonged celibacy. Second, the psychoneuroses proper were believed to result from experiences in childhood, of which sexual seduction was the most important in leading to psychological traumatisation. Freud (1894) evolved a sophisticated traumatic model and proposed that the 'psychic apparatus' of childhood was unable to cope with, or to understand, sexual exposure or seduction by an adult. However, as the child entered puberty and began to have a more adult experience of her own sexuality, she re-appraised the earlier sexual events which now became potentially comprehensible. This re-experiencing put events in a different light and became traumatic. The neurotic symptoms that were subsequently created can be seen to represent an attempt to deal with unbearable amounts of pain aroused by the re-experiencing.

Clinical example of Freud's model

There were some ingenious aspects of this theoretical formulation, and in current psychiatric clinics people are seen who seem to demonstrate well some aspects of Freud's model. There are women who report having been sexually traumatised before puberty. Although they may or may not have clear memories of their experience, as young adults another event occurs, commonly the beginning of an adult sexual relationship, which may cause them to suffer in a different and more intense way. Intense anxiety, depression, suicidal feelings and profound sexual inhibition may develop.

Freud's reconsideration

Despite this clinical cogency, Freud (1925) became uneasy about his theory for reasons relevant to the present-day discussion. He realised that what he was proposing meant that serious incestuous traumatisation occurred often enough to account for the widespread incidence of psychological disturbances. Later, he came to doubt that all the vast number of cases of psychoneurosis could have originated in incest. In addition, he came upon material in his own self-analysis which he knew would have led him to construct in another person a sexual seduction and traumatisation by the mother. As he did not believe that such a construction was literally true in his own case, he felt forced to consider that the images of his mother's sexual seductiveness were, in actuality, his own creations.

Consequently, as is well known, Freud (1900, 1925) came to alter his earliest theories of the causes of psychological illness. In his clinical histories, however, he never ceased to highlight sexual traumas as important in determining the development and content of neurotic illness. His advocacy of internal psychological processes proved no more acceptable to the medical and psychological world as a general theory of psychological disturbance than did his traumatic theory. He postulated that internal psychological processes in children have an inherent sexual nature and that the defence against these wishes results in neurosis.

Freud believed that he had discovered that sexuality, as a biological drive, played a large part in the development of children (Freud, 1905). The theory was based upon his knowledge of the capacity of children to have sexual fantasies which took diverse forms. These included sexual, sensual interests that were thought to be perverse in Freud's time. For example, interests in exhibitionism, oral and anal forms of sexuality and the admixture of sadistic and masochistic elements within sexuality. The idea that children had a rich fantasy life (which is certainly true) led to a distortion, such that the complaints of children and women that they had been subject to seduction, humiliation and attack were denied or ascribed to the victim's fantasies.

In some quarters, Freud is accused of having some responsibility for the high levels of denial about sexual abuse, neglect and lack of concern for children in society. It is possible that he might, by his authority, have enabled a much earlier acceptance of this reality. However, it is debatable whether Freud was a cause of the process of denial, or whether his was an ignored voice that could have altered these facts. The fate of Freud's hypotheses concerning the nature of neurosis had consequences for the lot of many young women in the first sixty years of this century who claimed that they had been sexually abused. Society, psychotherapists and psychoanalysts continued to ignore, or to be otherwise in ignorance of, the reality that children, especially girl children, were being sexually hurt on a very wide scale. Freud's abandonment of his sexual trauma theory (Freud, 1900) can be explained, in part, by his being controlled by patriarchal attitudes, which are evident in many of his views about female psychology. However, a general patriarchy does not explain why he started to expose the truth about adult sexual abuse of children in the first place.

This historical account suggests that there is something that opposes measured, rational assimilation of the subject matter. Just as denial, exaggeration or martyrdom for the victim, perpetrator or the discoverer may all act in an individual case, so such mechanisms have influenced society's response. It seems that crucial factors in the eventual acceptance of the extent and significance of childhood sexual abuse were the feminist movement and the acknowledgement that adults were capable of physical abuse to their own and to other people's children.

THE LONG-TERM PSYCHOLOGICAL EFFECTS OF CHILDHOOD SEXUAL ABUSE

Literature on the long-term psychological effects of childhood sexual abuse has identified multiple disturbances. These include disturbances of mood, self-esteem, sexuality and relationships. Attempts to construct a specific syndrome have been unsuccessful. However, long-term sequelae can include elements of post-traumatic stress disorder. Situational anxiety, depression and 'flashback' recall of the traumatic event are common, but neither inevitable nor characteristic. Flashbacks take many forms and often pick up a detail of the experiences which was used by the victim as a focus for distraction at the time. A preoccupation with recurrent and menacing images of the abuser's face, the most painful and feared attack, or a particular sensation of strangulation or pressure on the body may dominate. The recalled image may be striking because of the emotional coldness of the attacker's expression, or because of a sense of his cruelty and indifference. Such images may force themselves into the sufferer's mind at any time, although it is common for them to occur in a specific context, such as at the time of a sexual approach.

Mood disturbances include a vulnerability to depression and anxiety, with or without suicidal and self-harming behaviour. In younger women, self-harming features, such as parasuicide, substance misuse and self-cutting may be more dominant than long-standing depressive symptoms. Disturbance of self-esteem, a sense of worthlessness, a hopeless expectation of further abuse and a hatred of her own body including its shape, sensuality and sexual potential are often all intense, even when the level of depression is low.

Friendships and intimate relationships of survivors of sexual abuse can be distorted by depression, anxiety states, self-harming behaviour, sexual fearfulness and inhibition. The development and maintenance of relationships can also be disturbed by the unassuageable demand for reassurance and an obsessive need to recount the abusive experiences, or to describe the flashbacks. However, all these things may be suffered in silence and be accompanied by a life that appears colourless, unadventurous and inhibited.

Personality disorder is a well-known associated feature of childhood sexual abuse. The more that the clinical picture is affected by interpersonal and life-pervading problems, the more the diagnosis of personality disturbance will be used. The specific features of marked lability of mood, periods of intense destabilisation, rages and frequent extreme, short-lasting hates and loves, lead towards the application of the label of borderline personality disturbance.

This descriptive account of the psychiatric sequelae of childhood sexual abuse emphasises the diversity and lack of a unitary syndrome characterising survivors. Sexual abuse consists of a wide miscellany of events, occurring in differing contexts, at different stages of the victim's development and with greater or lesser degrees of accompanying physical or emotional abuse. This can explain, in part, the variety of outcomes seen following childhood sexual abuse. For example, a teenager who has grown up in a supportive, caring and stable family may be raped by a guest at a family wedding. This is sexual abuse within the family, but is different from the situation of a woman in adolescence who has been consistently sexually assaulted by a step-father with the suspected compliance of her mother, who herself physically assaults and emotionally rejects her daughter. Whilst rape in adulthood is likely to be associated with features of post-traumatic stress disorder, the prolonged sexual abuse of a child in a rejecting, chaotic and neglectful family is likely to give rise to a person with fragile resources, poor self-esteem, a proneness to mood disturbance and a damaged capacity for consistent emotional relationships. These disorganised families also have higher rates of substance abuse, alcohol abuse and other psychiatric illness. It is difficult to disentangle the extent to which the victim's psychological problems are the consequence of general disturbance in the family, rather than specific effects of sexual abuse.

A PSYCHODYNAMIC AND 'EXPERIENTIAL' ACCOUNT OF THE EFFECTS OF CHILDHOOD SEXUAL ABUSE

It is well accepted in psychoanalytic writing that different antecedents can result in similar psychological organisation, while similar traumas may result in disparate psychopathological structures. Over the last century, psychoanalysts have been divided on the emphasis that should be accorded to external or internal events in determining the onset, course and disposition of psychological disturbance. These considerations should be taken into account when working with adult survivors. If someone appears to be in psychological difficulties as a consequence of external events, then it may be difficult to find motivation for change. In principle, it is easier to undertake the hard work of change if the reason for needing to change is felt to be one's own. In addition, complex opposition to change can evolve in a person who believes herself to be the victim of another. After all, if the person's suffering is a result of the harmful, purposeful cruelty of the other, an apparent improvement may appear to exonerate the perpetrator.

The polarisation within psychodynamic thinking between external and internal events as responsible for psychopathology is strikingly evident in the attitude of psychotherapists towards childhood sexual abuse. The works of Alice Miller are widely popular and some of their appeal stems from the way in which they explain some of the sense of grievance and hurt that so many patients describe when they discuss their parents. Alice Miller proposes that patients are the victim of their parents and appears to agree with the simplistic aphorism that 'parents screw you up'. She would argue that other propositions of the role of internal factors, such as intense and innate envy or primary destructiveness, risk scapegoating the vulnerable individual.

'Father blaming' versus 'mother blaming'

These considerations address a controversial aspect of the psychodynamic approach to the effects of childhood sexual abuse and the possibility of moral hazards in espousing a psychodynamic viewpoint. Until recent years, a common proposition was that sexual abuse by a father figure can only occur with the complicity of the mother, either with active collusion, or by maternal absence or neglect. Harney (1992), discusses how this idea leads to a dangerous shift in the focus of responsibility for the occurrence and sequelae of sexual abuse: a shift from paternal abuse to maternal unavailability being the key causative factor. There is also a suggestion behind this that a wife owes her husband sexual gratification, and that if this is not forthcoming he is justified in fulfilling his sexual needs elsewhere.

Harney suggests that 'mother blaming' in psychoanalytic thought has contributed to the experience of child sexual abuse being ignored in the developmental theory of borderline personality disorder. The mother's role has been described as the more central in the development of borderline personality disorder, with little focus on the father's role. Although this may seem to emphasise the personality and role of the mother, it also implies that it is the mother who is ultimately responsible for *any* impairments in her child's development. Neglecting the impact of childhood trauma in a theory of borderline personality disorder may result in a failure to explore a history of childhood abuse in the psychotherapeutic treatment of such women. An understanding of this debate is important, because many women survivors of childhood sexual abuse do blame their mothers for a lack of supervision, or even complicity in the abuse:

'She must have known he was doing it to me'.

In psychodynamic terms this could be seen to link with the daughter's self-denigrating identification with the mother. The woman often sees her mother simultaneously as the victim, and yet also guilty of being in a weak, tormented relationship with the perpetrator. Survivors of sexual abuse often have enormous difficulties in preventing themselves believing that they are to blame for what has happened: 'I could have told him to stop', as an adult said about the abuse by her 15-year-old brother at the time that she herself was 6.

Childhood abuse and adult offending

Many reports and studies have linked childhood sexual abuse with a variety of acting out behaviours, such as promiscuity, delinquency, aggressiveness and inappropriate sexual behaviour. Links between childhood sexual abuse and later criminal behaviour have led to theories about the role of childhood sexual abuse in the development of deviant behaviour and in the development of an inevitable cycle of abuse (Widom and Ames, 1994). It has been suggested that being abused can lead to becoming an abuser (the 'cycle of abuse'), and this is something abused women may fear. Women who have been abused and who express such fears may have a confused self-denigrating identification with their mother, which may lead to the acting-out behaviours. These fears are important and need to be explored in terms of real risk, as well as within the transference in psychotherapeutic work.

Although survivors' concerns about this can be fuelled by talk of cycles of abuse, Widom and Ames's recent research (1994) has shown that victims of childhood sexual abuse are certainly not inevitably destined to become future abusers or offenders. Indeed, compared with other types of child abuse and neglect, the experience of having been sexually abused did not uniquely increase an individual's risk for later delinquent or adult criminal behaviour. Those who had experienced abuse (sexual, physical or neglect) in childhood were all more likely to be convicted of an offence in adulthood. The association with offending may not result from sexual abuse uniquely, but may be associated with the matrix of trauma and stress of the early childhood experiences, or with society's response to the event. Indeed, the broad range of outcome in individuals with a history of childhood abuse illustrates how protective factors can buffer an individual from long-term consequences. These factors may include characteristics of the abuse itself, of the abuser, the child or their environment. Further understanding of how protective factors operate has important implications for development of treatment.

Effects on future relationships

The child who has been abused often finds it impossible to integrate the abusive experience into other aspects of herself. The woman often believes herself to have been 'normal' in the intervening years between apparent forgetting of the abuse and subsequent recollection in adulthood. The suppression of memory seems to lead to a failure to assimilate into the developing self a gradually evolving perception, knowledge and understanding about relationships and sexuality. It is as though, in a sense, a 'blind eye' is turned to anything that has a sexual quality. This means that when adult sexuality becomes possible it is met by an immature psychological organisation which has not been through the gradual integration of sexuality and relationships that normally exists. Such a woman enters into an intimate sexual relationship with only the haziest notion as to what she might be experiencing and has a relatively dissociated state of mind, in which her own body and psychological experience are separated. Nonetheless, a wish to heal the trauma and to have a reassuring, comforting contact with the feared object, the man, may lead to repeated attempts to make a reparative relationship. Sometimes, the point of the relationship is to gain mastery of the sort of person who does abuse. Alternatively, the young woman may have no experience of a non-abusive relationship to call upon in choosing a partner. Hence, instead of gaining some reassurance about the possibility of being safe with a man, some women get repeated confirmation of the riskiness of men, leading to further splitting of the bodily and emotional needs.

MODES OF TREATMENT

The wide range of problems from which survivors of childhood sexual abuse can suffer means that the whole realm of psychological states and psychiatric syndromes may have to be considered. As emphasised previously, many survivors of childhood trauma necessarily seek help from the usual services. However, a wide scope of specific treatments is available. These include self-help manuals, instructional books, audio and video material, computer self-help programmes, community groups, volunteer counsellors, private counselling or psychotherapy, out-patient treatment programmes in the health services, day-treatment settings and in-patient units. Mental health workers should not forget that the outcome for survivors depends on a number of factors. If we return to our previous example of a teenager being raped at a wedding, a family who can hear and believe the circumstances of the assault and support their daughter can have an important effect in preventing the development of later difficulties. At different times in a woman's life, non-professional interventions, such as the understanding of a partner, can have a beneficial effect. However, long-term amelioration of the effects of childhood experience often can only occur with some form of psychological help. The aspiration of all people involved in mental health care must be to sensitise themselves and their colleagues to meet the special needs of survivors as their outcome is by no means inevitable. Having said that, few guidelines exist as to which particular kinds of help are most useful under any given clinical circumstance.

Feminist perspective and treatment modalities

In the same way that feminist thinking has had an influence on society's acknowledgement of abuse, services for women shaped by feminist principles have had an important impact on meeting women's needs. The sense of powerlessness, helplessness and hopelessness that can overwhelm a survivor may be reinforced by the experience of being in a male-dominated society. Other systems can reproduce this experience, e.g. a psychiatric in-patient setting. This is particularly relevant in patients who show features of borderline personality disorder, such as self-mutilation or violent outbursts. In a concrete way, there can be an escalation in attempts to control or contain such behaviours, which might lead to inappropriate admission to hospital or use of medication. The paternalistic structure of an in-patient ward and the inherent powerlessness therein may lead to a powerful re-experiencing of early trauma and an exacerbation of symptoms (Fromuth and Burkhart, 1992). In some situations hospital is necessary, but this example illustrates how service providers must think about how survivors might experience a service. The assumption that exploration of childhood trauma is always sufficient would also be wrong. This could lead to those women with serious mental health needs being deprived of intensive and appropriate treatment.

An extensive literature describes counselling and psychotherapeutic approaches to children, adolescents and adults who have been sexually abused. Sanderson (1990) describes a wide range of modalities and time frames that have been reported as useful in helping this group. She points out that, although controlled studies are lacking, it is evident from the clinical accounts that a range of treatments can be effective. She suggests dividing the therapies into those that address the emotional, cognitive and behavioural aspects of the survivors' problems. She advocates the need for changes in all three areas, declaring that a method that limits itself to one area alone is unlikely to be complete. Jehu (1988) presents a detailed account of cognitive-behavioural treatment and Grant (1991) provides an overview based on psychoanalytic theory. Both reviews highlight the importance of addressing all aspects of a survivor. The treatments focus on current problems, as it is these that tend to precipitate and perpetuate the distress, even though reference to past experience is necessary, in order to deal with them effectively.

Family, couple and group treatments

Treatment may be offered to the individual, a group, couple or family. The advantage of being in a group is that it allows members to overcome feelings of being alone with their experiences. Although sensible in principle, this may be difficult for the client or patient to accept because of the fear of public exposure and humiliation. For this reason, couple therapy with survivors and their partners has to be suggested cautiously, ideally after rapport has been achieved in an individual assessment. A woman in a stable relationship can be helped to gain more intimacy and support from her partner, if he is motivated and if the therapist can facilitate a safe setting in which the couple can develop greater mutual revelation and understanding.

Family therapy has been widely used as part of programmes for helping children and adolescent survivors, but it is important that the professional suggesting this treatment modality has a clear notion of what end is sought. Family therapy can also involve adult siblings, who may find it easier to support each other in this setting and thus to confront their parents with the facts of the abuse of one or more of their number. In this instance, the aim of a family meeting may be simply to give siblings an occasion to tell parents about the extent of their continuing pain and distress that has ensued from childhood.

For women who have not been able to establish a stable sexual partnership, couple work is not possible. For many survivors this is met in a long-term counselling or psychotherapeutic relationship. Within this it is hoped that they may be able to address their painful dislike of themselves and their body, and to mourn what has been taken from them by their childhood experience.

OBSTACLES ENCOUNTERED IN TREATMENT

The setting

The heterogeneity of problems experienced by survivors is mirrored by the plethora of services developed in a wide variety of settings. Whether professionals have a specific interest in or knowledge of this area, women who have had such aversive experiences have particular needs. When the symptoms and persisting negative effects of sexual trauma are not addressed, treatments may meet with limited success. It can often be the case that a mental health service facility will not be the context within which disclosure of childhood abuse will occur.

Psychodynamics of working with women survivors

There is a danger that the relationship between the sufferer and the professional may come to resemble a replay of the mother–daughter relationship that so often accompanies the abuse and which has been described earlier. Within this, the daughter may have felt intensely, though unreasonably guilty and ashamed, leading her to disguise, hide or disclose abuse in a partial or obscure manner. The mother may have been in ignorance, suspicion or helpless inaction about her daughter's experience. Mental health services professionals are susceptible to all the possibilities of denial, distortion and helplessness in the face of childhood sexual abuse, as are the parents, relatives and general population.

All too often, a professional with a special interest in helping survivors will be asked to see someone with a range and severity of problems that would, without the history of the abuse, be treated by the referring agency or worker. It is as though the history of abuse is assumed to disqualify able practitioners from conducting themselves with their usual competence. As we have described, people who have been sexually abused in childhood may be ashamed or even disgusted by themselves for having been the victims. They will regularly have felt unable to tell their family, close friends or partners, out of the obscure but powerful sense of having been incriminated by the abuse. A person who has felt overwhelmed and controlled by abusive experience can imbue similar feelings in helpers. Either they fail to reveal the history, and its importance for them in determining their beliefs, attitudes and distress, or they reveal it in such a way as to make others believe in their own sense of 'irrecoverability'.

Aspects of the mental health worker

Male professionals, who may be seen to have power and authority over them by women patients, may feel disqualified by their gender and apparent power from addressing the pain of women who have suffered at the hands of an adult male. Female professionals can also feel unable to handle the fear of denial or revulsion on the part of the sufferer. In addition, it follows that a significant percentage of women professionals have themselves suffered sexual abuse in childhood or adolescence or have been sexually attacked or harassed as adults. Such identification with the sufferer can be painfully felt by the professional.

Specialist or general services?

The particular dynamics of working with women who have been abused inevitably make an impact on the mental health services. It would be wrong to set up fully comprehensive mental health services specifically for these women. Some form of help will inevitably be required within many different locations and survivors may suffer from a wide range of disorders. The fear and uncertainty that disclosure provokes in the professionals has tended to lead to a sense of powerlessness which may result in inappropriate referral, determined not by the problem for which the person needs help, but by a single aspect of her history. Women survivors of childhood sexual abuse have the whole range of normal life experiences, including childbirth, caring for others and mental health problems, that other women have. It would not make sense to set up parallel services exclusively for women survivors who have disclosed their abuse.

However, specialist services are appropriate for two reasons:

1 To provide help for women who have found it impossible to go to an agency where they feel they will be disbelieved or discredited. Other women may be unable to return to a generalist agency because of new abusive experiences in a hostel or hospital ward. Or they may have been sexually abused in individual psychotherapy or counselling.
2 To develop a concentration of expertise to help sufferers, which can then be communicated to generalist settings. The aim is to increase the competence of workers in a wide range of services. Clinical research into the sequelae of childhood sexual abuse and into the methods of helping the survivors should also be developed.

TREATMENT SETTING

Specialist services have developed in many settings: National Health Services, the Social Services, the voluntary and the private sectors. Sometimes the services have been developed in a planned and integrated manner, but more often sporadically. Although initially a 'top down' structure seems more reasonable, this is not necessarily the most helpful. The provision of services in an apparently sporadic way may represent something that has grown in response to a real demand in the community. This source can be productive of a more sensitively designed utility, meeting the needs of a specific area, and might therefore be more appropriate. Importation of a model designed on theoretical principles, or evolved as a result of mainly political concerns (emanating from a scandal or crisis) may turn out to be designed more to cover over problems than to help. This may continue the social denial of the problem alluded to earlier.

CONCLUSION

A long period of silence and denial is being replaced by increased awareness of the impact of childhood sexual abuse on women. Historical analysis helps us to understand why the realisation about childhood victimisation is a recent phenomenon, and how failing to acknowledge its importance can continue to impinge on the needs of women survivors. The raised awareness has led to a growth in services, and although lacunae remain, the development continues. Further research is needed in this area to evaluate and improve what is already available. The historical perspective highlights that listening to women must be the focus in research, clinical work and the design of appropriate services.

> A thing which has not been understood inevitably re-appears; like an unlaid ghost, it cannot rest until the mystery has been solved and the spell broken.
>
> (Sigmund Freud)

CROSS-REFERENCES WITHIN THIS BOOK

Chapter 4　Girls in distress: an unconsidered issue
Chapter 12　Women and violence
Chapter 13　Women as abusers

REFERENCES

Finkelhor, D. (1994) 'The international epidemiology of child sexual abuse', *Child Abuse and Neglect*, 18 (5): 409–417.
Freud, S. (1894) 'The neuropsychosis of defense', *The standard edition of the complete psychological works of Sigmund Freud* (hereafter, *SE*), vol. III, London: Hogarth Press, 1958.
Freud, S. (1900) 'The interpretation of dreams', *SE*, vol. IV, V.
Freud, S. (1905) 'Three essays on the theory of sexuality', *SE*, vol. VII.
Freud, S. (1912) 'Types of onset of neurosis', *SE*, vol. XII.
Freud, S. (1923) 'The ego and the id', *SE*, vol. XIX.
Freud, S. (1925) 'An autobiographical study', *SE*, vol. XX.

Freud, S. (1930) 'Civilisation and its discontents', *SE*, vol. XXI.

Fromuth, M.E. and Burkhart, B.R. (1992) 'Recovery or recapitulation? An analysis of the impact of psychiatric hospitalisation on the child sexual abuse survivor', *Women and Therapy* 12: 81–95.

Grant, S.M. (1991) 'Psychotherapy with people who have been sexually abused', in J. Holmes (ed.), *Textbook of Psychotherapy in Pychiatric Practice*, London: Churchill Livingstone.

Harney, P.A. (1992) 'The role of incest in developmental theory and treatment of women diagnosed with borderline personality disorder', *Women and Therapy* 12: 39–57.

Jehu, D. (1988) *Beyond sexual abuse: therapy with women who were childhood victims*, Chichester: John Wiley & Sons.

Mullen, P.E., Martin, J.L., Anderson, J.C., Romans, S.E. and Herbison, G.P. (1993) 'Childhood sexual abuse and mental health in adult life', *British Journal of Psychiatry* 163: 721–732.

Mullen, P.E., Martin, J.L., Anderson, J.C., Romans, S.E. and Herbison, G.P. (1994) 'The effect of child sexual abuse on social, interpersonal and sexual function in adult life', *British Journal of Psychiatry* 165: 35–47.

Sanderson, C. (1990) *Counselling adult survivors of child sexual abuse*, London: Jessica Kingsley Publishers.

Showalter, E. (1987) *The female malady: women, madness, and English culture, 1830–1980*, London: Virago.

Widom, C.A. and Ames, M.A. (1994) 'Criminal consequences of childhood sexual victimisation', *Child Abuse and Neglect* 18: 303–318.

Chapter 12

Women and violence

Gillian Mezey and Elizabeth Stanko

INTRODUCTION

Over the past few years, women's concern about public danger has been acknowledged, as evidenced in a flurry of advice we receive as women 'to take care'. In police-issued and government-financed leaflets, we are first and foremost advised, 'whenever possible, avoid travelling alone'; and when in public, we are told how to walk, how to carry our bags, and how to look inconspicuous and in charge. Exacerbated by the salacious media accounts of sexual violence, our concern about sexual danger is an acknowledgement of what it means to be female and to be constantly reminded about being vulnerable to the so-called vagaries of men. As women, what are the mental health implications of *knowing* about sexual danger? What are the consequences of the constant reminders we receive about having to act and 'be sensible' in order to minimise danger? And if we experience sexual and physical violence, what are the repercussions on our mental and physical well-being?

Few connect our anxiety about danger in public with our experiences and anxiety about danger in our private lives. This chapter attempts to do just that. It explores the popular notion of 'fear of crime' and its special impact on the lives of women. It goes on to explore the mental health consequences of the forms of violence most people associate with danger: sexual assault and physical battering of women in the home. What this chapter suggests is that women's mental health is affected by our position *as women*. We argue that negotiating our secondary status in society has mental health consequences, which stem from the potential and the reality of sexual violence. Those working in mental health must take seriously the context and legacies of sexual danger to women.

WOMEN AND THE GENERALISED FEAR OF CRIME

Generally, fear of crime is taken to represent individuals' diffuse sense of danger about being physically harmed by criminal violence. It is associated with concern about being *outside* the home, probably in an urban area, alone and potentially vulnerable to personal harm.

Typically, the discussion of fear of crime is centred around things that take place outside the home. The most popular question that appears on victimisation surveys is: 'How safe do you feel walking alone in your neighbourhood [in this area] alone after dark [or at night]?' In responding, interviewees are assumed to be thinking of their personal safety with regard to criminal violence. Women report fear at levels that are three times that of men, yet their recorded risk of personal violence, especially assault, is, by all official sources, lower than men's. Indeed, there is a mismatch between women's and men's reported risk of violent criminal victimisation and their fear of falling victim to such violence. Those who admit feeling safest, young men, reveal the greatest proportion of personally violent victimisations.

There have been some attempts to explain why women might harbour such anxiety about their personal safety. Michael Maxfield, analysing the 1982 British Crime Survey, finds some evidence to suggest it is women's fear of sexual assault that 'reduces feelings of safety among young women' (Maxfield, 1984). Mark Warr (1984) argues that 'it may well be that [for women] . . . fear of crime is fear of rape'. Margaret Gordon and Stephanie Riger (1988), extending their earlier work, go further by naming women's fear of rape as 'the female fear'.

Limiting the explanation of our fear of crime to the fear of rape, as some criminologists have, directs our attention to the worst scenario of sexual violence, the violent invasion of rape. Most crime surveys categorise rape as the only understandable, abhorrent sexual intrusion that could reasonably frighten us. This means that ordinary events, such as receiving sexual comments on the street or from co-workers, which are experienced as threatening, often private encounters, are overlooked because they are not 'serious' enough events (i.e. not crime), and therefore do not contribute to our fear of crime (Crawford *et al.*, 1990).

Crime against women, as most now agree, is seriously under-reported and under-recorded. The findings of oft-cited government-conducted crime surveys have no way of estimating a 'dark figure' of women's victimisation (Stanko, 1988). Nor can we fully explain our fear of crime by examining crime data alone. Threats and crime we experience *inside* the home, many feminists have argued, are important in understanding our feelings of insecurity.

Despite their shortcomings in capturing 'family' crime, crime surveys frame the contemporary debate about violence and the fear of violence, because of the way they fail to take into account what we ourselves say about the dangers we face throughout our lives, and in particular the danger associated with violence within the home. Thus, when many discuss women's anxiety about crime, they are usually separating what is assumed to be public violence from that which is characterised as private violence.

Canadian Michael Smith (1988) explored how violence by intimates affects women's fear of crime and found that women who experienced severe forms of violence at the hands of intimates were significantly more fearful than women who had experienced minor violence and those who were not victimised.

The study of fear of crime neglects the domestic nature of a vast majority of men's violence to women which may contribute to our fear and anxiety about safety: we are treated as if we fear only the unknown male stranger. As English researcher Rachel Pain (1993) found, women, despite disclosing a variety of domestic and intimate assaults, do speak of potential violence as 'stranger danger'. Such concern about danger begins early in life, suggests Jo Goodey (1994): as schoolchildren, we have been socialised to take precautions, especially with strangers. Stanko's research on safety and violence-avoidance illustrates how early lessons in danger become part of a lifetime of negotiating danger, inside and outside the home (Stanko, 1990).

Both officially recorded crime and the vast hidden violence against women suggest that our assailants are most likely to be known to us. As part of the feminist strategy of naming sexual violence as a form of oppression, feminist researchers have set out to document women's experiences of sexual and physical violence. Importantly, they include a wide range of such experiences that are rarely classified as criminal offences, such as obscene phone calls, being followed on the street, being touched up on public transport, and sexual harassment. By exposing men's violence to women, they explain women's fear of crime as a realistic appraisal of endemic abuse. These studies have uncovered a significant incidence of serious sexual and physical violence among adult women. Often, women's fears translate into concerns about the physical environment: parking lots, public stairwells, and public transport, for instance, feature prominently in our assessments of personal safety. Feminist geographer Gill Valentine (1989) characterises women's fear as a 'spatial expression of patriarchy'. Fellow geographer Rachel Pain (1993) suggests that fear, for women, 'ought to be taken as more a pervading state of alertness than a momentary terror'. Women therefore voice concern about safety as a routine consequence of everyday life.

What feminist studies indicate is that the reality of sexual violence – whether from known or unknown men – is a core component of being female and is experienced through a wide range of everyday, mundane situations. What we define as sexually violating and threatening, moreover, is not confined to what is statutorily defined as rape. As Pauline Bart and Patricia O'Brien (1986) show, even some women who were 'legally' raped define their experience as attempted rape.

Women may also be intimidated in their own homes, not only by their partners or former partners, but also by neighbours, teenage children and their friends. Beatrix Campbell (1993) describes how women living on a so-called high-crime estate in the North of England experienced constant intimidation from local young men. While the women found some respite in their own networks for safety, many were harassed and threatened by these young men, whose vandalism, drunkenness, and joy-riding threatened many from the area. No doubt women's fears are also affected by the blight and abandonment of neighbourhoods neglected by economically hard-pressed local governments. Women may also experience racial harassment and racist violence.

As gender is the most significant predictor of fear of crime, and as fear of sexual violence is by far the greatest concern among the most fearful gender, it seems reasonable to state that fear of sexual violence accounts for a sizeable measure of all fear of crime.

As a consequence of fear, we police ourselves:

- by restricting our activities in public because of the anxiety about potential violence;
- in public and in private, by using more safety precautions than do men (Stanko, 1990).

We arm ourselves with a number of strategies and routines for our own safety (Gardener, 1988), but we are rarely acknowledged as having any awareness about safety or danger. Some commentators deny women's virtual curfew after dark, assuming that we would always choose to restrict our movements to our own homes. Research suggests that the differences in our circumstances, such as our class, race, disability, age, type of residence, sexual partners, as well as our relationships to motherhood and to employment, mean that our management of threat and danger varies, as do our options for avoiding men's abusive behaviour in public spaces.

For women, fear of sexual violence has resulted in restrictions on lifestyles and mobility. We take more precautions than do men (perhaps, given all the official statistics, men should be considered feckless!). Of course, not all men are violent. The work on masculinities, especially masculinity and violence (of which we are part) tells us much more. The fact is that many of us consciously and unconsciously anticipate the need to avoid men's violence, whether it be from a known or unknown assailant.

WOMEN'S EXPERIENCES OF VIOLENCE

All the research on violence supports an analysis that places the gender of the victim at the centre. The actual experience of violence is different for men and women (Stanko and Hobdell, 1993; Stanko, 1995). Both domestic violence and sexual assault are crimes predominantly directed against and affecting women. Although men can be victims of sexual assault, this is still rare enough to be regarded as a curiosity by social scientists and to be virtually ignored by law enforcers and policy makers. The 1990 Criminal Statistics noted that the proportion of violent crimes directed against women appeared to be increasing. Women were most likely to be assaulted in their own home or in another's home, unlike men who were more often assaulted outdoors: 32 per cent of all violence recorded against women was 'domestic', in 38 per cent of cases there was not enough information to determine whether or not it fell into this category (Home Office, 1992). Although domestic violence is regarded extremely seriously by the victims, women still appear to be very reluctant to report to the police. Similarly, women are more likely than men to be killed by their partner or spouse: in 1990, out of 226 female victims of homicide, the perpetrator was a spouse or lover in 43 per cent of cases, compared with 9 per cent of the men. Women were significantly less likely to be killed by a stranger (11 per cent) compared with 24 per cent for men (Home Office, 1992). Fear of crime is highest for elderly women although they appear statistically to be at lowest risk.

WOMEN'S RESPONSE TO SEXUAL ASSAULT: RESISTANCE OR SUBMISSION?

Rape is a violent crime and yet it is a crime that rarely results in visible physical injury, the violence may be threatened rather than actual and the main damage is to the woman's sense of self, her physical and psychological integrity and her ability to trust others. The emotional and psychological consequences of rape, for many women, leave open wounds that refuse to heal.

There is some evidence to suggest that, whilst non-violent resistance (in the form of pleading, persuasion or other verbal strategies) may be effective in warding off an intended sexual assault, physical resistance is less effective. Indeed, violent resistance appears to increase the likelihood of a completed sexual assault as well as physical injury to the victim. Nevertheless, resistance, even if ineffective in terminating the assault, gives the woman a sense of having been in control during the attack, whereas the woman who submits is tormented by a sense of profound helplessness which can persist for years as well as self-doubt as to whether her failure to resist had unknowingly transmitted a wish for sexual relations. Unlike women who 'submit' to the rape (the majority) and fail to deter the assailant, 'resisters' are rarely accused of collaboration and generally encounter a more positive and supportive response from friends, family and the criminal justice system. Most women fail to offer any active resistance during a violent assault. Many women are immobilised with fear. Their behaviour becomes focused on preventing any additional physical harm or injury, not antagonising their assailant and complying with his demands. Women who are socialised to suppress overt expressions of aggression are rarely able to override such inhibitions in a life-threatening situation and defend themselves in an effective way. Moreover such resistance may not interrupt the intended attack and may even antagonise the assailant or encourage further aggression (Carter et al., 1988).

Women's lack of effective resistance during a rape attack is reminiscent of the passivity of many victims during a violent assault, and in extreme cases may manifest itself in overdependence on the aggressor, similar to the state of frozen watchfulness identified in battered children. During an attack the victim becomes highly attuned to the moods and behaviour of the assailant in order to be able to anticipate and thus avoid further injury. In extreme cases women will thank the rapist after he frees her, she may be ambivalent about retribution and finds it extremely difficult to express anger, because of the pervasive sense that, whatever the preceding hurt and violation, she has been allowed to live. This phenomenon is well recognised as a pathological transference reaction, the 'Stockholm Syndrome', among hostages, whose interests lie in calming and appeasing the terrorist and who may eventually develop very intense feelings of love and gratitude for them, if they survive the ordeal.

THE LEGAL RESPONSE TO VICTIMS OF SEXUAL ASSAULT

The consequences of such behaviour in legal terms is that the woman's passivity during the rape, her apparent acquiescence to the rapist's demands, and her ambivalence about pursuing legal retribution can easily be misinterpreted so as to undermine her credibility as a witness and her claim to have been raped. She will appear to have consented to sex and through her lack of resistance, will be regarded with additional scepticism, particularly in the face of a defendant who asserts consensual intercourse. Thus, non-resistance to a violent sexual assault has important legal and social repercussions: blame, disbelief and greater difficulty in achieving a conviction in court (Adler, 1987).

Many victims of crime, particularly of sexual and familial violence, are blamed for what has happened. The 'Just World Hypothesis' (Lerner and Miller, 1978) describes a basic belief that people get what they deserve and deserve what they get. Thus, if a woman is raped, this must be either because she is an inherently 'bad' woman (who in practice, is often a woman who doesn't fit the traditional female stereotype), or because an apparently respectable woman has uncharacteristically behaved in such a way as to get herself raped. Either way the victim loses out.

If responsibility for the rape is attributed to the victim's personality or behaviour, the rapist appears less blameworthy and the illusion of a predictable and just world order can be preserved. Adherence to a belief in a 'just world' has important practical and legal implications, reducing a jury's willingness to convict in cases where the victim is regarded as more blameworthy and thus more deserving of a sexual assault (Adler, 1987). Thus, virgins are regarded as more legitimate complainants than prostitutes; women who resist their assailant are more plausible than women who 'submit'; and women who are raped by strangers are more likely to get a conviction than women who have some prior acquaintance with their assailant. The victim's presentation in the courtroom also plays a significant role in the final verdict: one of the most significant factors affecting the final verdict is whether the jury like the look of the witness or not, whether they can identify with her, and whether she fits into their view of how a genuine rape victim should behave.

The numerous myths and misconceptions about rape are shamelessly peddled in the courtroom, generally without any attempt to counterbalance this with evidence from expert witnesses. Thus a woman's submission and apparent compliance during an assault is commonly presented as evidence of her consent to sexual relations. Her failure to report the rape immediately to the police may be interpreted as a calculated attempt to subvert justice and fabricate the story. The woman's sexual history is still presented in court, in spite of legal restraints, generally in order to undermine her credibility as a witness, and to make her appear as someone who, in any case, would be unlikely to sustain any real damage through 'one more' sexual encounter.

Although rape trauma syndrome can be offered as circumstantial evidence of a rape having taken place, in some states in the USA, its admissibility in the British courts has been vigorously opposed. The opposition is on the grounds that this would unfairly weight the case against the 'innocent man' unfairly accused and that, in any case, the so-called expert would not be giving the jury any information that would be outside the knowledge of the ordinary man (Frazier and Borgida, 1985).

WOMEN'S PSYCHOLOGICAL REACTIONS TO SEXUAL ASSAULT

The experience of violent crime shatters certain basic assumptions about one's own vulnerability, the safety of the world, the trustworthiness of other people and the predictability of the future. Compared with natural disasters, crime directly challenges the victim's relation to their fellow man and is more likely to be interpreted as a deliberate malevolent act, than as an accidental one. Within crime, certain factors may make recovery more difficult, for example a rape by a trusted friend or acquaintance will challenge the victim's judgement and her ability to control such events in the future, in a more fundamental way than a rape perpetrated by a stranger. The victim of acquaintance rape may find it difficult to persuade herself that the next person she puts her trust in won't do the same thing to her again. Victims of acquaintance rape appear to experience more difficulties in re-establishing long-term intimate relationships. They blame themselves more and experience more guilt than women raped by strangers. Stranger rape can be more readily, and probably more successfully, separated from ordinary everyday interactions and relationships, than can acquaintance rape. These psychological effects are exacerbated by the fact that women raped by acquaintances are less likely to have their claims processed by the police and are less likely to achieve a conviction in court than women raped by strangers.

The woman's distress and shame as a result of being raped may be compounded by the negative and critical reactions of her friends, family, her social network and the criminal justice system in a process known as secondary victimisation. For some women these secondary effects can be more damaging and humiliating than the attack itself.

Although there are considerable methodological difficulties in studying the effects of criminal assaults such as rape (mainly due to under-reporting and the difficulty in studying a representative sample), there are a number of studies that have found rape to be associated with higher rates of depression, generalised and phobic anxiety, and post-traumatic stress disorder. Studies have also indicated substantial impairment in work, relationships, social functioning and self-esteem, often for many months following rape (Resick et al., 1981).

The general picture of recovery suggests a spontaneous resolution of symptoms in the four to six weeks following a rape attack. Initial recovery proceeds regardless of psychiatric intervention. Indeed, there is little research evidence to date that crisis intervention in the immediate aftermath of a sexual assault does much to modify the natural course of recovery or to prevent the emergence of long-term psychiatric disorder. Clearly, there are different rates of recovery between individuals which depend on a number of factors. Vulnerability factors which appear to predict greater problems with recovery include a past history of victimisation (including previous rape (Miller et al., 1978) and childhood sexual abuse), past psychiatric illness, drug or alcohol abuse and a history of psychosocial disturbance. Recovery may also be affected by the woman's age, socioeconomic status, past personality, the nature of the assault and her social support system (Hilberman, 1976). Delay in reporting the rape may impair recovery, although results are contradictory. The frequency of physical and psychological complaints and absenteeism at work, in victims, has considerable personal and social costs, as well as an economic impact. A thorough understanding of the impact of rape is therefore needed in order to intervene effectively.

PSYCHIATRIC SEQUELAE OF RAPE

Depression

Frank and Anderson (1987) compared recent rape victims four to six weeks after the rape with a similar group of women who had not been raped. They found that recent rape victims had significantly higher rates of depression (38 per cent v. 16 per cent), generalised anxiety (82 per cent v. 16 per cent) and drug abuse (28 per cent v. 3 per cent). Atkeson and colleagues (1982) followed up 115 rape victims and compared them with a group of women who had not been raped. Initally, the rape victims had significantly higher levels of depression than women who hadn't been raped, and just over a quarter remained depressed at one-year follow-up. Women with prior psycho-social problems had an increased risk of becoming depressed. In their national survey of over 2,000 women, Kilpatrick and colleagues (1985) found that, compared with non-victimised women, victims of completed rape were nearly nine times more likely to have made a suicide attempt and twice as likely to be diagnosed as having a major depressive illness.

Generalised and phobic anxiety

Rape-related phobias relate to three main areas: first, rape-associated fears such as fear of the dark, fear of strange men, fear of the sexual act; second, fear of the consequences of rape, and third, fear related to the woman's sense of her own vulnerability. The pattern of fear appears to change over time so that vulnerability fears increase as rape-associated fears decrease. Calhoun *et al.* (1982) found a rapid drop in anxiety levels in nearly all women who had been raped, regardless of therapeutic intervention. About a quarter of women had recovered by three weeks post-rape and did not require further treatment. The level of distress three weeks after the rape was the factor that best predicted continuing distress after three months. Without further counselling or treatment, there was no significant reduction in distress from three months to three years after the rape.

Physical health

In a study of over 2,000 women, based on one work site, 57 per cent reported having been the victim of a physical assault, a burglary or a rape since the age of 14. Of these, a third had been raped. Rape victims had increased rates of medical consultation up to two years after the event, which was twice as long as that seen in victims of burglary (one year). Victimisation was a more powerful predictor of medical consultation than other life stressors studied (Koss, 1988).

Post-traumatic stress disorder

Rape represents a markedly distressing event, which is often life-threatening, and in certain cases gives rise to symptoms characteristic of post-traumatic stress disorder. The main symptoms of post-traumatic stress disorder are persistent intrusive re-experiencing of the trauma in the form of flashbacks and dreams, avoidance of situations reminiscent of the trauma, a sense of numbness and unresponsiveness to the environment, and symptoms of increased arousal such as poor concentration and sleep. Steketee and Foa (1987) found that more than 90 per cent of women could be diagnosed as having post-traumatic stress disorder immediately after the rape. One controlled study found that over 80 per cent of women were still reporting re-experiencing and avoidance phenomena three years after the rape. Numbing of responsiveness, reduced involvement with people, and in former interests such as sexual activity, have also been noted.

The evidence, however, suggests an initial rapid recovery, so that within four to six weeks the majority of women no longer appear significantly different from a similar group of non-victims. On the other hand, for some women, symptoms of post-traumatic stress disorder may persist for years after the original assault. In a national survey of adult women, 16.5 per cent were still diagnosed as having post-traumatic stress disorder over an average of seventeen years following the rape (Kilpatrick et al., 1987).

Among victims of crime in general, three elements make a significant individual contribution to the development of crime-related post-traumatic stress disorder. These are perception of life threat, actual injury and being the victim of a completed rape as opposed to an attempted rape (Kilpatrick et al., 1989). If all three features were present a woman was more than eight times more likely to develop post-traumatic stress disorder than were victims of other forms of crime. This holds true even if elements of violence and dangerousness are controlled for, which suggests that there are other elements present in a rape attack which are particularly harmful.

Responses to domestic violence

The repeated and systematic use of violence against women by their partners is a serious problem, not only for the victims themselves, but because of the resulting health, social and public-policy implications (Tuck, 1989). Domestic violence has been defined as 'an act carried out with the intention or perceived intention, of physically injuring another person' (Straus et al., 1980). It includes actual and threatened physical violence, psychological abuse and sexual assault, which is repetitive and increasingly difficult to anticipate or avoid.

Battered women are forced into continued association with their tormentor, with whom they may have an ambivalent, 'love–hate' relationship. Social processes lock the woman into a battering relationship and may then contribute towards attributing her apparent passivity to masochism. The notion of the good wife and mother, of the woman as responsible for the happiness of her husband and family and the smooth running of the home means that the woman sees the violence as her responsibility and evidence of her personal inadequacy.

There is a general unwillingness of social, health or criminal justice agencies to respond to women's requests for help, and a lack of safe accessible emergency accommodation for women who need to escape a battering partner. These problems are reinforced by the continuing inequality of access by women to educational and work structures, which ties them into financial as well as emotional dependence on their partners and reinforces their feelings of inadequacy and the futility of resistance.

'Battered woman syndrome' is recognised as a variant of post-traumatic stress disorder (Dutton and Painter, 1981). However, the nature of the precipitating trauma is unusual in that it consists of repeated and long-term violence rather than a single circumscribed incident. The features of battered woman syndrome, which was described in the 1970s (Walker, 1979), include emotional, psychological and behavioural deficits, which arise in response to repeated acts or threats of violence. The syndrome emphasises the woman's hopelessness, helplessness and despair. Battered women become incapacitated by the violence so that their coping strategies are progressively rendered ineffective and eventually extinguished (Hilberman and Munson, 1978). This terminal state has been likened to the animal model of learned helplessness in the face of inescapable shock. Such is the growing acceptance of the battered woman syndrome, that its existence has been recognised by the American courts and seems to be gaining some acceptance in British jurisdiction.

Other mental health consequences of domestic violence include depression, generalised anxiety and fearfulness, stress-related symptoms, physical complaints and suicidal thoughts and attempts (Bergman and Brismar, 1991; Pagelow, 1981). Post-traumatic stress disorder can be a further mental health consequence: Houskamp and Foy (1991) assessed 26 women who had been in physically violent relationships and found that 45 per cent of them met the DSM-III-R standardised diagnostic criteria for post-traumatic stress disorder. The probability of developing post-traumatic stress disorder was highly correlated with the frequency and severity of violence received.

The majority of women are reluctant to disclose their experiences to family friends or health professionals, such is the sense of shame and stigmatisation associated with being a 'battered woman'. Many women who experience violence in the home are faced with insurmountable difficulties in avoiding the violence and leaving the battering relationship. These difficulties relate, at least in part, to the psychological deficits caused by the battering, the woman's isolation, the lack of safe accommodation in the community and her fear of retaliation by her partner, as well as the economic hardship many women face without continuing financial support from their partners (Binney et al., 1981). Some women are able to leave their partners, although little is known about how well they cope in the community, or whether these psychological and behavioural deficits are permanent and persist when the immediate threat of violence has been removed.

Although much early psychiatric research in domestic violence came from American researchers, certain British initiatives, such as Erin Pizzey's work with women in the Chiswick Refuge, and the development of numbers of refuges for victims of domestic violence, have been influential in raising awareness of the difficulties experienced by women attempting to escape battering relationships (Pizzey, 1974). Sociological studies of women who have left battering relationships emphasise the economic and social difficulties faced by women after they leave a relationship, particularly when there are children involved. Follow-up studies consistently report inadequate housing, a fall in the standard of living, high rates of unemployment, difficulties in arranging childcare, lack of family and social support, loneliness and isolation (Hoff, 1990). The difficulties in surviving in the outside world may result in a number of women ultimately returning to their battering partners.

The Domestic Violence and Matrimonial Proceedings Act passed in Britain in the 1970s had some effect on the handling of cases of domestic violence within the criminal justice system. However, the problem has continued. The National Association of Victims Support Scheme's recent report (NAVSS, 1992) recorded an increase in the number of victims of domestic violence seeking help from the organisation and recommended certain new training initiatives to deal with a particular need. Whilst some have suggested that a more effective criminal-justice response, including cautioning or arresting the perpetrator, would act as a deterrent (Walker, 1985), the Women's Aid Federation has suggested that the prosecution of violent partners alone is not enough. More work is needed to tackle long delays in bringing such cases to court and the problems women have in accessing legal aid.

CONCLUSION: IMPLICATIONS FOR GOOD PRACTICE

Research consistently shows that violence and its threat are an acute reality for many (most) women. At home and in many so-called safe spaces, domestic violence and sexual assault are interwoven within women's heterosexual relationships with men. All the research suggests that men nearest and dearest to women pose the greatest danger. Women are also targets for sexual harassment and pestering on the street and at work, and may be subjected to attack because they are, or are perceived to be, lesbian; because they are women of colour; or because they are not able-bodied. So being female – in spite of our many differences – has profound implications for living our lives with the anxiety about confronting physical and sexual danger. In essence, experiencing subordination means having to negotiate it.

There are a number of concerns about the relevance of current psychiatric theory and practice to the needs of women. Concern centres on the traditional 'medical model' and the paternalistic relationship between doctors (generally male) and patients. For many women, this relationship replicates and legitimises the inequitable power distribution in their past relationships. There is concern that some women's apparent mental disorder may in fact be a legitimate and understandable response to social and interpersonal oppression, and that psychiatry ignores the cause whilst pathologising and treating the individual.

The sexual abuse of female psychiatric patients by their carers is widely documented and can have a devastating psychological and emotional impact on the victim (Mezey, 1994). Such behaviour, as well as being unethical, represents a clear breach of trust and violation of professional boundaries. Female psychiatric patients appear to have higher rates of past sexual victimisation than other women (Palmer, 1993). It is ironic that women who seek help for problems arising out of earlier abusive experiences may then be subjected to a repetition of those experiences by the very people entrusted with their care. Professional training bodies must place clear prohibitions on sexual contact between patients and their carers, as well as raising awareness of the issue.

Women may also be more vulnerable to experiences of sexual assault, harassment and intimidation by fellow patients within psychiatric institutions (Bartlett and Mezey, 1995). The MIND 'Stress on Women' campaign has highlighted a failure of psychiatric institutions to protect women patients or to deal sensitively with allegations of sexual harassment and abuse (see Chapter 16). The policy of running down sex-segregated wards, in the interests of 'normalisation', may unwittingly increase discrimination in its failure to recognise the risks involved to many female patients, or to take into consideration their wishes and concerns.

There should also be greater recognition of many women's wishes to be seen by women professionals and of the importance of offering them some choice over the gender of their therapist. We need to be sure that mental health professionals are not simply mirroring and reproducing a system that encourages low self-esteem, dependency and low aspirations in women. The underachievement among women in a non-psychiatric population does not justify the continuation of these practices in an institutional setting. The expectations that psychiatrists hold about the level of recovery and functioning in psychiatric patients must be the same for women and men. Clearly, psychiatry on a wider basis must eradicate sexual stereotyping by the medical establishment. There is an urgent need for social and political measures that will increase the health of women, such as the provision of shelters for battered and abused women, as well as for recognition of the extent of violence to women in general.

Finally, we must recognise that women feel the effects of being potential targets of sexual violence. Fear of crime is a declaration about women's position in society *vis-à-vis* men. While we must provide women with mental health services that are sensitive to the effects of serious physical and sexual violence, we must also confront the detrimental effects of living within a social climate within which women fear for their safety.

CROSS-REFERENCES WITHIN THIS BOOK

REFERENCES

Adler, Z. (1987) *Rape on trial*, London: Routledge & Kegan Paul.
Atkeson, B.M., Calhoun, K.S., Resick, P.A. and Ellis, E.M. (1982) 'Victims of rape; repeated assessment of depression symptoms', *Journal of Consulting and Clinical Psychology* 50: 96–102.
Bart, P. and O'Brien, P. (1986) *Stopping rape*, New York: Pergamon Press.
Bartlett, T.C. and Mezey, G. (1995) 'The extent of violence among psychiatric in-patients', *Psychiatric Bulletin* 19: 600–604.
Bergman, B. and Brismar, B. (1991) 'A five year follow-up study of 117 battered women', *American Journal of Public Health* 81 (11): 1468–1488.
Binney, V., Harkell, G. and Nixon, S. (1981) *Leaving violent men: a study of refuges and housing for battered women*, London: Women's Aid Federation, England.
Calhoun, K.S., Atkeson, B.M. and Resick, P.A. (1982) 'A longitudinal examination of fear reactions in victims of rape', *Journal of Counselling Psychology* 29: 655–661.
Campbell, B. (1993) *Goliath*, London: Methuen.
Carter, D.L., Prentky, R.A. and Burgess, A.W. (1988) 'Victims: lessons learned for responses to sexual violence', in R. Ressler, A.W. Burgess and J.E. Douglas (eds), *Sexual homicides: patterns and motives*, Lexington, MA: Lexington Books.
Crawford, A., Jones, T., Woodhouse, T. and Young, J. (1990) *The second Islington crime survey*, London: Middlesex Centre for Criminology.
Dutton, D. and Painter, S.L. (1981) 'Traumatic bonding: the development of emotional attachments in battered women and other relationships of intermittent abuse', *Victimology: An International Journal* 61 (4): 139–155.
Frank, R. and Anderson, B.P. (1987) 'Psychiatric disorders in rape victims: past history and current symptomatology', *Comprehensive Psychiatry* 28: 77–82.
Frazier, P. and Borgida, E. (1985) 'Rape trauma syndrome evidence in court', *American Psychologist* 40 (9): 984–993.
Gardener, C.B. (1988) 'Access information: public lies and private peril', *Social Problems* 35: 384–397.
Goodey, J. (1994) 'Fear of crime: what can children tell us?', *International Review of Victimology* 3 (3): 195–210.
Gordon, M. and Riger, S. (1988) *The female fear*, New York: Free Press.
Hilberman, E. (1976) *The rape victim*, New York: Basic Books.
Hilberman, E. and Munson, K. (1978) 'Sixty battered women', *Victimology: An International Journal* 2 (3): 460–470.
Hoff, L.A. (1990) *Battered women as survivors*, London: Routledge.
Home Office (1992) *Criminal Statistics of England and Wales*, London: HMSO.
Houskamp, B.M. and Foy, D.W. (1991) 'The assessment of post traumatic stress disorder in battered women', *Journal of Interpersonal Violence* 6 (3): 367–375.

Kilpatrick, D.G., Best, C.L., Veronen, L.J., Amick, A.E., Villeponteaux, L.A. and Ruff, G.A. (1985) 'Mental health correlates of criminal victimisation: a random community survey', *Journal of Consulting and Clinical Psychology* 53: 866–873.

Kilpatrick, D.G., Saunders, B.E., Veronen, L.J., Best, C.L. and Von, J.M. (1987) 'Criminal victimisation: lifetime prevalence, reporting to police and psychological impact', *Crime and Delinquency* 33 (4): 479–489.

Kilpatrick, D.G., Saunders, B.E., Amick-McMullan, A., Best, C.L., Veronen, L.J. and Resnick, H. (1989) 'Victim and crime factors associated with the development of crime related post traumatic stress disorder', *Behaviour Therapy* 20: 199–214.

Koss, M.P. (1988) 'Criminal victimisation among women: impact on health status and medical service usage'. Paper presented at the American Psychological Association, Atlanta, GA (unpublished).

Lerner, M.J. and Miller, D.T. (1978) 'Just world research and attribution process: looking back and ahead', *Psychiatry Bulletin* 85: 1030–1051.

Maxfield, M. (1984) *Fear of crime in England and Wales*, London: HMSO.

Mezey, G.C. (1994) 'Sexual victimisation in the workplace', in T. Wykes (ed.), *Violence and healthcare professionals*, London: Chapman & Hall.

Miller, J., Moellar, F., Kaufman, A., Divasto, P., Patnak, D. and Christy, J. (1978) 'Recidivism among sex assault victims', *American Journal of Psychiatry* 135: 1103–1104.

NAVSS (1992) *Domestic violence. A report of a national inter-agency working party on domestic violence*, London: NAVSS.

Pagelow, M.D. (1981) *Women-battering: victims and their experiences*, Thousand Oaks, CA: Sage.

Pain, R. (1993) 'Crime, social control and spatial constraint', unpublished Ph.D. thesis, University of Edinburgh.

Palmer, R.L., Colmán, L., Chaloner, R., Oppenheimer, R. and Smith (1993) 'Childhood sexual experiences with adults. A comparison of reports by women psychiatric patients and general practice attenders', *British Journal of Psychiatry* 163: 499–504.

Pizzey, E. (1974) *Scream quietly or the neighbours will hear*, Harmondsworth: Penguin.

Resick, P.A., Calhoon, K.S., Atkeson, B.H. and Ellis, E.M. (1981) 'Social adjustment in victims of sexual assault', *Journal of Consulting and Clinical Psychology* 49:705–712.

Smith, M.D. (1988) 'Women's fear of violent crime: an exploratory test of a feminist hypothesis', *Journal of Family Violence* 3: 29–38.

Stanko, E.A. (1988) 'Hidden violence against women', in M. Maguire and J. Pointing (eds), *Victims: a new deal?* Milton Keynes: Open University Press.

—— (1990) *Everyday violence*, London: Pandora Press.

—— (1995) 'Gendered criminological policies: masculinity, femininity and violence', in H. Barlow (ed.), *Crime and public policy*, Boulder, CO: Westview Press.

Stanko, E. and Hobdell, K. (1993) 'Assault on men: masculinity and victimisation', *British Journal of Criminology* 33 (3): 400–415.

Steketee, G. and Foa, E.B. (1987) 'Rape victims: post traumatic stress responses and their treatment', *Journal of Anxiety Disorders* 1: 69–86.

Straus, M.A., Gelles, R. and Steinmetz, S.K. (1980) *Behind closed doors*, New York: Anchor.

Tuck, M. (1989) 'Introduction', in *Domestic violence*, London: HMSO.

Valentine, G. (1989) 'The geography of women's fear', *Area* 21 (4): 385–390.

Walker, L.E.A. (1979) *The battered woman*, New York: Harper & Row.
—— (1985) 'Psychological impact of the criminalization of domestic violence on victims', *Victimology: An International Journal* 10: 281–300.
Warr, M. (1984) 'Fear of victimisation: why are women and the elderly more afraid?' *Social Science Quarterly* 65: 681–702.

Chapter 13

Women as abusers

Estela Welldon

My feelings of arousal in certain situations with O., my 18-month-old son, started a couple of weeks ago. I have touched him twice in response to those feelings. After having spoken to my husband, the PSW [Social Worker] and the NSPCC I have been jolted out of it. I now recognize when I am aroused but I will not act on those feelings inappropriately. When he is toddling around I feel that he is my son, my baby and I love him as such. I would not hurt him physically and I do not want to hurt him psychologically either. I have a daughter, my feelings for her have always been those of a loving mother–daughter relationship.

This paper attempts to address our need for the recognition, accurate diagnosis, adequate management and proper treatment of women who abuse. I shall offer: a working definition and classification of the term 'female abuser'; a brief summary of my own work on differences and similarities between male and female perversion; some social, psychological, economic and cultural factors; an account of the female developmental context; an index of suspicion in terms of predictability and risk; techniques of assessment taking into account early psychological development and family tree; emotional contexts which may facilitate the abuse of children; preventive measures and suggestions for treatment.

I use the term 'perversion' as a technical, psychoanalytical concept without moral connotations. In perversion, the aim is the release of sexual anxiety through compulsive behaviour, which includes unconscious hostility towards the other person or object, for example a 'flasher' is overwhelmed by increasing sexual anxiety accompanied by hostility, which is only released by exhibiting his genitals to a strange woman in order to shock her. This release is quickly superseded by shame and guilt, which re-create sexual anxiety. These actions are defensive manic mechanisms, a sort of psychic survival 'minikit' for individuals who suffer from a masked chronic depression, which has impaired their capacity for full emotional-genital gratification.

This presentation is based on the psychological clinical findings of women referred for assessment to the Portman Clinic over a period of four years with the presenting problem of physical or sexual abuse towards their own and other children. These findings follow on from a decade during which thirty of the women whom I assessed triggered concern about the possibility that they were abusers. Referral of women with these problems increased after the publication of my book *Mother, madonna, whore: the idealization and denigration of motherhood* (Welldon, 1988).

Some of these women are presently receiving treatment individually, or in groups, at the Portman Clinic. Others are seen for consultation, and yet others are brought by other agencies and professionals for consultation. Many are self-referrals who have previously failed to obtain appropriate professional help.

Apart from the phenomenon of 'battered babies' which is now well known, other psychopathological traits associated with motherhood have been ignored or undiagnosed. It is also important to point out that the recognition of battered babies didn't come from the professionals dealing with women with psychological problems, but from experienced paediatricians who could no longer ignore the suffering of babies they were treating. A similar situation exists at the present time with 'Munchausen syndrome by proxy', a 'discovery' made by Professor R. Meadow who again is a paediatrician. It has been extremely difficult for society to acknowledge that women can sexually or otherwise abuse their children, and this has left children unprotected.

The women concerned are from many, and varied, walks of life and incredulity and disbelief are the main reactions encountered by victims when they try to disclose sexual abuse by women. Such a reaction is met in professionals, as well as by potential or actual female victimisers. A conspiracy of silence triggers off worse despair, and a sense of desolation and isolation is created in both victims and perpetrators. The stereotyped view that 'women are victims and men abusers' has been the socially accepted formula. The acknowledgement of female perversion was absent, because motherhood has been glorified and equated with good mental health. It has been wrongly assumed that women, in becoming mothers, feel free of conflict and totally fulfilled.

After years of clinical experience, I have had to acknowledge that female perversion exists, although the mental mechanisms are different from those found in men. The reproductive functions and the organs attached to men and women are used for perversion; the man has the penis to carry out his perverse activities, while the woman has the whole body to pursue them, since the female reproductive-sexual organs are more widely spread. The different psychopathology originates from the female body and its attributes, including fecundity. Women commit their perverse actions against themselves or what they regard as an extension of themselves, their babies/children, while men direct their perverse activities outwards using their penis. It is a false premise that what applies to male perversions applies equally to females, although the function of the perversion for the individual, in terms of release of anxiety, may be similar.

DEFINITION OF THE FEMALE ABUSER

Clinically, the female abuser demonstrates a perversion of the 'maternal instinct' in which she, at times of stress, experiences strong and powerful physical sensations including sexual attraction towards children; her own and/or others. She tries to stop herself from acting out the thought, since she knows it is wrong, but the urge physically and/or sexually to attack the object of her desire/hate proves irresistible, and hence she succumbs. When committing the action there is a sense of elation and release of sexual excitement, but these feelings are immediately superseded by shame, self-disgust and depression.

DIFFERENCES BETWEEN MALE AND FEMALE PERVERSIONS

From what has been said previously, the hypothesis is that in women suffering from perversions the aim is directed towards themselves, their bodies or their babies. This is in contrast with men where the target for the sadistic action is directed towards an outside object. This has been discussed in detail elsewhere (Welldon, 1993), and so here I will point out the essential features of female perversion and the female abuser.

Female perversions include bulimia, anorexia, self-mutilation, sexual and physical abuse of children and incest with children of both sexes. A significant percentage of the patients we see (and this refers to both men and women), were themselves the victims of sexual abuse as children. Furthermore, the histories of women who are perpetrators of physical and sexual abuse of children are often preceded by self-abuse and/or sado-masochistic relationships.

Psychological, emotional, social, cultural and biological factors are deeply intertwined in the production of female perverse traits. Society gives almost total power to mothers over the early care of their children, and at times is quite unprepared to deal with situations where mothers may require help. I believe that we have all had experiences confirming the above statement. At the sight of a woman screaming at, slapping or physically abusing a child in a public place, we hesitate as to what to do and usually decide to keep quiet because of fear of being told by the mother 'mind your own business, this is my child'. When a woman feels completely unable to obtain any help, she may fall back on inappropriate and perverse behaviour. She feels powerless and unable to cope with a raging baby, and her perverse behaviour as a mother may paradoxically be seen as the only power available to her, through her exclusive emotional and physical authority over her baby.

Women are usually physically and emotionally attached (negatively or positively) to the 'objects' of their abuse, namely their babies and bodies.

Another sociocultural phenomenon worth mentioning is the expression of basic emotions, such as anger and crying, according to gender (Bernardez, 1987). Men are encouraged to show anger since this is associated with being in charge, in authority and self-assertive. Women are inhibited from showing anger and encouraged to cry because by this they show vulnerability, frailty and weakness, which men find difficult to resist. At present there is a new fashion to encourage men to cry, but I doubt if changes in women towards being able to express anger would be so well received. Usually, as soon as women shout or show their anger in any way, men are ready to flee, perhaps a reflex response linked to a childhood experience of their mother screaming at them. Some women, unable to show in any authentic way their sense of frustration, impotence and helplessness to any adult, have no other alternative but do so when alone with their children who are completely at their mercy. The other option is to turn the anger inwards, become even more depressed and harbour dreams of revenge.

FEMALE DEVELOPMENTAL CONTEXT

There are different normative developmental phases in a woman's life which require understanding, sensitive care and a great deal of adaptation. With regard to female sexual development one must always bear in mind the capacity for fecundity. Excessive demands and/or neglect during childhood can result in a range of psychopathologies and the production of perverse traits (Welldon, 1991). These may appear at various stages, prompted by stress which opens up old emotional wounds that have been kept at bay in order to defend against the original intense pain. Psychic survival is ensured by a fragile scaffolding of internal and external silence, which may collapse when faced with new adversities. The origins of such disturbance could date to birth, for example if the gender of a girl child was not welcomed by her family, perhaps even being a source of great disappointment. These 'unwanted' girls have a second chance during adolescence. Adolescence can either make it or break it.

Zilbach (1993) focuses on the mother–daughter relationship based on 'reciprocal identification', moving away from classical theory in which the relevance for the girl is to make the switch from attachment to mother to attachment to father. 'The girl's identification with her mother is as important as her attraction and turning towards her father.' Still, the role of the father during a girl's adolescence is crucial in her assertion of herself as a woman, particularly if things have gone wrong before. Her father has to be able to reassure the girl of her femininity without being either dismissive or seductive. Otherwise, self-abusive behaviour can settle in, which might include eating disorders, self-attack or promiscuity which, if not properly understood, could lead to prostitution.

Montgomery and Greif (1991) noted the association of female masochism and anorexia nervosa as another instance in which the hostile unconscious attitudes of parents and grandparents, for example to a new unwanted female baby, may manifest themselves. The authors reckon that such attitudes are at least partly responsible for actions taken by the sufferer with the aim of fulfilling her parents' unconscious wish to get rid of her. They point out that all the pain, cutting and self-harm (including suicide), are attempts to repair the cohesiveness of the self in the face of overwhelming anxiety associated with annihilation and dissolution.

It is likely that young women who have experienced early emotional deprivation, a failed completion of self-assertion during adolescence and a growing dissatisfaction with themselves and their own bodies, will find enormous internal difficulties in achieving healthy, satisfactory, mature emotional relationships. Instead, they might easily enter into relationships with men where a sado-masochistic pattern emerges. It is extremely difficult for these women to leave these relationships, and if they do manage to give them up it is usually only in order to start a new relationship which will soon acquire the same characteristics as the previous one. This is because the brutish partner represents an internal part of herself which is the object of the woman's self-hate. She might now no longer need to attack her own body, because her partner is unconsciously assigned to perform this role.

A comprehensive and thorough study of self-mutilation in female remanded prisoners was carried out by Wilkins and Coid (1991) and Coid *et al.* (1992). Although the psychopathology of the women differed from the patient population of the Portman Clinic, their findings concerning early emotional deprivation are similar to ours, with abnormal psychosexual development and 'polymorphous perversity', in which varied and different perversions exist. They concluded that self-mutilation was often experienced as a symptom-relief mechanism accompanied by 'great pleasure or excitement', describing patients who obtained sexual arousal and orgasmic release. I, too, have encountered women who have resorted to extremely painful and dangerous practices, such as bonding and self-hanging, as a means of controlling their mounting desire to attack their own offspring. They also admit sexual gratification achieved through these practices.

Self-abusing actions are the expression of inflicted humiliation which has been introjected into negative self-attributes, with self-loathing at the extreme end of the scale. These are the precursors of the abusing behaviour to others, indicating the enormous ambivalence of love and hatred towards the female body and its attributes. Heterosexual intercourse with sadistic characteristics is the rule. Although on the surface submissive, compliant and passive, the woman may harbour various dreams of retaliation. An example would be to get pregnant as an expression of revenge against the man who is so undermining and contemptuous to her. Or, if left alone feeling isolated and despondent, the young woman might want to have a child who will keep her company and who will provide her with unconditional affection. These motivations are not usually considered by those who equate motherhood with a healthy and mature development. Thus the cycle of abuse commences.

My own hypothesis is that motherhood is sometimes chosen for unconscious perverse reasons.

> The woman would know that in achieving motherhood she is automatically achieving the role of master, that of being in charge, in complete control of another being who has to submit himself or herself not only emotionally, but also biologically, to the mother's demands, however inappropriate they may be.
>
> (Welldon, 1988)

Perversion of motherhood is the end-product of serial abuse or chronic infantile neglect, and must be seen as the product of emotional instability and inadequate individuation brought about by a process that involves at least three generations. This is a useful concept which helps us to move towards neutrality during clinical assessments since, at times, listening in a non-judgemental way may prove to be difficult. The examiner, regardless of gender, is faced with two main reactions; first disbelief and second, an overwhelming identification with the abused baby/child.

Some of the differences between men and women are independently corroborated by Bentovim (1993), when he speculates about the reasons why women constitute such a small proportion of abusers, despite the fact that girls are abused four or five times more commonly than boys. He postulates that, in their socialisation, girls tend to internalise their response to abusive experiences, developing a low sense of self-esteem, together with self-mutilation and anorexia nervosa, whereas abused men externalise and project outside their experiences of abuse.

In any case, women seem to suffer more from their own abusing actions, and to be more aware of the deep psychological wounds and long-term consequences that they produce. They seem to take more responsibility for them and to ask for professional help which, as observed, is not easily available (see also Matthews, 1993). These characteristics – a degree of responsibility, the existence of psychic pain, flexibility in the 'choice' of perversion and the attachment displayed in female perversions but absent in their male counterparts – may account for the apparently better prognosis in women. Detection by the police is rare except in cases in which a mother is accused of aiding and abetting sexual abuse by the father.

CLASSIFICATION OF FEMALE ABUSERS

Female abusers can be divided into the following categories:

1. Intrafamilial abuse by the mother alone

This refers to abuse by a mother for reasons related to her own psycho-pathology.

2. Intrafamilial abuse by a single mother

Many single mothers, who have children from either one or different part-ners, find themselves alone. These women may have been victims of sexual abuse themselves, lack self-assertiveness or self-esteem, feel depressed or de-spondent and valueless, and have very poor-quality relationships. With regard to men, it is not unusual for some to leave the household after parent-ing one or more children, because of the responsibilities associated with parenthood. Men in this position often find another partner, and a repeating pattern is begun.

Women left alone in this way may consider the children responsible for the absence of a man. They feel sexually abused by their partners, ostracised, unable to socialise, despondent and depressed. One solution for women facing such predicaments, is to fall into despair and start abusing their chil-dren in order to obtain some comfort in frustrated lives. I do not agree that the motivation for these women in initiating sexual abuse with their children is just to 'achieve non-threatening emotional intimacy', as stated by Math-ews *et al.* (1989). I believe that this abuse contains a hidden and unconscious revenge since blame is apportioned to the children for their mothers being left alone.

3. Intrafamilial abuse by the stepfather with compliant mother

At this point, I would like to alert professionals to an observation deriving from my clinical work with victims and perpetrators of both sexes, which links mothers with male paedophiles. It is important to state that there is a distinction between incest perpetrators and paedophiles, although at times they are spoken of interchangeably.

Some other women, left alone in the way described above, continue their search for male companionship and, being unable to meet them in the usual ways because of being housebound, advertise in lonely hearts columns. They place adverts giving detailed and rich descriptions of their children, since they want to be open about what they consider to be handicaps in their domestic lives. Little do they know that this advert may obtain exactly the opposite results, as it will be quite a bait for male paedophiles in search of easy solutions. Paedophiles eagerly read these columns, readily answer the adverts and in no time make their way into the domestic scene. Women in this position are taken by surprise. They can't believe their 'luck' because this man, for the first time, is so nice to the children. Women do not even mind whether or not they have sex, because often their previous experiences were so very unsatisfactory. A new relationship starts, and marriage follows. Eventually, the 'incest' or sexual abuse comes into the open and paedophiles may appear on the record as incest perpetrators because it happened inside the family although, in fact, they have been paedophiles from the beginning.

4. Intrafamilial abuse by both parents, with mother's participation

This is usually part of a sado-masochistic pattern, with a very dependent, depressed and submissive woman, described by Mathews *et al.* (1989) as 'male coerced'.

5. Extrafamilial abuse by a woman alone

Women in this category may have florid psychopathology, equivalent to that of male paedophiles. The abuse sometimes goes unreported because they seek work with children in residential places where the abuse is unnoticed.

6. Extrafamilial abuse by a woman with partner(s)

The most notorious case is that of Myra Hindley.

FEMALE ABUSERS AND DANGEROUSNESS

According to Scott (1977): 'Dangerousness is an unpredictable and untreatable tendency to inflict or risk serious, irreversible injury or destruction, or to induce others to do so. Dangerousness can, of course, be directed against the self.' This is a well-known definition, considered both practical and useful. Beneath the deceptive simplicity there lies a hidden wisdom and complexity. Incidentally, it is worthwhile noting that the last sentence of the definition is usually omitted from authors who quote it. Such an omission is, in my view, unacceptable because it denotes a lack of understanding of a developmental process that may prove to be essential in the assessment of predictability of female dangerousness, specifically in women who abuse.

Index of suspicion; predictability and risk

It is difficult to conceive of predictability when society cannot contemplate the problem, and thus is totally unprepared to deal with an emergency involving a female abuser. Once more I am reminded of Scott (1977), who remarked: 'Prediction studies should aim not to replace but to complement the clinical approach, and vice versa.'

Possible indicators of future female dangerousness to others, considering the previously described clinical findings, would include self-harm. This is not to say that self-abuse will necessarily be superseded by child abuse, but the knowledge that these two conditions could be associated might facilitate better assessment.

Scott (1977) has already dispelled the myth that women are less dangerous than men because they are physically weaker, and he mentions the fact that mothers are as likely to batter their babies as are men. However, I strongly disagree with his contention that 'women more rarely cross the threshold into dangerousness, but when they do, perhaps by substituting stealth for strength, they offer the same difficulties of prediction and treatment as do men'. I believe that the important differences between males and females could help us in the prediction, assessment and management of female dangerousness. These could be used in a positive way to promote further understanding and prevention of these particular conditions.

An example can be seen in the case of Beverley Allitt, the 24-year-old nurse who admitted to having killed children while they were under her care. Her history included severe and long-standing self-mutilation (noted whilst she was a student nurse). At the time of her trial she was suffering from anorexia. Had the new concept of female perversion been taken into account, a job involving 'mothering' duties could have at least been discouraged, and would indicate that thorough screening should always take place for women who apply for caring positions with children under their care.

Being a woman, she may not fit in with our perception of a serial killer which, of course, she is. The actual dangerousness in the Beverley Allitt case is devastatingly obvious, and we must ask: What are the determinants for these horrific killings? What has been overlooked and even neglected? Could this violent behaviour have been predicted earlier on? Are there circumstances that establish an increased chance for this dangerousness? Furthermore, is this dangerousness intrinsically female? If so, why? How can we use this awful experience to learn possible ways of improving our means of detecting and assessing dangerousness accurately, so preventing future criminal behaviour?

PERSONALITY PROFILE AND DIAGNOSTIC APPROACH

It is important to develop a personality profile that could lead to the accurate diagnosis, prevention and better treatment of these conditions.

The inability to obtain professional help may be due to:

(a) the patients' enormous difficulties due to shame, or
(b) the professionals' difficulties in listening, due to a marked response of disbelief, helplessness, as well as a tendency to call 'problem' women hysterical, manipulators, inadequate, attention-seekers.

The diagnostic approach must include the following: Was the patient a wanted baby? Was she taken care of by her mother, and what was the value of femininity in the family? There should be a record of mother's and grandmother's previous pregnancies, abortions, miscarriages, stillbirths, cot deaths or any other child's death; gender and age of the 'lost' infant (this can lead us to clues regarding the patient's sense of individuation and separation, and the possibility of a 'quick replacement pregnancy'). One must also ascertain whether there is a history of known incestuous activities in the family.

There must be a history of educational and sexual developments and relationships. With regard to pregnancies, are her babies/children wanted or 'accidents'? Has any of them been singled out from birth? Are any of them considered to be different from the others? Does she feel 'funny','odd' feelings about a particular child or other children? Was the particular abused child singled out from birth? What is the gender of the child? Did he/she represent another child, such as the product of a quick replacement pregnancy following the death or miscarriage of a previous child/pregnancy? Or was there a brother/sister that the patient felt her own child resembled? Did she consider abusing that child for a long time prior to the actual abuse or was it sudden and unexpected? Was the abuse taking place when the woman was feeling unable to convey to anyone her own sense of despair and desperation, or when she was in distress or feeling extremely isolated, helpless or moody? Was this a chronic condition, or was it aggravated by superimposed conditions?

The assessment should also include the presence of sexual arousal or sexual gratification which they might have obtained while the abuse is taking place. (This could be asked as 'did you feel surprised about sensations in your body accompanying the abuse? Was this over as soon as the action was over?') Women experience a great sense of relief to be asked this question, since the sexual satisfaction fills them with shame and disgust.

Another important characteristic to be elicited is the degree of emotional attachment that they feel towards the children involved in the abuse. Also included should be the question of whether they are able to stop themselves from acting out these sadistic fantasies, and if so, how. Could they talk to anybody about this? Do they have access to emotional or practical resources?

The consultation should also include other common findings in the history of these women already referred to; for example the presence of self-abuse and the lack of emotional and practical resources during pregnancy and early mothering, as well as associations with uncaring and violent men in sado-masochistic relationships.

TREATMENT USING GROUP THERAPY

Some patients, who come from very large families with financial deprivation and emotional overcrowding, are likely to respond better to an initial individual approach of a limited period of time. These initial meetings are with two aims in mind: first, to relieve patients of unbearable and increasing anxiety about their own guilt following disclosures, which could include their own self-abuse or abuse to others; second, to consider whether the patient/client is suitable for a further treatment which would include group therapy.

At the Portman Clinic (see Appendix for address), we have become increasingly aware that group analytical therapy is often the best form of treatment, not only for severely disturbed perverse patients, but especially for sexual abusers and sexually abused patients, and some reasons for this will be described. Secrecy is a key issue in incest. It has prevailed not only in the one-to-one situation of abuse, but also through family collusion, and group analytical therapy breaks through these patterns of secrecy. The family–social microcosm of a group also affords a much better understanding of problems since they are so deeply related to violence and antisocial actions occurring within family dynamics.

By treating the victims and perpetrators of incest, and including perpetrators and victims of both genders within a group, there are unexpected qualities of containment and insight to be gained which are virtually impossible in a one-to-one situation. Female perpetrators at first experience a sense of bewilderment to have fellow patients with similar problems. They feel a tremendous sense of relief in being able to talk to others about those 'horrid' urges. Newcomers may attempt, on arrival, to blame Social Services and other outside agencies for 'interfering' by taking away their children, leaving them feeling empty and dispossessed.

To start with, the other women, their 'seniors' in the group listen to them with much empathy, but soon afterwards, when they sense that the newcomers are ready to face realities, they confront them with much sensitivity. They help them to admit their own sense of responsibility for the situation that they find themselves in. They are also able to discuss and understand their relationships with cruel men. They can make explicit the presence of nasty habits that affect their personal appearance. The women in the group see themselves constantly changing and make generous remarks about one another, obviously obtaining a great deal of satisfaction from helping one another in a womanly comradeship.

The interactions between males and females, perpetrators and victims, in the group are very intriguing. Female perpetrators may observe how different their attitude towards their victims is, as opposed to their male counterparts, and they are able to help male perpetrators become deeply aware of the vast consequences of their actions. The male perpetrators become aware that their actions are not just limited to physical effects, but can also inflict deep psychological wounds on their victims. Second, the victims, who may at the start be quiet and compliant, have much anger to express, anger that they have never felt able to display before, and this is fundamental for them in achieving any real change. Anger is expressed in two different ways; first in a straightforward manner leading to self-assertion and second, in a vengeful way in which the person is still intertwined with the original relationship. Thus, when the victim claims she can now express anger against the perpetrator, but in a twisted and vengeful way, we can see that she is still a partner in the old incestuous process.

The composition of the group also makes it impossible for the members to single out groups according to stereotypes, or to produce and reinforce splits. Incestuous mothers maintain a symbiotic relationship with their child(ren) and do not allow any process of separation and individuation. In contrast, therapeutic groups offer separation/individuation processes by virtue of identification with more senior fellow patients. Group members thus grasp how unable they are to see themselves as separate human beings, but only as parts of their parental figures. For example, every member experiences a powerful sense of belonging to the group and witnesses others, and themselves, developing into individuals with increased respect and self-esteem. At times they are not only allowed, but encouraged, to express anger and frustration which has been kept hidden for long periods of time. This encouragement comes especially from other 'old' members who have gone through similar feelings.

Professionals can greatly help certain categories of patients to achieve self-awareness and a healthy outlook through group therapy. This has worked well even with such an apparently diverse and antagonistic group as one containing both perpetrators and victims of incest. I will now conclude by suggesting that this has an unexpected reverse side to it which we professionals would do well to note.

Workers of all sorts involved in cases of incest frequently find it difficult to maintain a detached professional stance. They tend to take sides, usually becoming emotionally bound to the victims. They may feel punitive towards the perpetrators. In their distress, they lose their understanding of the dynamics of what is happening. For example, they sometimes become so indignant that they fail to see that victims who become perpetrators experience a conscious or unconscious desire to avenge the pain inflicted upon themselves. These victim-perpetrators believe that they are creating a situation in which justice is satisfied, although they are actually identifying with their aggressors. In somewhat similar ways, professional workers often identify with the victims.

At any rate, there is a strong tendency for the workers in incest cases to re-enact within their professional network the splits, denials and projections which are so characteristic of the experience of family members caught up in the dynamics of incest. The therapeutic group can allow some distance and disentanglement from such dynamics.

CONCLUDING REMARKS

Power in society is unequally distributed. Women's exclusive power is in the domestic sphere, where abuse is hidden away, whereas men have access to public power, with transgressions into the open having the 'natural' concomitant of humiliation and punishment. The outcome of the split affects both individuals and society in general, since women are seen to be the victims and treated with sedatives, while men are always seen as perpetrators, faced with 'penalisation' and punishment.

This leads to a perpetuation of seeing women as victims, never allowed to disclose dreams of revenge, or abuse of power and an extreme need to be in control.

New awareness of, and deeper insights into, women's psychopathologies are now available, and should be used in a positive way to promote further understanding and prevention of the conditions that I have described. More adequate resources should be available to provide appropriately for mothers and babies. This should be aimed at preventing further abuses of domestic power which cause much pain, suffering and distress to both mothers and babies in the short run, and society in general in longer terms. Thus, close co-operation between all those professionals who care for either mothers and/or babies is needed to secure both accurate diagnosis and adequate provisions.

ACKNOWLEDGEMENT

Edited for publication with the assistance of Cleo Van Velsen, Consultant Psychotherapist, Maudsley and Bethlem NHS Trust.

CROSS-REFERENCES WITHIN THIS BOOK

Chapter   3   Motherhood and mental illness
Chapter   4   Girls in distress: an unconsidered issue
Chapter 11   The impact of childhood sexual abuse
Chapter 12   Women and violence

REFERENCES

Bentovim, A. (1993) 'Why do adults sexually abuse children?', *British Medical Journal* 307: 144–145.
Bernardez, T. (1987) 'Women and anger: conflicts with aggression in contemporary women', *Journal of the American Medical Association* 33: 215–219.
Coid, J., Wilkins, J., Coid, B. and Everitt, B. (1992) 'Self-mutilation in female remanded prisoners: II. A cluster analytic approach towards identification of a behavioral syndrome', *Criminal Behaviour and Mental Health* 2: 1–14.
Mathews, R., Matthews, J.K. and Speltz, K. (1989) *Female sexual offenders: an exploratory study*, Orwell VT: The Safer Society Press.

Matthews, J. (1993) 'Working with female sexual abusers', in M. Elliott (ed.), *Female sexual abuse of children*, New York: Guildford Press.

Montgomery, J.D. and Greif, A.C. (1991) *Masochism: the treatment of self-inflicted suffering*, Madison, CT: International Universities Press.

Scott, P.D. (1977) 'Assessing dangerousness in criminals', *British Journal of Psychiatry* 131: 127–142.

Welldon, E.V. (1988) *Mother, madonna, whore: the idealization and denigration of motherhood*, London: Free Association Books (American Edition, Guilford Press, 1992).

—— (1991) 'Psychology and psychopathology in women: a psychoanalytic perspective', *British Journal of Psychiatry* 158 (suppl. 10): 85–92.

—— (1993) 'Forensic psychotherapy and group analysis', *Group Analysis* 26: 487–502.

Wilkins, J. and Coid, J. (1991) 'Self-mutilation in female remanded prisoners: 1. An indicator of severe psychopathology', *Criminal Behaviour and Mental Health* 1: 247–267.

Zilbach, J. (1993) 'Female adolescence: toward a separate line of female development', in M. Sugar (ed.), *Female adolescent development*, New York: Brunner/Mazel.

Chapter 14

Women and primary care

EDITORS' INTRODUCTION

Links between mental health professionals and health centres and GPs' surgeries are of great interest in considering how to meet the particular mental health needs of women. Women present to GPs with more psychological symptoms, and yet are less likely than men to be referred on to specialist services: thus provision of mental health services in primary care promises great advantages for women. Access to a range of mental health professionals in the primary-care setting allows GPs to respond to problems in a much more varied way. Many women present with symptoms that are strongly related to their social circumstances and their experiences: medication may not always be the most appropriate, or the only course of action. Many GPs have excellent counselling and psychotherapeutic skills, but are unlikely to have the time to employ them for all suitable patients. Thus, the increased provision of mental health services in primary-care settings offers a considerable opportunity to reach groups of women whose needs would not otherwise have been addressed.

In the first section of this chapter, Roslyn Corney and Geraldine Strathdee examine the mental health needs of women who present in primary care and a range of ways of responding to these needs. The range of mental health problems found in primary care is first described. The authors then discuss ways of improving mental health services for women by developing them within primary care, to make them more accessible and to increase their diversity. Recent evidence suggests that working links are increasingly being established between GPs, other primary-care team members and specialist mental health workers and substantial advantages have been reported for these schemes. In the second section of the chapter, Mary Burd, a community psychologist, describes a model of good practice involving psychologists working within primary care.

Developing primary-care services for women

Roslyn Corney and Geraldine Strathdee

THE EXTENT OF PSYCHIATRIC MORBIDITY IN PRIMARY CARE

The extensive psychiatric morbidity in primary care was first identified by Shepherd and his colleagues in 1966. In a large-scale study of fifteen London general practices, they found that 14 per cent of patients consulted at least once during a twelve-month period for a condition diagnosed as entirely or largely psychiatric in nature. Later studies have indicated that a further 10 to 12 per cent of mental health problems in primary care are 'hidden' or go unrecognised by GPs (Goldberg and Blackwell, 1970). Thus in total, 25 to 30 per cent of patients have a significant psychological component in their presentation. In around 9 per cent of the population there is a more chronic picture, with symptoms persisting for at least one year or requiring maintenance treatment. Only one in twenty patients presenting to their GPs with psychological problems is referred on to secondary mental health services.

Other studies indicate that the GP is the professional most often contacted for psychosocial problems (Corney, 1990; Goldberg and Huxley, 1992). They are often the first point of contact for patients and families in crisis. GPs and other members of the primary-care team (practice nurses, community nurses and health visitors) are ideally placed to undertake preventive measures to reduce the number and severity of episodes of mental illness, particularly as they have ongoing contact with a number of high-risk groups in the community: the bereaved, the chronically ill, carers, women in the postnatal period and mothers with young children. Ninety-eight per cent of the population is registered with a GP, and almost three-quarters will see their doctor in any one-year period, so that it is very important to make effective use of this degree of patient contact.

Severe mental illness

There is much evidence that a major part of the treatment for those with chronic and severe illness also takes place in primary care. Early work was done by Murray Parkes and colleagues (1962), who followed up a cohort of patients diagnosed as having schizophrenia discharged from London mental hospitals. They found that over 70 per cent had seen their GP in the year after discharge and half of them had consulted more than five times. In the same period, less than 60 per cent had attended hospital out-patient departments, and of these most had been seen less than five times. Johnstone (1984) studied a similar group of discharged patients and found that a quarter were seeing only their GP. Effective care by the GP is therefore very important for this group of patients, but may require the back-up of the psychiatric services, if often only in an advisory capacity.

With the closure of the large psychiatric hospitals, the role of the GP will become even more important (Kendrick, 1992). As Table 14.1 shows, this is likely to increase further with community care reforms and the implementation of the 'care programme approach' (Department of Health, 1990).

Gender differences

Gender differences in the prevalence of minor psychiatric morbidity have been widely demonstrated in community surveys, although these studies are not without difficulties and inconsistencies (Jenkins, 1985). In general, studies have indicated that the prevalence of minor psychiatric morbidity, particularly anxiety and depression, is consistently higher in women – up to twice as much, and especially between the ages of 20 and 45. Theories for the increase in minor psychiatric disorders found in women include biological susceptibility and a variety of psychosocial factors. A number of studies

Table 14.1 The impact of community care on the GP workload

Community care strategy	Impact on GPs
Closure of large psychiatric hospitals	Greater number of patients with long-term disorders on list
Fewer hospital beds	More patients treated in the community
	Less access to respite facilities
Shorter length of stay	More acute illness treated at home
	Increased intervention with psychotropic medication
First point of contact for the severely ill	Increased crisis intervention
	Increased Mental Health Act application
	Support role for families and carers
Decrease in specialist responsibility	Enhanced care co-ordination/case-management role
	Increasing role of GP in care programme approach

lend support to the importance of social roles. These are discussed in detail in Chapter 1.

Surveys in primary care have shown that GPs diagnose twice as many episodes of mental illness in women as in men. This is likely to be due to a number of factors apart from actual morbidity. General practice surveys indicate that women attend more frequently than men. This difference occurs particularly in the childbearing years, which is also the period when women are most likely to complain of depression, and it is not accounted for purely by pregnancy and gynaecological consultations. It has also been found that women are more likely to recognise a psychiatric problem in themselves (Horowitz, 1977), and are more likely to consult their doctors with psychological and emotional problems (Briscoe, 1982; Corney, 1990).

A different explanation for female over-representation in mental health statistics is proposed by feminist researchers and others, who suggest that women are more likely to be labelled as mentally disordered than men. Some evidence suggests that this might be the case, as with Marks *et al.* (1979), who found that GPs more readily detect psychological problems in women than in men. Milliren (1977) studied older patients and found that male GPs diagnosed women as suffering from anxiety symptoms more often than men. Thus, some of the observed difference in the prevalence rate found in primary care may be artefactual, produced by more reporting of illness among women and by GPs being more likely to diagnose women as having psychological problems.

DEVELOPING SERVICES IN THE COMMUNITY

Despite the fact that twice as many women as men are identified by their GP as suffering from mental illness, these figures are not reflected in referrals to out-patients. Men are more likely to be referred by GPs to psychiatrists in hospital than women (Goldberg and Huxley, 1992). This has also been found in other areas. For example, in hospital drug-dependence settings three times as many men are receiving treatment as women, but in community-based clinics the imbalance is redressed and referrals are similar. This does not happen in other countries such as the USA, where women do not have to pass through the filter of primary care to get psychiatric treatment. With direct access, women have always formed the largest percentage of patients seen by mental health professionals (Weissman and Klerman, 1977).

The reasons for this disparity in referral to secondary care in this country are not known. A contributory factor may be access difficulties (both in terms of travelling and the presence of dependents). It is possible that GPs may find it easier to treat women themselves, they may take their problems less seriously, or they may regard the secondary-care psychiatric services as being less likely to help women. The latter may sometimes be an accurate perception. Many of the women's problems will be linked to social and interpersonal difficulties, such as poverty, single parenthood or domestic violence (Williams *et al.*, 1993). These may be more amenable to social interventions or counselling rather than psychiatric treatment.

Whatever the reason it follows that, if we are to improve services to women, we must increase and strengthen services at the community and primary-care level. Research conducted in child and adult psychiatry, and also in drug-dependency settings, has consistently demonstrated that when services are moved to the community the referral bias disappears and women are referred in true proportion to the prevalence of their problems. Brown *et al.* (1988), comparing referrals to a hospital psychiatric clinic in Camberwell with referrals to clinics in the primary-care setting, found that 70 per cent of the psychiatric referrals to primary-care clinics were of women, a similar percentage to known prevalence rates of mental illness in the community. Tyrer in Nottingham (1984) and Browning and colleagues in Bristol (1987) found similar results.

It is not, however, enough to develop purely psychiatric services within the primary-care setting. Psychological distress in women is often closely linked to psychological and social problems. These may be effectively helped by other workers, such as social workers or counsellors, or by less formal sources of help such as the extended family, effective peer groups or voluntary services and self-help groups.

WORKING MODELS WITHIN THE PRIMARY-CARE SETTING

Although previous studies have suggested generally poor collaborative relationships between members of the primary-care team and both specialist psychiatric services and social and voluntary agencies (Clare and Corney, 1982), recent evidence suggests that a number of working links are currently being established. The trend over recent years has been for GPs themselves to employ different mental health workers and/or to participate in collaborative schemes whereby these individuals are attached to, or liaise with, the practice.

The new contract for GPs (Chisholm, 1990) provided opportunities for increased collaboration, as it removed restrictions on the range and number of staff salaries for which reimbursement may be obtained under the ancillary staff scheme. In addition, other workers such as counsellors were employed for a time using health-promotion money, although restrictions have now been placed on the use of these revenues. With the advent of fundholding, GPs can use their budget to develop services offered within the practice, and many practices have indicated that developing psychological services is a priority area.

A recent study conducted by Thomas and Corney (1992) suggests that attachment schemes and the direct employment of mental health workers are now relatively widespread. They contacted every general practice within six randomly selected health districts in England. Half of the 261 practices had a specific link with a community psychiatric nurse, 21 per cent with a social worker, 17 per cent with a counsellor, 15 per cent with a clinical psychologist and 16 per cent with a psychiatrist. Other studies show an increase in the number of community psychiatric nurses and psychologists working in primary care over the 1980s.

Research has also shown that psychiatrists are increasingly moving towards working in primary-care settings. Strathdee and Williams (1984), surveying psychiatrists in England and Wales, found that one in five psychiatrists spent time in a primary-care setting, while a study in Scotland found a higher percentage (Pullen and Yellowlees, 1988). Psychiatrists may work within general practices using a variety of models: liaison, attachment and shifted out-patients. The liaison model means that psychiatrists will see relatively few patients themselves, but offers the most opportunity for case discussion and education of members of the primary-care team.

A questionnaire survey in 1992 of Social Services Departments in England and Wales provided additional evidence of links with social workers, finding that 62 per cent of local authorities had one or more schemes for attachment to or liaison with general practice in operation. The majority of these considered that work carried out was mainly in the field of mental health (Corney, 1995).

Advantages of these schemes

GPs normally have limited time available for each patient and are therefore restricted in the help they can offer. However, the greater variety of mental health professionals working within primary care means that women can receive a much wider range of help than was afforded by the previous possibilities of drug treatment, support from the GP and referral elsewhere. This can include various therapies: for example, counselling (given by counsellors and others) or cognitive therapy or behavioural therapy (from clinical psychologists or others). Social and practical assistance may also be crucial, either for the woman herself and/or her children and other dependents. This may be given by practice nurses, social workers or others.

With GP attachments and liaison schemes, women can see a counsellor or psychologist within a familiar environment, with little stigma attached. Advantages of this are seen in the fact that attendance at appointments for counselling in general practice is higher than at a marriage-guidance clinic or a psychiatric out-patient clinic. Similarly, one of the problems in referring patients to psychiatric out-patients is that many patients fail to turn up for the first appointment (Illman, 1983).

Training the primary-care team

The large numbers of patients attending their doctor, health visitor or practice nurse with psychological problems mean that only a small proportion can be referred on to others, and therefore the skills of all primary-care workers, including receptionists, need to be developed. All staff need training to increase their awareness of psychological and social problems in their patients, as well as their understanding of the different ways in which this distress may be manifested. Evaluation of training courses specially designed for GPs has shown that improvement does result, with GPs becoming more skilled in both identification and management (Gask, 1992). In addition, health visitors given brief training in counselling techniques were shown to bring about an improved outcome with women diagnosed as having postnatal depression (Holden *et al.*, 1989). Staff also need training to increase their awareness of areas which may particularly affect women's mental health, such as rape, sexual abuse and harassment, and ways in which the resulting distress may present.

One major advantage if mental health workers are attached to primary care is that both parties can start to work in close collaboration. If good working relationships are established, then mutual learning and development of skills can occur. The supportive role of the mental health worker may be particularly important in this context, as most primary-care staff receive little in the way of help in disentangling their own feelings, avoidances, prejudices and emotional responses. Whilst workers in some caring professions, such as counselling and social work, have supervision sessions built into their work, few other health professionals in either primary or secondary care have these opportunities.

With closer involvement, GPs and other members of the primary-care team can learn about each other's specific skills, interests and abilities, but such arrangements are unlikely to work well without time allocated for regular meetings to discuss the involvement of different professionals with particular patients. There is the possibility that roles may overlap and need to be clarified. Much research is currently underway to try and define which problems or disorders are most likely to respond best to medication, and which to psychotherapeutic techniques, of which a range of approaches is available. This is likely to be very applicable to primary care as the range of possible therapies increases, and an exchange of information between practices as to successful working models is essential. Jenkins (1992) reviews some ways in which different primary-care team members are currently involved in working with patients with mental health problems and discusses the successful integration of these with secondary-care services.

One way of developing services to small or single-handed practices is for these practices either to share the services of specialised mental health staff, or to employ a nurse facilitator. One study used a nurse facilitator who worked on a sessional basis for five or six practices. The facilitator's role was to develop a directory of mental health resources in the area, which included counselling services, drop-ins, day centres, weekend and luncheon clubs. The nurse also developed practice policies for the treatment and care of patients (Jenkins, 1992).

VOLUNTARY SERVICES

This chapter focuses on primary-care services, as other community-based services are discussed elsewhere in this book. However, it is important that the services based in primary care are not exclusively those offered by health workers and other professionals. GPs and other staff need to encourage the setting up of support groups, self-help groups and befriending schemes. These schemes may sometimes be able to offer more assistance to women in distress than those run by paid workers; e.g. volunteers may have experienced the same problems as the women needing help, or come from the same cultural background. They may be able to offer more long-term help and more practical assistance. Women receiving help may also be able to offer something in return, thereby having the potential to increase the self-esteem of both parties.

Many women with mental health problems find it more acceptable and less stigmatising when day care is provided not in psychiatric hospitals or day centres, but with support through a network of existing local facilities. Examples might include: sports groups in local leisure centres, local luncheon clubs, drop-in and befriending schemes through community or church centres, local women's or voluntary groups, skills training such as adult literacy, cooking or assertiveness training in local adult education centres. It requires the integration of statutory services with such normal and voluntary sector provision to ensure a wide range of appropriate facilities.

These vitally important voluntary schemes must receive support and encouragement from professionals. Users' views can be obtained to find out where these schemes are best based, and whether strong links with primary-care services will increase (or decrease) their acceptability and accessibility

INCREASING ACCESSIBILITY TO WOMEN

In general, primary-care services are very accessible to women, particularly if compared with traditional secondary-care services. There are fewer barriers to seeking help and self-referral is the norm. The service is usually non-stigmatising, especially in comparison with community mental health centres or psychiatric hospitals. Psychiatrists working in clinics in the primary-care setting have described how their greater accessibility and the less stigmatising environment have led to the referral of patients who had previously avoided contact with the secondary services for many years. This 'avoidance' applies particularly to women, individuals diagnosed as suffering from schizophrenia and paranoid patients (Strathdee *et al.*, 1990).

At all ages, women are more likely than men to call the GP out for a home visit, excluding requests for home visits for children. Women with young children or an elderly parent may find it more difficult to get to the surgery and are less likely to have the use of a car. In addition, women may find it difficult to make arrangements to be seen alone without the presence of dependents. Mental health workers and others need to extend their facilities so that they can offer more home-based care. Particularly in inner cities, with large populations of ethnic minorities, there is likely to be a need for advocates and/or translators to help communication. In some communities women have few opportunities to learn to speak English, because of the strong emphasis on their remaining at home. They may come to consultations with their children as interpreters, which is usually inappropriate and may be detrimental to the care of both parties.

Choice of sex of worker

In recent years the importance of recruiting more female doctors, particularly GPs, has increasingly been recognised. There is evidence that women prefer to consult a doctor of their own sex, especially for specifically female conditions (Cooke and Ronalds, 1985a). The relative lack of women doctors in the inner city is a cause for concern; as few as 13 per cent on average (Cooke and Ronalds, 1985b). The concentration in these areas of ethnic minorities, for whom cultural factors make it difficult for women to consult male doctors, means that it is paramount to recruit more women GPs, psychiatrists and mental health workers.

Thus, many existing facilities do not address the particular needs of women when providing services. The following list summarises factors which need to be taken into account in order to ensure good care for women.

- Locally accessible services (by public transport, buggy-friendly).
- Community-based clinics.
- Availability of home-based care.
- Access to a crèche.
- Baby /granny /carer sitting.
- Choice of sex of workers (including GPs).
- Choice of help – professional, non-professional, advocacy, self-help.
- Use of community resources for day care.
- Focus on life circumstances rather than symptoms.
- Carer/relative support groups/respite care.

- Provision of women-only residential facilities, wards, respite and crisis houses.
- More shared child facilities/family units.

COMMUNITY MENTAL HEALTH CENTRES

One of the disadvantages inherent in basing all community mental health services within general practices is that it may entail placing too great a reliance on the skills, attitudes and priorities of GPs. Thomas and Corney's study found a tendency for some practices (particularly the larger rural practices), to have many links with mental health workers while others had none or few. Thus patients on the lists of highly collaborative practices may receive better service(s), at the expense of patients at other less accessible or amenable practices. If resources are primarily channelled into developing multidisciplinary teams based in primary care, patients registered with GPs who do not wish to collaborate will be penalised.

The problem is made more acute because it is in areas of multiple deprivation that primary-care teams are less likely to be well developed. Many inner-city GPs operate either as single-handed practitioners or from poor-quality accommodation, and are therefore less likely to be able to employ mental health staff, or to have these attached to the practice. It is precisely into such areas that chronically mentally-ill individuals are most likely to drift. It is also important to consider the small part of the population who are not registered with a GP (approximately 2 per cent), and schemes are necessary to target this group. Many of those unregistered are the homeless and a high proportion of these have been found to be chronically distressed or mentally ill (Weller *et al.*, 1987). Many women become homeless after experiencing some kind of physical and/or sexual abuse and there are signs that homelessness is increasing among elderly women. In addition, homeless women have been found to be more likely to have mental health difficulties than homeless men and to have been hospitalised in the past (Williams *et al.*, 1993; see also Chapter 9 of this volume).

Not all community developments have been based in primary care, and in recent years there has been a marked increase in the number of community mental health centres (CMHCs) set up. Teams of mental health workers based in these centres accept and encourage self-referrals as well as referrals from elsewhere. CMHCs are perhaps most appropriate in areas where general practices are poorly developed (i.e. inner cities), or in those areas where there are higher concentrations of the severely mentally ill.

PRINCIPLES OF GOOD COMMUNITY MENTAL HEALTH CARE

It can therefore be seen that services based in primary care provide a unique opportunity to try and address the mental health needs of women living in the surrounding community. The extent of the psychological morbidity affecting women has been described, both in this chapter and elsewhere in this book. It is clear that a majority of these women will present in some way to primary-care services, but they are less likely than men to be referred on to secondary care. For this, as well as other reasons specific to women detailed above, it is important to develop integrated models of care, with mental health specialists working alongside GPs. Information about helpful strategies and ways of working needs to be disseminated to other practices, and there is likely to be a role here for more centralised planning policies.

We would agree that all community mental health services should be based on the principles proposed by MIND (see Chapter 17). The principles of good community psychiatric care were expressed as far back as 1953, stating that good care needs to be integrated, co-ordinated and provide continuity. We believe that these principles can only be put into effect if primary care is incorporated centrally in any services developed. In Great Britain we are unique in the strength of the primary-care infrastructure. Community mental health centres and teams have often developed in parallel to, rather than being integrated with the existing strong primary-care community base. It is crucial that efforts are made for a closer integration between all community facilities.

REFERENCES

Briscoe, M. (1982) 'Sex differences in psychological well-being', *Psychological Medicine* Monograph Supplement 1.

Brown, R., Strathdee, G., Christie-Brown, J. and Robinson, P. (1988) 'A comparison of referrals to primary care and hospital out-patient clinics', *British Journal of Psychiatry* 153: 168–173.

Browning, S., Ford, M., Goddard, C. and Brown, A. (1987) 'A psychiatric clinic in general practice: a description and comparison with an out-patient clinic', *Bulletin of the Royal College of Psychiatrists* 11 (4): 114–117.

Chisholm, J.W. (1990) 'The 1990 contract: its history and its content', *British Medical Journal* 300: 853–856.

Clare, A. and Corney, R. (1982) *Social work and primary health care*, London: Academic Press.

Cooke, M. and Ronalds, C. (1985a) 'Women doctors in urban general practice. The patients', *British Medical Journal* 290: 753–755.

—— (1985b) 'Women doctors in urban general practice. The doctors', *British Medical Journal* 290: 755–758.

Corney, R. (1990) 'A survey of professional help sought by patients for psychosocial problems', *British Journal of General Practice* 40: 365–368.

—— (1995) 'Social work involvement in primary care settings and mental health centres: a survey in England and Wales', *Journal of Mental Health* 4: 275–280.

Department of Health (1990) *The Care Programme Approach for people with a mental illness referred to specialist psychiatric services*, HC(90)23, London: HMSO.

Gask, L. (1992) 'Training general practitioners to detect and manage emotional disorders', *International Review of Psychiatry* 4: 293–300.

Goldberg, D. and Blackwell, B. (1970) 'Psychiatric illness in general practice', *British Medical Journal* 2: 439–443.

Goldberg, D. and Huxley, P. (1992) *Common mental disorders*, London: Routledge.

Holden, J.M., Sagovsky, R. and Cox, J.L. (1989) 'Counselling in a general practice setting: controlled study of health visitor intervention in treatment of postnatal depression', *British Medical Journal* 298: 223–226.

Horowitz, A. (1977) 'The pathways into psychiatric treatment: some differences between men and women', *Journal of Health and Social Behaviour* 18: 169–178.

Illman, J. (1983) 'Is psychiatric referral good value for money?', *BMA News Review* 9: 41–42.

Jenkins, R. (1985) 'Sex differences in minor psychiatric morbidity', *Psychological Medicine* Monograph Supplement 7.

—— (1992) 'Developments in the primary care of mental illness – a forward look', *International Review of Psychiatry* 4: 237–242.

Johnstone, E., Owens, D., Gold, A., Crow, T. and MacMillan, J. (1984) 'Schizophrenic patients discharged from hospital', *British Journal of Psychiatry* 145: 586–590.

Kendrick, A. (1992) 'The shift to community mental health: the impact on general practitioners', in R. Jenkins, V. Field and R. Young (eds), *The primary care of schizophrenia*, London: HMSO.

Marks, J., Goldberg, D.P. and Hillier, V.F. (1979) 'Determinants of the ability of general practitioners to detect psychiatric illness', *Psychological Medicine* 11: 535–550.

Milliren, J. (1977) 'Some contingencies affecting the utilisation of tranquillisers in the long term care of the elderly', *Journal of Health and Social Behaviour* 18: 206–211.

Murray Parkes, C., Brown, G. and Monck, E. (1962) 'The general practitioner and the schizophrenic patient', *British Medical Journal* i: 972–976.

Patmore, C. and Weaver, T. (1991) *Community mental health teams: lessons for planners and managers*, London: Good Practices in Mental Health.

Pullen, I. and Yellowlees, A. (1988) 'Scottish psychiatrists in primary health care settings: a silent majority', *British Journal of Psychiatry* 153: 663–666.

Shepherd, M., Cooper, B., Brown, A.C. and Kalton, G.W. (1966) *Psychiatric illness in general practice*, London: Oxford University Press.

Strathdee, G., Brown, R. and Doig, R. (1990) 'A standardised assessment of patients referred to primary care and hospital psychiatric clinics', *Psychological Medicine* 20: 219–224.

Strathdee, G. and Williams, P. (1984) 'A survey of psychiatrists in primary care: the silent growth of a new service', *Journal of the Royal College of General Practitioners* 34: 615–618.

Thomas, R. and Corney, R. (1992) 'A survey of links between mental health professionals and general practice in six district health authorities', *British Journal of General Practice* 42: 358–361.

Tyrer, P. (1984) 'Psychiatric clinics in general practice, an extension of community care', *British Journal of Psychiatry* 145: 9–14.

Weissman, M. and Klerman, G. (1977) 'Sex differences and the epidemiology of depression', *Archives of General Psychiatry* 34: 98–111.

Weller, B., Weller, M., Coker, E. and Mahomed, S. (1987) 'Crisis at Christmas, 1986', *Lancet* i: 553–554.

Williams, J., Watson, G., Smith, H., Copperman, J. and Wood, D. (1993) *Purchasing effective mental health services for women: a framework for action*, London: MIND Publications.

A model of teamwork in the community

Mary Burd

FROM THE GENERAL TO THE PARTICULAR

Corney and Strathdee have made the case for high-quality mental health service provision by the primary health-care team. What follows is an account of a primary-care psychology service which, although not specifically set up for women, has been predominantly used by them.

DESCRIPTION OF A MODEL

The Tower Hamlets Primary Care Clinical Psychology and Counselling Team has been evolving since 1981 and now has fifteen psychologists and counsellors. Its initial growth was influenced by an inaccessible, centralised hospital psychiatric service. Apart from the community psychiatric nurses (CPNs) and a crisis team, there was little devolution to a community-based service. This proved fertile ground for the development of a primary-care psychology service responsive to the needs of patients and their referrers. The team is based in primary care, with its members becoming an integral part of primary health-care teams working in a variety of ways and at different levels in the organisation, including direct work with clients, supervision, teaching and training, organisational interventions and research (Burd and Donnison, 1994).

Members of the team work in partnership with eighteen primary health-care teams (two-thirds of the GPs) and also provide a district-wide disability counselling service, and bilingual mental health counsellors – one each for the Bengali and Somali communities. A team member works with the East London Homeless Primary Health Care Team (HHELP; see Appendix for address), which is experiencing an increased uptake of its services by young homeless women. In response to a specific request, two sessions a week are provided for the Community Women's Health Team, who provide well women clinics, contraceptive advice and also run the day-care abortion service. Our aim is to help members of the team think about the psychological component which may influence the presentation of women to their service; e.g. a woman who repeatedly requests terminations. We also offer direct clinical work to their clients.

The main focus of the team's work is the provision of a clinical service.

The work also involves providing formal and informal support to a wide range of other health professionals and the voluntary sector. This takes the form of clinical supervision and organisational consultancy, including team-building, to enable groups of people such as primary health-care teams to work more effectively. We believe that this support can help to reduce the stress experienced by local health workers, many of whom are women. In addition to the normal range of problems, many of their clients have to cope with living in a deprived inner-city area, with appalling housing conditions and high unemployment, which all contribute to high levels of distress. Up to a quarter of the population comes from ethnic communities and requires services that are sensitive to race and culture, particularly with reference to women (Mahtani and Marks, 1994; MacCarthy and Craissati, 1989).

THE GENERAL PRACTICE CONSULTATION

Years of research have demonstrated that consultation with a health professional is a complex activity (Roter and Hall, 1992). For example, when a woman patient walks through the door of her health centre or general practice, both lay and professional models of distress will influence the forthcoming interaction. The eventual outcome will depend on the capacity of both the woman and the health professional to reach a shared understanding.

Traditionally, models of illness have been conceived of in terms of either mind or body, and this has been influential in medical counselling and psychotherapy. Our work however, is based on an understanding of the interdependence of the biological and psychosocial aspects of the person (Erskine and Judd, 1994). This is particularly relevant to our work with women, as this interdependence may be more difficult for them to maintain because negative cultural stereotypes of womanhood concerning sexuality and reproduction mean that women may have unrealistic expectations about their bodies. This divergence has been extensively explored by feminist psychotherapists such as Orbach (1986) and has implications for how, when, and even whether, women present for psychological help.

WORKING IN PARTNERSHIP

If the psychologist is able to become a trusted member of the team, it is through the informal contact and regular discussions which take place within the practice that she or he can gradually increase the doctor, nurse or receptionist's psychological understanding of, and empathy with, patients and their problems. Simple measures such as identifying and naming the problem and thus demonstrating the doctor's capacity to 'bear' it can be therapeutic. Discussion with the psychologist may enable the referrer's anxiety about a patient to be identified and contained, facilitating re-evaluation of urgency and a more gradual approach to referral which involves the client in the decision-making. The psychologist can also have a role in helping GPs or nurses in their work with patients with chronic physical illness. For example, advice or information on psychological approaches to diabetes or cancer may enable them to work more effectively with these patients.

There are a variety of roles that the psychologist may have within the primary-care team itself, including mental health educator, broker of psychological referrals and, at times, psychologist to the team. It is, of course, not a one-way process. GPs frequently have extensive knowledge of both the history and current circumstances of their patients, which can allow the work to proceed more rapidly. A partnership model means that liaison and joint work continue after referral, beyond assessment and through to discharge, providing an essentially nurturing environment. We would argue that this may go a long way to enhancing a woman's sense of self-esteem. This can very easily be damaged, particularly with a mental health problem, by referral to what may be experienced as an impersonal out-patient department. Offering clinical sessions in a health centre ensures accessibility, familiarity and virtually no stigma, enabling women to receive the specialised help they need.

WORKING DIRECTLY WITH CLIENTS

Psychologists working in primary care take referrals from the whole team, as well as self-referrals and referrals from social services and the voluntary sector. They will use a variety of interventions which may include problem-solving, cognitive therapy, psychoanalytic psychotherapy, systemic work, group work and family therapy. Although psychologists are not able to prescribe medication, the treatment of choice may often be one of the above combined with drug therapy.

Clients' problems

Problems can be varied and complex, ranging from panic attacks to more severe long-term mental health problems. The service offered will mirror that of primary care in that it is generic – cradle to grave – and provides continuing care. Interventions will usually be short-term, but the opportunity is there for a client to do some work and then return at a later date, either to look in more depth at the original problem or to work on a new problem, having gained confidence from the initial encounter.

CONFIDENCE THAT THE MODEL WORKS

As clinicians, we have a responsibility to attempt to measure the effectiveness of the care we provide and we regularly audit our work as to the

number of clients on our books, length of interventions and range of problems. There has been widespread research by clinical psychologists which
demonstrates the effectiveness of many of their interventions (Watts, 1990).
To date, we have looked at patient satisfaction, which showed 95 per cent
satisfaction with practical details of the service provided, length of intervention and improvement in presenting problems, although this is obviously
subjective (Bucknall, 1994). We regularly meet with our referrers, not only to
monitor their view of how we provide the service, but also to ensure that our
assessment of clients' progress is matched by theirs. Psychologists in primary
care have shown that both consultation rates and prescription rates for psychotropic drugs can be reduced by psychological interventions (Robson *et
al.*, 1984).

The constantly increasing demand for all elements of our service at least
gives face validity to the idea that our enterprise is addressing some of the
psychological needs of the local community. We are encouraged in this by
the fact that we are maintaining our current level of funding and continue to
attract new sources of revenue.

FINANCING THE MODEL

Because the service has developed opportunistically, finance has come from
a variety of sources. In a constantly changing market, what may appear
fixed at one moment, can change radically the next. The current resourcing
is: 28 per cent from the mainstream mental health budget (District Health
Authority), 17.5 per cent from Family Health Service Authority and GP
reimbursement, 37 per cent from the London Implementation Zone and
17.5 per cent from short-term funding.

The development of the clinical service has been supported by GP contributions, but this has inevitably led to a two-tier service in which, in general,
only patients of those practices that contribute to the costs receive a service.
This present situation is unsatisfactory as it does not provide an equal service for all. However, if more funds were made available to replace the GP
contributions, extra resources would also be required to fund more psychologists and counsellors to give the same level of service to all practices.
However, some of our provision is district-wide, particularly the consultancy
and training element, and some rolling group programmes. We are now
actively working on new initiatives such as a walk-in clinic and project work,
particularly addressing the needs of young mothers and supporting women's
projects in the voluntary sector. We see ourselves as a mainstream service
but our varied funding, despite many headaches, has enabled some flexibility
and creativity in what we do.

ACKNOWLEDGEMENT

I would like to acknowledge the contributions of Marta Buszewicz and 'The Team' in preparing this section.

CROSS-REFERENCES WITHIN THIS BOOK

Chapter 2   Women's mental health in the UK
Chapter 6   Planning services for black women
Chapter 12   Women and violence
Chapter 15   The user's perspective: our experiences and our recommendations

REFERENCES

Bucknall, A. (1994) 'Evaluation of client satisfaction questionnaire', *Clinical Psychology Forum* 63: 22–25.

Burd, M. and Donnison, J. (1994) 'Partnership in clinical practice', *Clinical Psychology Forum* 65: 15–18.

Erskine, A. and Judd, D. (eds) (1994) *Psychodynamic therapy in health care: the imaginative body*, London: Whurr Publishers Ltd.

MacCarthy, B. and Craissati, J. (1989) 'Ethnic differences in response to adversity: a community sample of Bangladeshis and their indigenous neighbours', *Journal of Social Psychology and Psychiatric Epidemiology* 24: 196–201.

Mahtani, A. and Marks, L. (1994) 'Developing a primary care psychology service that is racially and culturally appropriate', *Clinical Psychology Forum* 65: 27–31.

Orbach, S. (1986) *Hunger strike: the anorectic's struggle as a metaphor for our time*, London: Faber.

Roter, D.L. and Hall, J.A. (1992) *Doctors talking with patients: patients talking with doctors*, London: Auburn House.

Robson, M., France, R. and Bland, M. (1984) 'Clinical psychologists in primary care: controlled clinical and economic evaluation', *British Medical Journal* 288: 1805–1808.

Watts, F.W. (1990) 'Efficiency of clinical applications of psychology: an overview of research', in *The Manpower Advisory Services Review of Clinical Psychology Services*, Cheltenham: MAS.

Chapter 15

The user's perspective: our experiences and our recommendations

Mary Nettle and Andrea Phillips

INTRODUCTION

Andrea and I were asked to contribute our experiences to this handbook on women's mental health. We were especially pleased to have the user perspective included, as we feel it is vital to any understanding of community care to listen to those who have been personally involved; as it were, 'on the receiving end'. We do wish to stress, however, that this contribution is the direct result of work with other women users across the country. Our stories are unique because they belong to us. At the same time, they are typical and we hope many women will be able to relate to what has happened to us.

This chapter contains a synthesis of women's views as revealed in conversation with Kathryn Abel and Sophie Davison. As such, it is a perspective on the woman user's position and does not deal with all or many of the important aspects of user concerns. All mental health service users are disempowered when they enter the mental health system, but women, particularly those from minority groups, may become invisible. We may sink without trace under a blanket of psychiatric drugs designed to help us cope with partners, children or other life circumstances. Very little notice is taken of what we think about ourselves, our self-esteem; rather, we are chemically enabled to cope.

Both of us have been supported throughout our experience by caring workers, often working in an uncaring organisation. We all need to look after ourselves and to work together to change the status quo that finds the only solution in a 'chemical cosh'. As users, we know that this kind of view is short-sighted and that chemicals, whilst having their place, are no substitute for sensitive, caring and holistic approaches to the problems of daily living that are faced by mental health service users.

We have chosen to illustrate these sorts of concern by describing our real-life experiences as women using the mental health services.

MARY'S STORY

Mary was 25 and just married when she first came into contact with the mental health services:

'It was unusual in those days that I didn't simply go down the long-term valium and GP pathway that so many women in my position might. I had been married for about six months and was working in market research at a well-known company. There was a lot of pressure on the company budget and they decided to make redundancies. At the time I had been flattered and really quite chuffed to be the only member of staff at my grade not to be laid off. However, it soon turned out to be a very mixed blessing. They expected me to do extra work and the pressure on me was really tough from that point. It's such a common problem these days with all the redundancies. Women in part-time employment feel particularly vulnerable to redundancies and seem prepared to make sacrifices and compromises to keep their jobs. I had lost many of my friends and I think I became overworked and isolated. One day I just cracked. I became hysterical. It was out of the blue; I had never been unwell before. I didn't understand what had hit me. They sent me home and I went straight to my GP.

'He was a single-handed, "old-school" doctor who felt my real problem was that I wanted to have children and should be at home looking after my husband rather than out at work. I felt isolated, confused and disorientated; above all, I wanted to know what was happening to me. The doctor prescribed me valium and I was given an unusually large dose. I think he had written out the prescription wrongly. Neither the pharmacist nor the chemist questioned it. I was turned into even more of a zombie. The GP wasn't bothered that the valium knocked me out and that I was unable to work. His attitude was that I shouldn't be working in the first place. I'd attended with my husband and he had a good job. I should be at home anyway.

'I kept taking the tablets. The accepted truth is that one often feels worse before one gets better, and that you must keep taking the pills you are given – "a doctor knows best". Soon I was unable to eat, talk, get up, dress. Finally, my husband got worried and a psychiatrist came to visit me at home. That was very unusual in retrospect. It was a relief that somebody saw how ill I was and that they visited me at my own home. Unfortunately, this doctor's approach was rather crude. He told me that I "needed to come into hospital for a few days for a rest". He didn't tell me what kind of hospital. Most people have the impression that a hospital is bright, busy, airy and clean. That wasn't what I encountered at all. All he need have said was that the place looked awful, but that it was filled with people who really understood and cared. Doctors don't realise what it's like going into a mental hospital. They are so used to it. They are not patients. It was horrifying. I never saw that psychiatrist again. My "few days rest" turned into a three month admission.

'I had further bad experiences that I associate with being a woman. Once when the hospital doctor was questioning me, I saw a cockroach on the floor and commented on it. My husband was with me. He saw it too, but the doctor accused me of seeing things and my husband, was so frightened by what was happening that he agreed with the doctor and, of course, he took his word. It felt like I was ganged up on. It seemed less and less relevant, the questioning. So often it seemed as if there was going to be an opportunity to talk and yet it really turned out to be a chance for the staff to confirm their own views about me. They came to the conclusion that my problems stemmed from a combination of my being Catholic and taking the contraceptive pill, and that I was likely to be feeling guilty. And that what I really wanted was to have a baby; therefore, that was the root of all my problems. It was so humiliating; I felt they had missed the point entirely. I wasn't being listened to.

'Later my experience improved. When I became ill again, I was seen immediately by a GP who'd had personal experience of mental illness. Because he'd been there himself he had a better idea of my circumstances and took them into account when thinking about my problems. I was allocated a social worker and a Community Psychiatric Nurse (CPN); both of whom were men. I was never offered the choice and I'm not sure if that mattered. I had a very good relationship with the male social worker. We had a real rapport. He looked at me as a person and not as a diagnosis and that's what mattered. It would have been nice to have had a choice about who gave me my depot injections though. I was just randomly allocated a male CPN. I never thought any of the choices were mine. I was very passive and the way things were set up seemed to encourage that passivity. I didn't ask and so people thought I didn't want or need to know. There were some improvements, like the opening of the day hospital. However, it was typical of those in rural areas, situated miles away from where people actually lived. We were bussed around "like the insane" in a little white van from 8 a.m., when I was first picked up, until 10 a.m. when I'd finally arrive at the centre thirty miles away. That sort of bad organisation makes it seem like little thought or care has gone into its planning. Similarly, the psychiatric hospital itself was miles away and fairly inaccessible by public transport. Luckily my husband had a car.

'Perhaps the most traumatic times have been to do with my husband. He is an alcoholic. He says that it was my illness that drove him to drink. Because he was always working, unlike me, and a "middle-class executive", he was always listened to. Even the social workers and community nurses seemed to turn a blind eye to what was happening with him at home. He wasn't violent or anything, but I put up with a lot. I put up with so much and nobody ever suggested that it might be contributing to my illness. He was busy telling me that I was the one who had made him ill. Finally, he went in for a detox. He was put on the same ward where I had been an in-patient. Despite the fact that my husband was no longer able to look after me, no-one on the ward then felt able to offer me any help or support; I was no longer the patient.

'I feel that part of my problem with my husband is directly related to being a woman. I felt unable to tell them how difficult I was finding it, coping with an alcoholic partner. My official carers didn't seem to notice. They thought that as he was my husband he was also a carer with my best interests at heart, and his judgement, therefore, went unquestioned. I feel somehow I got lost in the system, trapped in it. I was taking lithium and I think that contributed to my inability to get myself help. If I hadn't been in the system, I would have done the sensible thing and left him years ago, the thing that ultimately would have been about looking after myself. I think mental health workers may be more likely to interfere with women's lives than men's – that's my experience. My husband, for example, was able to refuse consistently the few services offered to him over the years. I found it impossible to refuse things. A false sense of paternalism may be to blame: do people feel that women may need more looking after in a particular and not necessarily helpful way? Perhaps that's just something in my nature or in women's nature; to do what they are told more easily. I do think, however, that women are expected to need help more readily by the services. But that shouldn't mean any old help is OK. For a long time it wasn't recognised that the support my husband was assumed to be providing me with was inadequate.

'Sometimes, even if you know what kind of help you want and are able to articulate it, the services either don't exist in your area, are not funded by the National Health Service, or are "deemed inappropriate". I've found art therapy, aromatherapy, massage and individual counselling of great benefit in coping with the stresses of day-to-day life, but I can't afford to pay for them and they are very limited on the NHS. In the past, I've been told that the real reason I feel in need of these other therapies is just because I don't want to take my medication. It feels difficult to have a say in your own treatment. I need to talk to people and to be listened to. I think a lot of women find they need to talk, perhaps more than men, because they are more used to expressing their feelings in that way. Perhaps they find it easier to talk about things and they may gain more from it. When I went to see my female consultant psychiatrist recently, she was about to retire and she finally admitted that she had always known my husband was partly responsible for making me ill. I always thought his word was more respected than mine. It was a huge relief to hear that. She was adamant that his behaviour had influenced my outcome from the very beginning. I don't think I would have been encouraged to stick with him in the same way if I had been the husband and not the wife. I don't know.'

ANDREA'S STORY

Andrea's first contact with services for mental health problems was when she was 17 and took an overdose of sleeping pills.

She had been brought up an only child and had a difficult relationship with her father, who she describes as emotionally and psychologically abusive, an oppressive and dominating man who had a physically intrusive relationship with her which fell just short of sexual abuse. She was a chronically shy, vulnerable and sensitive adolescent. In retrospect, she thinks her school reports picked up the difficulties she was having but nothing was ever done about it and she was never given the opportunity to talk to anyone about her difficulties.

The overdose she took at 17 was never discussed, and her parents and GP decided between them that it was 'accidental', without trying very hard to talk to her. She began to believe that her problems must be trivial and unimportant. She now feels strongly that she would have liked to have been given the opportunity to discuss her feelings and the difficulties leading her to overdose.

Andrea was first admitted to a psychiatric hospital soon after leaving home when she was at teacher training college. Just before that she had been feeling unwell for a couple of weeks and the GP called. He started her on phenobarbitone but never called again to follow her up. He did not try to explain the treatment or what was happening. At the time she would not speak to him or turn round, but she feels that things would have gone better if he had taken the time to try and talk to her and to listen. Andrea says she has always had male GPs and therefore has never been able to talk to them. She sees her current male GP for physical problems only and keeps her psychological problems completely separate. The gender of her workers is very important to her. She has never been able to talk to men. For many years it did not occur to her that there might be a choice of worker. The best help she got was when she had a female psychiatrist and CPN.

After she started teaching she went into group psychotherapy and spent two years in a mixed-gender group run by a female and a male registrar. She feels that many people complain about not having access to talking treatments, whereas she did, but was not able to make use of it. She said virtually nothing for two years. In retrospect, she believes she needed one-to-one therapy with a female therapist. Andrea took an overdose just before the group came to an end; she felt attached to the female registrar, but was upset that she felt she had not put anything into the group herself, or got anything out. The female registrar came to see her after the overdose and took her on for individual therapy over the next two years. She feels the therapy went well as she had already had two years to get used to the therapist and to build up trust. Had it been a new therapist, it might have taken two years just to build up the trust and she would once again have got nothing from it. She began to learn ways of thinking and talking about her problems.

During the psychotherapy, Andrea was having a very difficult time with her relationship with her mother. She had to travel an extremely long distance after work, late at night and on public transport, to get to the therapy sessions and had to wait in a crowded pub to catch the bus home. She began suffering from chronic migraines on the days after therapy and had a lot of time off work as a result of both the migraines and depression. Eventually, she gave up her teaching job, at least in part because of this. She feels that no-one realised the effort required to get to and from the therapy and wishes something could have been provided more locally. Shortly before therapy ended, she took an overdose, as she still felt she had problems communicating about her depression.

She was nearly offered medical retirement from teaching, but the process was not completed, because of a misunderstanding. In 1983, she moved to Swindon to work for the civil service for five years. She felt terribly lonely and isolated in Swindon and began to have problems at work. Then began a series of admissions to hospital. She took a couple of overdoses and was admitted to the intensive care unit. In retrospect, she feels she was brushed aside because she was a single woman. Her experience, and that of other women she has known, is that single women are neglected and taken less seriously than women who have husbands and young children whose welfare the system cares about. She began to feel that she was repeatedly discharged because she couldn't be helped and the bed was required for someone who needed it more. She was very isolated and withdrawn and felt that no-one made an effort to try and get to know and understand her, confirming her feelings of lack of self-worth and rejection. She was not given a community worker for some time despite multiple admissions and overdoses. At least twice, Andrea was discharged to her father's care without being consulted. She had not been living with him prior to admission and did not like being discharged to him.

Later, Andrea joined a church house group where she met her husband. At that time, she was on lithium and other medications and she and her husband decided to have children, so they went to see her consultant. She feels that the consultant became more interested in her when she was engaged and getting married. Prior to that she had seen a succession of different junior doctors. It is thanks to the support of the female consultant over the last twelve years and the female CPN (for eight years) that she feels she has stayed married and had children.

With the support of her consultant, she came off lithium and antidepressants in order to get pregnant and began to attend the day hospital. When she was four to five months pregnant she began to experience very distressing pains in her back and legs and became very worried that the baby might be a girl and be 'like her'. Her great-grandmother had died with 'religious mania' in an asylum and her mother had suffered from depression, so she felt that severe depression ran through the female line of the family. Because of these fears, she did not want the baby and became suicidal. She was admitted to hospital when she was six months pregnant.

The baby was induced at eight months because of concerns about its growth, as Andrea had not been eating. She feels it was thanks to the effort that the consultant and CPN put into liaising with the midwife in charge of the postnatal ward that she was able to keep the baby. Andrea was kept in hospital during a period of negotiation. Apparently, the midwife had said that people 'like her' should not 'be allowed' to have babies. At first, she did not want the baby and took no interest in her. She was admitted back to the psychiatric ward, with the baby, into a makeshift mother and baby arrangement. Fortunately, one of the nurses happened to be a midwife. This nurse was helpful but could not be with her all the time. Andrea had to do a lot of the caring for the baby on her own and found it very hard. She needed far more practical help with the baby, especially at night, and feels that things might have been better if it had been a specially designated mother and baby unit rather than a makeshift arrangement. She had ECT which helped her a lot but did affect her memory.

During the time she was in hospital, the civil service initiated a process of medical retirement for her. At the time, Andrea felt desperate in herself and found worrying about her job so stressful that, in order to get rid of the problem quickly, she wrote to the civil service to resign. Despite knowing how very ill she was, they stopped the retirement proceedings immediately. In retrospect, Andrea feels she was deprived of her rights and might have benefited from an advocate, or someone with power of attorney to act in her best interests. Six years later, Andrea took up the matter successfully.

Eventually, Andrea returned home with her baby daughter and her CPN called quite often. She feels the CPN and psychiatrist considered her a 'success story' because she had been discharged, but she did not feel 'one hundred percent'. It took her about a year to have any feelings for the baby and she found her very difficult to care for, despite her being a very good baby. She feels that she needed far more practical help at home. A nursery nurse at her home would have been helpful in developing a relationship with her child, especially for the first month. Because her husband was working at home, it was assumed that she would get all the encouragement she needed. However, this was not the case as he had to work. Andrea felt very isolated. It never occurred to her to ask to attend the day hospital. As it was not offered, she assumed that her problems were not considered serious enough for it. In any case, there would have been no-one to care for the baby.

After her first child, Andrea was invited by her consultant to talk to student midwives about her experiences. She enjoyed doing this and thought it a very valuable initiative to educate midwives about mental illness so they might improve their understanding of women in her position. It also boosted her self-esteem. Maybe she had something to 'offer back' by way of a thank you. Three years later she saw the consultant about having another baby. Andrea and her husband had taken the long-term view that they would regret not having children and Andrea did not want her daughter to be an only child like her. She had her second child, a son. With her daughter she had lived in constant fear, for the first three years, that she would be taken away and the same was true when she had her son. Now that they are 8 and 5, she has finally stopped worrying about them being taken into care.

When her son was six months old Andrea was once more admitted to hospital and again received ECT, but has had no admissions since. During the last five years, although she has not actually been admitted, she has felt a strong need to go into hospital at times; however, no-one would have been able to care for the children and they would have had to be fostered. For this reason, her husband has been very opposed to her going into hospital and this has made her feel very guilty. If she had been able to go into hospital, she feels it would probably have taken her three months to get better, whereas at home it took her six months or more each time.

When the children were small, Andrea would have liked both more medical and more practical help at home. On one occasion when she rang the CPN for help, the CPN told her that what she needed was childcare and that she should phone the health visitor. Andrea felt let down. She had not phoned for that reason; she wanted help for *her* mental health problems, not just childcare. The health visitor then told her to ring social services for childcare and she had to explain that she could not face telling her story to a stranger. Eventually, the health visitor rang for her and she managed to get three days a week childcare for six months which was, in fact, a great help. However, at that time she still wanted medical help in her own right, but was not offered the opportunity to attend a day hospital and felt unable to ask for it if it was not offered. She feels that currently hospital is the only option for crisis care, but that it is not an option open to her, because of her children. When unwell, she needs to be somewhere that is not 'home'.

The local mental health resource centre has a women's day every week. When the children were small the nursery was too difficult for her to get to and from by public transport, because it was on the other side of town. Now the children are at school, transport arrangements for the day hospital would make it impossible for her to pick them up. She would prefer to be given money to pay her own childminder; then the children could be cared for in their own home.

About eighteen months ago Andrea took an overdose. It was an impulsive reaction to a passing remark by her husband and she was admitted to a general hospital. The next day she was seen by a registrar who asked if she needed hospital and when she said 'no', the registrar agreed.

Andrea felt quite unable to say yes, if the doctors did not offer it directly to her.

Personally, Andrea only feels able to speak to female workers and has found having a female consultant useful. She has also valued the continuity of care provided by her consultant, as it takes her a long time to build up trust, although recently she has had no continuity with CPNs.

One particular problem that Andrea is grappling with now, is what to say to her daughter about her mental illness. Recently, her daughter has frequently asked why Andrea takes pills and she tells her that she takes them 'to stay well'. Andrea is reluctant to tell her daughter very much. She does not want her to be burdened, feel responsible for her, or have to make allowances for her, as Andrea always had to do for her own mother. What she feels is that she is the parent and must meet her daughter's needs, rather than her daughter having to meet hers. Another fear is that she may frighten her daughter, because depression runs in the female line. She feels that it may be that by not talking about her feelings she is giving the same message to her daughter that she received from her parents: that you must never talk about 'bad' feelings.

GENERAL RECOMMENDATIONS

In the following paragraphs, we have distilled the more important aspects of good service provision as we see it, and have presented them as a series of recommendations to service planners and mental health workers. The most consistent feature to emerge from this process is that women need more choice. Trust plays a crucial role in providing the framework for this choice, so women feel safe to ask for what they need. Women want to make informed choices about particular aspects of care. For example, whether or not women are cared for by particular relatives; the conditions of their discharge; the gender of psychiatrist, CPN and other workers, and mental health workers must trust them to make such choices. In addition, some women wish to be given the opportunity to say thank you and to shape the service they must use; some users want to put something back into the services they consume.

Staff approaches that improve service provision

Ask women what they want. A woman's self-esteem may acutely colour her ability to ask for things and make her needs known. A better understanding of some women's extremely poor self-esteem and their feelings of worthlessness might prevent this being misinterpreted as lack of engagement and motivation. Many women do want people to find out about their lives and to know about their personal details, perhaps more than men, but they don't want this fact to be taken for granted, and, therefore, to have their lives interfered with unduly. The choice that women want can only be provided if the health care worker understands and knows about a woman's life. All too often attention is paid to those around women, e.g. children and partners, rather than looking to their needs as an individual. Women may need special help not to get 'lost' amidst their family commitments; they may be unable to extricate themselves from traditional roles of responsibility, and partners often need support to accept a revised role for the woman. In addition, carers, partners and dependants must be catered for carefully in service provision. Women may need particular help to explain their illness experiences to their children. Some women can be especially compromised by overbearing or blatantly illness-provoking partners. These possibilities have to be explored by all mental health care workers in consultation with their clients.

Recommendations for future services

The need for women-focused provision in the service should be fully recognised and adequate training provided for this. An holistic approach to all mental health service users must be encouraged so that users are treated first and foremost as individuals. In this way, they will have the right to as full a range of life experiences as care workers would wish for themselves. This includes thinking about the person not just as a set of symptoms. Training for mental health workers should reflect this and focus on attitudes to various important aspects of the individual: how people think about race, gender, sexuality, and how that individual relates within their environment, for example how parenthood or marriage might influence a woman's experience.

Although we do not recommend women-*only* services, those women who wish should have access to safe, women-only space at the local level. At a national level, we anticipate potential problems with this approach. Women-only services could be seen as a form of 'ghettoising' women. In addition, very good women-only services in one locale may give service providers elsewhere the impression that they need not think about women, and it may even encourage general psychiatric services to be run down.

RECOMMENDATIONS IN SPECIFIC AREAS

Mental health workers:

Women in particular recognise that people are important and buildings aren't.

- Everyone should have access to an approachable consultant and CPN.
- Continuity of psychiatrist, CPN and other workers is very important in building trust and being able to discuss feelings.

- Everyone should be supported by their consultant, CPN and other workers in being given the opportunity to lead a fulfilling family life.
- Every woman should be given the choice to see female workers.

Mental health facilities

Women need better and more extensive use of non-hospital-based services. Many community facilities are cheaper than the hospital.

- Services should be local and accessible and not require travelling long distances alone on public transport, especially at night.
- Thoughtfully organised services with advice from women users as to what they really find beneficial, for example as well as crèches and nurseries women should be provided with resources to make their own local arrangements.
- If the woman chooses, mental health workers should visit women at home more often, rather than just at times of crisis. This would allow for a better understanding of their circumstances.
- It is important to understand and to combat the social isolation of many women; for example by providing accessible day care and more support in the community early on.
- We would like women to be given financial power and enabled to take control of some resources.

Women with children

- Good liaison between agencies, especially between psychiatric services and maternity services.
- Better education of midwives and maternity staff about mental illness to remove prejudice and preconceptions and increase their understanding.
- Local and accessible mother and baby facilities which support mothers with children of all ages.
- Help with childcare in order to attend day hospitals and other community resources or for admission to hospital. Give women resources directly so that children can be cared for at home or in a familiar environment.
- Practical help with childcare should complement and not replace medical and psychotherapeutic help for the woman in her own right.
- Greater awareness of the support needed by women in telling their children about mental illness.
- The needs of women with older children should be taken seriously.
- Hospitals should have places suitable for children to visit.
- Acknowledge women's fear of having their children taken into care.

Women at different ages

- Adolescent girls' problems should be taken seriously and they should be given the opportunity to talk about their distress. Schools should make provision for this and have good referral mechanisms to other agencies.
- Single women's needs should be taken more seriously.

THE FUTURE

More and more, mental health service users are involved in teaching the service how crucial a part they can play in the planning and provision of good mental health care. We recommend that all stages of mental health service planning should include representation from female and male users. In addition, users should be encouraged to be involved in service delivery. Good practice models, for example advocacy and user groups are already in existence and these can interact fruitfully to inform the planners and providers of users' desires. They may be important in gaining recognition, especially for vulnerable groups of women, such as the sexually or physically abused and those who are single parents. In order to participate fully in the planning and delivery of services, user groups require support and resources so that they may take an equal part in the process. There is a great need to encourage and enhance user networks and user consultants and to ensure their active participation in women's mental health service planning and in the future quality monitoring of those services.

CROSS-REFERENCES WITHIN THIS BOOK

Chapter 7   Women, lesbians and community care
Chapter 14   Women and primary care
Chapter 17   Campaigning for change

FURTHER READING

Breggin, P. (1993) *Toxic psychiatry*, London: Fontana Paperbacks.
Johnson, L. (1989) *Users and abusers of psychiatry: a critical look at traditional psychiatric practice*, London: Routledge.
Millett, K. (1991) *The loony bin trip*, London: Virago.
Wallcraft, J. and Read, J. (1992) *Guidelines for empowering users of mental health services*, London: COHSE/MIND Publications.

Chapter 16

Shanti

An intercultural psychotherapy centre for women in the community

Maggie Mills

Women in our society are nature's carers. They expect, and are expected, to nurture others. Women who come for therapy hardly use the pronoun 'I' in the first weeks, and it is unusual to hear them say 'My needs are . . .' or 'What I really want is . . .' Instead, they worry about the well-being of all the people they are close to: their children and partner, their parents, relations and friends, even their boss. Looking out for the well-being of others, usually at the expense of themselves, is absolutely ingrained in women. This role defines them culturally and personally, so that psychological health for women is defined as caring for others, as a substitute for being properly cared for themselves.

The lifelong neglect of their own desires is hard to shift therapeutically, bringing forth feelings of inadequacy, selfishness and guilt (Mills, 1993). There is a double bind here too: carers are traditionally the strong ones, so if women fail in this already lowly role (wife, mother, low-paid or unpaid worker), they are left with nothing. Women are seen as the emotionally literate ones who understand feelings, yet when they actually manifest distress, anxiety and depression more frequently than men, they are labelled as the weak ones – the mentally ill. Throwing off society's dictate – a prescription which has been so well internalised – presents a real psychic conflict to women. Moreover, in reality, it also entails a shift in power, since women *are* marginalised economically, often against a backdrop of social deprivation and victimisation.

So the provision of resources specifically for the psychological well-being of women does need to be addressed by service providers and policy makers. But where and how should they start? This chapter gives an account of a fairly unique service called Shanti, which has been created for women. It is an intercultural, psychodynamic psychotherapy centre in the inner-city community setting of a Brixton housing estate (see Appendix for address). Originally a pioneering project for Inner City Partnership, it is a free service within the NHS (WLCC Trust), although clients do not perceive it as having institutional links. It is open every day and offers limited evening working. Its staffing includes a co-ordinator and a crèche worker, and three full-time equivalent psychotherapists actually made up of two South Americans, one British-born black therapist and two British-born white therapists. Their backgrounds encompass social work, psychiatric nursing and clinical psychology, although all also have an independent psychotherapy training. The nature of the multi-racial team is enhanced by volunteers working under supervision, students on placement and trainees on Shanti's one-year course in intercultural psychotherapy.

Shanti got started eight years ago by spending several months researching carefully what local women actually wanted. Tenants' associations, the sandwich queue in the local M & S, women's refuges, one o'clock clubs, bingo and other local meeting places were all visited by workers who simply went and listened to what women said. The views of local professionals were also sought. Outreach, action research is essential in the start-up of a community service.

There seemed to be a large unmet need. Women wanted a safe, anonymous, user-friendly place where they could come and talk comfortably about their distress and their difficulties. The predominant message was that many women were battling on in their family lives with no resources for themselves. They were well aware that something had to change in their lives or they would go mad, and meanwhile they described themselves as just about hanging on, often by their fingertips. This is how they described what they felt (Reader, 1993):

> It wasn't just in the odd black moments I felt bad. It was in every aspect of my life. I couldn't do anything; I was bursting into tears, I was not sleeping, it was interfering with the relationship with my daughter because I was so wound up with what was going on, I couldn't cope with the basic things – it was totally devastating.

> Before, I didn't even want to get out of bed. I couldn't get on with things. I used to just sit here like a blob and watch television and not have the energy to do anything.

> I used to feel so numb: engulfed really by my depression. I couldn't cry, I couldn't move, I couldn't do anything at all.

> I'd take a day off work and just spend it under my duvet; just not moving.

What women wanted was to feel comfortable, valued and listened to. Many (nearly 40 per cent) had tried conventional, more formal, health services but, for different reasons, seldom felt they had got what they needed. A major difficulty for those who had encountered previous psychiatric care is that it is hard to feel comfortable, valued and listened to when you hardly ever see the same professional twice. Social oppression itself prevents many women obtaining help, and they can feel excluded by reason of ethnicity, class, sexuality or age. As for psychotherapy, women in the community found such services as there were quite inaccessible. Often they would have been thought 'unsophisticated' – some notion that a high level of education was traditionally required for such an undertaking, or even that by virtue of their lifelong histories of emotional deprivation, they were 'untreatable'.

Given that some 60 per cent of the clients coming to Shanti have an ethnic-minority background, there was justified mistrust about whether the issue of internalised racism could be addressed, particularly in the usual set-up of a white professional treating a black client. Also, for a lot of women, there was disquiet about how a eurocentric therapeutic philosophy could ever be adapted to their needs. But, as Francis (1993), one of the co-founding psychotherapists in Shanti, points out, Brixton is not entirely a black or working-class community:

It has middle class enclaves as well as end of the road council estates with a high drug and crime rate ... It is a truly strange conglomerate of people. If you feel different within your own community, it often feels more comfortable to live within a community known to be full of difference. It is then possible to feel less alien.

Shanti's first task was to build a centre for women's mental health that at least did not alienate clients – a service for 'outsiders', deliberately set up outside the conventional care system. It chose to do so by acknowledging that women often get a raw deal in society, so that, where women therapists work with women clients, there is some sense of an identity of feelings and experiences. This can reassure clients and provide a therapeutic willingness to hear, empathise and understand them. As one client said in a follow-up interview after therapy was completed:

It gave me a lot of confidence seeing all those women at Shanti ... different races, sizes, voices, problems, working and being happy. It's a wonderful thing there, you see light people and dark people – and you will always fit in with someone. It helped me also that my therapist was black and I am too. My own family were light: I never belonged. Seeing the women at Shanti – capable, working, doing things, active, well and able to help each other, it made me feel better and gave me the feeling I could do it ... And I did!

Therapeutic benefit can come from the safe feeling many women experience with a women-only space, and the attachment women make to the centre and its ethos. The aim was an integrated political and therapeutic stance, not a federation of individual therapists. Clients said in after-therapy interviews that they knew Shanti would always be there. It felt as if someone still cared and there was something to go back to if need be.

It does help in therapy to feel that a therapy centre and/or therapist is with you *contra mundum* in the struggle to acknowledge and retrieve any sense of powerfulness. At an intercultural centre, the client must be offered the choice of a therapist from a similar ethnic background. The issue is always explored at initial interview and then the client may be referred on to another therapist. The Centre's policy is explicit:

> The way people act and think, the images and structures that continue to make women feel put down or excluded thereby making them feel power-less, will be actively challenged amongst the staff, the women who use the service and other organisations with whom Shanti has contact. Shanti will provide a space where all women can feel welcome, make changes, grow and become confident, and in so doing take control of their lives.
>
> (Statement of Intent, 1988)

It has been necessary to adapt psychodynamic understanding and practice to the political and social reality of largely under-resourced clients. Light-touch, non-interpretive counselling was felt to be inadequate, given the high rates of psychiatric morbidity demonstrated by Shanti users and the abuse, neglect and losses that often made up their early life histories. The therapy of choice, clearly a 'talking therapy', had to be one that would attend to early losses, problematic early attachments, intimacy and the nature of close relationships. Psychodynamic psychotherapy does address emotional memories and fantasies in some depth.

Examining the histories of a hundred consecutive users in the second year of clinical practice at the Centre (Reader, 1993), it was found that 91 per cent of women were clinically depressed on the Present State Examination (Wing *et al.*, 1974); 62 per cent had depression and anxiety; 15 per cent experienced psychotic episodes; and 20 per cent had made serious suicide attempts. Nearly 80 per cent of users had experienced more than two years of psychiatric disorder in their lives. As for their personal history, half of Shanti's users had experienced one major change of caretaker before they reached 13, and 65 per cent of the parental partnerships were discordant or broken. Sixty-one per cent of users reported emotional or psychological neglect during childhood which was not associated with physical or sexual abuse, where the rates were 44 per cent and 34 per cent respectively. Not surprisingly, 59 per cent expressed negative evaluations of two early caretakers. A third of the users received no emotional support from family, friends or those they worked with, so that many women were extremely isolated and socially unsupported. About half the women coming to Shanti were already parents, and 60 per cent of them reported experiencing difficulties in their parenting role.

It is understandable that consumer-led demand was for an opportunity to talk to someone who could help women explore, understand and contain difficult feelings, particularly when their past lives reflected considerable at-tachment difficulties and they described themselves as currently still strug-gling with their close relationships. But it was also important that the therapeutic environment should reflect as little as possible the conditions in society that demoralise women. Therapy is not administered on prescription: women must positively want it, and being able to make the first approach to the centre themselves gives them the power to make their own choice to engage in the process or not, rather than being shuffled on in the system.

Clients self-refer by walking in off the street – the Centre is a ground-floor, homely flat which is easily accessible yet private, and staff are always welcoming. Crèche facilities, to obviate the hassles of childcare, are essential. Women are also encouraged to refer themselves by telephone and nearly half the clients do this. If a statutory agency or GP wants to refer their patient, they are welcome to suggest she visit or call herself. Some care workers accompany a prospective client on the first visit. The procedure is informal, no referral letter is required, all disclosures are dealt with in absolute confidence, and there is hardly any bureaucratic interchange between professionals over a woman's head – case conferences, circulated records or the like, although if GPs or other referring agencies want to check up or share information with a therapist, they are welcome to contact the service directly. Shanti's records, however, whilst open to the client, are never circulated. One client said on follow-up:

> Shanti was very unthreatening, nothing to do with a hospital. I wouldn't have gone. I was relieved it was like in someone's house and only women and very friendly. It didn't make you feel you were a freak or a mentally ill person, which from my previous experience was very important to me.

It is so important to hear a woman's own experience and how her inner world is constituted from her own lips. Telling her story is validating for her, whereas bearing a referring diagnostic medical or social label is not. In the same way, clients are invited to give their own accounts of their self-identity in terms of their ethnicity. All of this helps women to feel they are likely to be listened to. Having been open eight years, the centre has a word-of-mouth reputation in the area, and women send along friends and relations, which is the real test of consumer confidence and satisfaction. Post-treatment evaluation found that over 90 per cent of clients said they would recommend the centre to a friend. Shanti is able to treat many women who are not known to formal services at all.

This painstaking attention to the interface between the therapeutic service and the process of engagement is the first essential in good clinical practice, yet it is the one most often neglected by more traditional service delivery. For example, it is arrogant to assume that the current NHS practice of requiring clients to fill in a pre-assessment six-page questionnaire is a necessary test of motivation. To be truly user-friendly, even small details are important. In Shanti, artwork on the project's walls has been carefully accumulated over the years to reflect the diversity of women's lives so that new clients can find a useful image to identify with.

Some women, although clearly in distress, just may not be ready emotionally to do the often-painful work that psychotherapy requires. Because there is no prescription, women can explore what developmental stage they are at during the initial assessment interview to which all prospective clients are entitled, without feeling a failure if they decide not to take up a therapeutic contract with an agreed focus for the psychological work. Some women return in the future, some have the economic or other resources for Shanti not to be the appropriate venue, while others decide for referral on to some other therapeutic option, which may be suggested by Shanti staff, who often serve as informal gate-keepers to any number of different local services. But the locus of control is always left with the client. This kind of approach is likely to ensure that women use local services appropriately, which is a plus for the NHS Trust in which Shanti is situated, and means efficient service delivery.

All this careful planning means that women who do engage are very well motivated for change. Being in pain is itself a condition likely to galvanise the psyche, so it is quite counterproductive for clients to be chemically 'coshed' with medication or self-anaesthetised with recreational stimulants or serious substance abuse. The Centre aims for clients to be as drug-free as possible, explains why, and instead offers containment and support for the unbearable anxieties that drugs have been keeping at bay. It is important to point out that American research finds time-limited psychotherapy as effective as antidepressant medication in alleviating symptoms and preventing relapse (US DHHS, 1993). There is tolerance for psychotic and immediately post-psychotic clients attending out-patients, although non-compliance is common. If clients have persistent substance abuse, then local detoxification programmes need to precede therapy.

Experience in Shanti suggests that high levels of engagement in treatment can be achieved with this client group if attention is paid to ways of holding and reducing their initial anxieties. In the eight years Shanti has been open, no client has committed suicide. Attempts of varying severity have occurred and sometimes therapists visit clients on in-patient wards and continue treatment when they are discharged. Not surprisingly, clients with delusions and compulsive thoughts were the only ones not to show statistically significant symptom-reduction after treatment, although 50 per cent showed some improvement. Brief work is clearly not the treatment of choice for psychosis, but with the extremely worrying (and worsening) situation some severely ill clients are experiencing in getting any post-discharge care in the community at all, it is inevitable that Shanti finds itself engaged on a 'maintenance' basis in containing distress and anxiety with some women, rather than being able to embark on the usual work – intensive and in-depth.

Once embarked on a treatment contract, nearly 80 per cent of clients complete right to the end, but in the initial engagement phase, the issue of how long clients had to wait for an assessment is crucial. Waiting lists with initial contact not made after three weeks or so are useless. Women cannot feel contained and trusting if they wait too long to be seen and feel let down before they have begun. Also, more therapeutic change is possible when women come in considerable distress. Unfortunately staff resources in Shanti are inadequate to cope swiftly with the demand, which can lead to forty to fifty women waiting in the system. Periodically, therapists concentrate on assessments to reduce waiting time, as the Centre has demonstrated time and time again that long queues mean potential clients get lost and do not present themselves for an initial interview if forced to wait too long. Once accepted for therapy, clients find a wait easier, although it is hardly to be regarded as good practice. Obviously, matching demand to resources is the principle for good clinical practice, as well as knowing as clearly as possible what kinds of clients are most likely to benefit from psychotherapy offered in the community.

The Centre completes around 150 full therapies a year, by which is meant brief time-limited work confined to once-weekly individual therapy lasting sixteen weeks. Each individual session lasts fifty minutes and is costed at £24.30 (1994 prices). Assessment interviews are also completed, since a thorough assessment is essential for brief work and important to allow an agreed focus for the therapeutic work to develop (Balint and Balint, 1961). Refresher sessions are offered on an informal basis when required. Since, with time-limited contracts, the issue of ending is worked with throughout, the opportunity for clients to have a follow-up a few months or weeks after termination is especially important as clients can continue to feel quite raw emotionally. This is a difficulty with doing brief work and the Centre's research evaluation concluded that a follow-up session should always be offered.

Work done by therapists in groups includes group analytic therapy, supervision, trainee teaching within Shanti, and external group work with local voluntary organisations and statutory services. This group work constitutes about 1,700 therapist contacts a year. The Centre also acts as a resource for women's issues, mental health advice and liaison with other services – for example, solicitors, refuges, well-woman clinics, housing pressure groups, crèche care and parenting workshops. Concerned as she must be with inner reality, it is not the psychotherapist's task to give practical help herself in these areas. However, it is important to share something of the same world-view with clients, given the hardness of their lives, and it can be very important to help clients get in touch with appropriate sources of support.

The essential dilemma is how to provide quality intervention and prevention in enough quantity to begin to meet the demand. Time-limited psychotherapy as offered at Shanti is not, however, a reluctant compromise. It is offered as a worthwhile therapeutic enterprise in its own right, not as a second-best therapy for under-resourced clients because it is free at the point of delivery and relatively cheap to provide. An independent research study by the King's Fund evaluated its efficacy (Reader, 1993), and its findings endorse this approach and help put paid to the middle-class notion that only several years of intensive psychodynamic psychotherapy is really any use. Research shows that the maximum benefit to be derived from psychotherapy occurs in the first twenty-five sessions (Howard, 1986). Surveys of psychotherapy in American community mental health centres find that the median treatment length is thirteen sessions. So Shanti's treatment duration, adapted from Malan's brief workshops at the Tavistock Clinic (Malan, 1961), is respectable.

So far this chapter has dealt with the first issue of good clinical practice, namely engagement. It has indicated that the needs of women are not always appreciated in an NHS service staffed predominantly by men in the higher echelons, and that distressed and under-resourced women may not feel confident enough to access mainstream services. Our experiences also indicate that women from ethnic-minority communities do need black-on-black therapy to facilitate their psychological growth, so this should always be on offer. However, they should always be entitled to expect a sensitivity to the issues of intercultural work, even when their therapist has a different ethnic background from their own. Finally, it should be said that many women prefer a women-only space, whether or not this is for reasons of protection and safety to do with childhood sexual abuse, or with ongoing domestic abuse and violence in adulthood (nearly 40 per cent of clients report this experience).

It is important to consider the nature of the therapeutic model that has evolved in Shanti, together with the quality of work achieved in terms of client process and client development and outcome. Does Shanti facilitate personal change in its client group? (Describing *how* the 'talking' is done is not the province of this chapter and no case history accounts are offered.) Genuine change for clients is possible without it being necessary to create a complete transference neurosis and work it through in the classic analytic tradition (Hildebrand, 1986). After all, Freud was convinced that it was possible to help people understand something of their psychic problems in a very brief time (his early patients got brief psychotherapies) and through that insight to initiate major changes in their lives. The therapist has to work on the problem/s that seems central to the patient and be fairly single-minded about a focus. If brief therapy is to be successful, some significant shift in affective communication is experienced around sessions 4/5 and research shows important psychic changes happening again around session 12 (Orlinsky and Howard, 1986). Few women in Shanti have ever successfully negotiated separation from anyone important in their lives, which have often been full of painful partings, so the issue of termination is always kept in mind.

Shanti's research findings indicated that the achievement in therapy of insight, self-affirmation and self-perception that was reality-based was the best predictor of women's psychological well-being two years after the work ended. In brief therapeutic encounters, something of an 'observing ego' emerges, so that when things go well the experience gets internalised and the woman is enabled to get on with things by herself, with the therapist as the catalyst for change. The theoretical model for brief psychotherapy must be a developmental one (Mills, 1993). The question is how little therapy – rather than how much – is necessary to help a woman feel in control of her life again – or possibly take control for the first time and be able to make creative choices for herself in her working and personal life. If brief work is successful then it is usually the case that after therapy ends the process of sorting out difficulties goes on, with habits of self-enquiry now an established part of a client's psychological repertoire, together with the ability to think more realistically about feelings and responses in ongoing relationships.

Since Shanti's evaluation was carried out two years after the clients' therapy had ended, the Centre learnt that for many women real change, which they themselves attributed to the therapeutic work, only actually started to happen in their lives *after* the therapy. The analogy, with apologies if the metaphor seems a masculine one, is perhaps this: rather than the therapist taking the engine apart like some mechanic, what happens in brief therapy is more like when the blocks or chocks in front of an aircraft's wheels – which stop the plane flying – are taken away. In this way, women lose that terrible sense of stuckness in their lives so that one day, in their own good time, they will move down the runway of their own volition, and fly.

When new services in the community are established, it is essential to carry out an independent investigation of the efficacy of any project, and to assess whether reported personal change is attributable to the therapeutic efforts of the Centre being evaluated. Clinicians (Andrews, 1993) might expect to find benefits of symptom-reduction or disappearance, as well as an improved ability to work and relate. Ideally, risk factors in personality vulnerability that might lead to relapse should be reduced or better contained, while continuing improvement after termination is essential.

On follow-up, 83 per cent of clients reported improvements in self-esteem, and 73 per cent demonstrated social support networks that were improved in quality and/or were more extended. For those women who had children, roughly half the sample, over two-thirds reported improvements in their abilities as parents. One-third of women had improved their work situation – having got a job, or obtained a better one since before they came to Shanti (this in the context of 44 per cent being unemployed when they first came to the Centre). In addition, many women had started to engage in adult education courses either at access or degree level.

In terms of symptom reduction, 70 per cent of clients were improved on the GHQ and 91 per cent on Beck's self-administered questionnaire on his depression inventory. Symptom improvement on the PSE-derived psychiatric interview was significant for depression and anxiety, suicidal ideation and symptom severity impairing everyday functioning. Eating disorders and substance abuse also showed significant remission. All these findings were statistically significant. These findings for Shanti (Reading, 1993) compare favourably with other community mental health services using treatment methods that are psychodynamically oriented and serve under-resourced women, such as Nafsiyat (Kareem and Littlewood, 1992) and NEWPIN (Mills and Cox, 1991).

Areas of personal change included practical issues; coping and awareness of own needs; self-confidence; resolution of childhood feelings in the family of origin; managing the emotional side of current relationships; ability to cope with psychic pain and loss. There was also evidence for psychic phenomena derived from a continuing use of therapy, such as dreams, insight and the realistic rather than fantasy appraisal of important life situations. Seventy-seven per cent of women showed a positive outcome and in 89 per cent of such cases the change was judged attributable, or at least partly attributable, to Shanti. For thirteen women there was no change, and one woman's condition had deteriorated.

In looking at the usefulness of therapy, it is possible to make a distinction between long-term changes and immediate consumer satisfaction. Users mentioned safety and the containment of difficult feelings; the relief and ventilation of pain; the experience of being with a therapist who had valued and accepted the client and, last, the sharing of understanding of lifelong difficulties in the context of the therapeutic relationship. These benign factors need not be the province of psychoanalytic psychotherapy, the treatment offered at Shanti, but would be important for any worthwhile clinical service.

Shanti's clients differed, of course, in the extent to which they were able to use the therapy to make positive changes in their lives. Success was more likely where clients finished their contracts and had felt properly held in the Centre. This seemed true even in the presence of a predominantly negative transference. Previous counselling, surprisingly, had an adverse effect. Clients had sought to continue self-exploration and development in a variety of therapies and alternative treatments after their involvement with Shanti was over, and, as explained earlier, this is seen by the Centre as a good outcome, not as a failure of brief work. No one individual background variable predicted a good or poor outcome, but those with multiple early adversity/ deprivation did less well. It should be noted that the opportunity to talk to someone about very private matters, particularly childhood sexual abuse, which women in the initial survey had said they wanted, turned out to be an important area for success. Where women had no resident confidante to turn to (and less than 20 per cent of women lived in a traditional family pattern), the insight gained during therapy was linked to a positive outcome.

The experience of intercultural working would require a chapter in its own right. Positive outcomes, however, were just as likely no matter whether black-on-black, or white-on-black therapy had been undertaken. This certainly reflects not just ethos but also the initial care Shanti takes to get the therapist right for the client during the assessment stage. So, where women from ethnic minorities were seen by a white therapist, they had as the focus for therapy an issue that could feasibly be dealt with in an unmatched relationship. The crucial importance of black-on-black work, however, is not to be downplayed by these findings.

While we know the Centre works well for its women users, how may its image be affected within other referral and professional care agencies by its 'outsider' stance, reflecting perhaps the experiences of the 'nomadic' cultures it was set up to support? Are more efforts at liaison required? It is important also to establish what is the optimum clinical size of the service in the face of continuing demand, and to develop some realistic measures of the effectiveness of Shanti in comparison with other Trust agencies. The Centre would welcome the opportunity to achieve a cross-comparison cost appraisal, which is beyond the capability of one relatively small service on its own. What other aspects of service should Shanti perhaps be developing? A one-year training programme particularly for ethnic minority students is running. Another worthwhile development that was tried was a befriending service within Shanti, which had ex-clients willing to offer help and support to other users. Such social action offers a genuine reciprocal relationship to befriender and user alike and offers one way for women who have become empowered through their psychotherapy to continue their own personal development.

Shanti recognises that many women in the community seek contact with others to reduce their isolation and some friendly support and communication which stops short of intensive psychotherapy. Befriending might be a service for women who have to wait a long time for therapy or, equally, it could offer containment and support to post-psychotic clients who get little after-care now in conventional mental health provision. Referrals came both from Shanti and from other agencies. Potential befrienders were paid expenses, and could arrange a contract with their client that was flexible in term of hours and of meeting their client's needs. Meetings often took place at home or outside the Centre. Both users and befrienders reported satisfaction with such arrangements.

The training itself, initially of ten weeks' duration, consisted of a personal group and a formal seminar on difficult issues likely to be encountered in the work. In the initial contact work and matching supporter to client, befrienders supported each other in relieving anxiety until some confidence built up and regular monitoring and supervisory work (which is essential) was carried out by the Shanti staff running the scheme. Organisation and monitoring of such a service is time-consuming and proved to be so at Shanti. The ultimate goal would be for the befrienders themselves to take over the work and the organisation completely.

Shanti will continue to experiment in finding ways to meet the differing needs of women in the community. The psychodynamic psychotherapy service remains its central core: popular in the community and securely funded from the local NHS trust. Final evidence, however, for the success of this model of mental health care in the community for women will come from its replication in other parts of Britain.

CROSS-REFERENCES WITHIN THIS BOOK

REFERENCES

Andrews, G. (1993) 'The essential psychotherapies', *British Journal of Psychiatry* 162: 447–451.
Balint, M. and Balint, E. (1961) *Psychotherapeutic techniques*, London: Tavistock.
Beck, A. and Beck, A.N. (1972) 'Screening depressed patients in family practice', *Post-Graduate Medicine* 5: 81–85.
Francis, S. (1993) 'Power, culture and psychiatry: the work of Shanti Women's Intercultural Psychotherapy Centre'. Paper presented to the 5th International Congress on Mental Health Nursing, London.
Hildebrand, P. (1986) 'Brief psychotherapy', *Psychoanalytic Psychotherapy* 3: 1–12.
Howard, K. (1986) 'The dose-effect relationship in psychotherapy', *American Psychologist* 41: 159–164.
Kareem, J. and Littlewood, R. (1992) *Intercultural therapy*, Oxford: Blackwell.
Malan, D. (1961) *A study of brief psychotherapy*, London: Tavistock.
Mills, M. (1993) 'Psychotherapy for women', *Journal of Mental Health* 2: 89–93.
Mills, M. and Cox, A. (1991) 'Evaluation of Newpin', *Journal of the Royal Society of Medicine* 8: 217–220.
Orlinsky, D. and Howard, K. (1986) 'Process and outcome in psychotherapy', in S. Garfield and A. Bergin (eds), *Handbook of psychotherapy and behaviour change*, Chichester: Wiley.
Reader, L. (1993) 'Evaluation of a psychotherapy service for women in the community (SHANTI)', unpublished final report to the King's Fund.
US DHHS (1993) *Depression in primary care: treatment of major depression*, Rockville: ACHPR Publications.
Walker, M. (1990) *Women in therapy and counselling*, Milton Keynes: Open University Press.
Wing, J. (1974) *Measurement and classification of psychiatric symptoms*, Cambridge: Cambridge University Press.
Wing, J.K., Cooper, J.E. and Sartorius, M. (1974) *Description and classification of psychiatric symptoms*, Cambridge: Cambridge University Press.

Chapter 17

Campaigning for change

Liz Sayce

INTRODUCTION

History is full of examples of women being defined as 'mad' for different reasons than men, and of receiving very different forms of treatment. For instance, in the nineteenth century active female sexuality was seen as a sign of derangement and some women were sent to the asylum because they sent their visiting cards to men to whom they were attracted (Ussher, 1991). Rehabilitation programmes have more often encouraged men than women into paid employment. But it was not until the late twentieth century – with the introduction from the 1970s of women's therapy centres and projects for women experiencing violence – that campaigning activity in Britain began to try specifically to change attitudes to women's mental health, and not until the 1980s that different groups of women – black and white, young and old, lesbian and heterosexual – began to get their different experiences of mental health seriously discussed.

A major focus of this chapter is on strategies for campaigning for change, both at a local and at a national level. Other chapters have discussed current needs and problems in service delivery and have set out some desirable goals for change. In this chapter, the main aim is to describe how to make change happen: by identifying clear priorities, arming service users with information so that they can pursue their own rights, influencing public and professional attitudes and persuading local and central services planners to place women's mental health high on their agendas.

This chapter is written from the perspective of the large UK voluntary-sector organisation, MIND (National Association for Mental Health – see Appendix for address). MIND works to promote the rights and interests of people diagnosed mentally ill and to improve public understanding of mental health issues. This discussion draws particularly on experience gained in the MIND 1992–1994 campaign, 'Stress on Women'. It is hoped that the lessons learnt can be generalised to provide inspiration and guidance for all those who are working to improve services for women who experience mental distress.

PLANNING A CAMPAIGN

Building on previous campaigns

The first rule of campaigning is not to waste scarce resources in re-inventing work that has already been done. Achievements in women's mental health over the last twenty-five years have been considerable, although the gains have not always been preserved.

During the 1970s and 1980s, inspired by the emerging women's liberationist view that 'the personal is political', specific work on women's mental health took off with the following results:

- a re-think of women's psychology, emanating initially from the London Women's Therapy Centre (e.g. Eichenbaum and Orbach, 1983);
- the birth of further local women's mental health projects, some addressing the different needs of black women, lesbians and other groups;
- the rapid growth of service-user organisations, which put women's issues on their agendas;
- the beginning of a consensus in favour of community care, which allowed some limited space for the development of local women's services.

Some coalitions between service users and workers generated successful campaigns: for instance, WISH (Women in Special Hospitals) provided advocacy with and for women in secure provision; and the Southwark Women and Mental Health Forum succeeded in getting the issue of abuse of women in psychiatric hospitals seriously discussed by NHS staff and managers.

These developments were not without their opposition. During the Thatcher years projects for women, and especially for black women or lesbian women, were ridiculed by the press as 'loony left'. This led to an atmosphere of defensiveness in local authorities: many disbanded their women's committees (in favour of less threatening 'equalities' committees); funding for women's projects was insecure, and sometimes only available to projects focusing on 'families'. Those projects that flourished did so through the commitment of groups and individuals rather than through the clemency of the policy climate.

Moreover, it was clear that double standards persisted. For instance, men are permitted by society to express far more anger than women before a psychiatric response, such as prescribing medication, is considered – a fact that in 1993 prompted adverse comment from the Princess of Wales:

Pills will tend to make a woman more passive, 'to help her conform to the norm'. But whose norm is it? Isn't it normal not to be able to cope all the time? Isn't it normal for women as well as men to feel frustrated with life?

Isn't it normal to feel angry and want to change a situation that is hurting?

(Turning Point Conference, 1993)

Responding to need

A campaign will only succeed if a body of people want to put energies into it. In the early 1990s there was a growing call from women for action on mental health. At that time, there was no national focus for work on women's mental health. The important issues being raised by women were simply not reaching mainstream policy debates. National mental health policy concerned itself with whether the law should be changed to increase control and supervision of users living outside hospitals. Proposals for community supervision orders, and later for supervised discharge, repeatedly conjured up examples – almost always male examples – of people who might need compulsory supervision in the community. Black mental health groups feared that any such measure would be applied particularly to black men. Meanwhile, a parallel policy debate about rationing was being concentrated on the need to target resources for people with 'severe and long-term mental illness' rather than those disparagingly referred to as 'the worried well'. Examples of the latter nearly always happened to be women, for instance women with 'neurotic disorders', who at times appeared to be considered unworthy of any service.

Women seemed to be well and truly off the agenda. At the 1991 MIND Annual Conference a strong call came from women to run a campaign to change that.

Identifying women's views of what should change

Campaigns are only successful if they strike a chord with the people they affect: if they select the issues that people think important.

Our initial review of the literature on women and mental health in Britain revealed a familiar picture of a mental health service in which women predominate among the users (by a factor of about 3:2) and front-line care staff, but are in a minority of decision-makers. Men make up 73 per cent of consultant psychiatrists, 78 per cent of directors of social services and 58 per cent of senior/general managers in the NHS. UK women receive about thirty million prescriptions for psychiatric drugs per year – slightly more on average than one prescription for every woman in the country. Women are clearly receiving a significant share of the nation's mental health resource, but are they getting what they feel they need?

To address this question the MIND campaign began by consultation with different groups of women who were using or had used mental health services: black women, women from different ethnic groups, lesbians, old and young women, women with and without children. Although as some women saw it, they *had* happened on a good service or found what they needed eventually, there were three main areas of complaint which arose again and again.

Problem 1. Ignoring hidden distress

> I'm a survivor of sex abuse and I get flashbacks about my abuse, and I fear men. When I went to hospital I longed to talk to someone about this but no one seemed to have the time and they just gave me drugs and told me I was depressed. I felt like saying 'you'd be depressed if you'd gone through what I have'.
>
> (User surveyed by Southampton MIND's Stress on Women group)

Repeatedly, women told us that the mental health services seemed to concentrate on symptoms, rather than causes and to see the woman in terms of her diagnosis, rather than the depth and richness of her life. The experiences that the women saw as contributing to their distress (including abuse and neglect in their own childhoods, miscarriages and domestic violence) were often never revealed to mental health staff who, the women felt, had not made space available for them to talk about these hidden and sometimes taboo aspects of their lives.

Treatment was seen to be too much about methods of controlling symptoms and not enough about understanding and empowering:

> They just gave me drugs.
>
> (Service user)

> A crazy system of rewards and punishments was put into operation. If I gained x amount of weight, I might be allowed certain so-called privileges – things that for any other person would be basic human rights and taken for granted, such as using the lavatory alone, having a bath in privacy and having visitors.
>
> (Service user)

Some women felt that they could have recovered faster from their problems if the response had addressed their underlying distress. For instance, one woman who had been sexually abused in childhood said that she had spent years in and out of psychiatric hospital before eventually finding a counsellor who enabled her to come to terms with her past and stop needing to use psychiatric services. Given that British research shows that 50 per cent of women who see a psychiatrist remember being sexually abused in childhood, it appears that an approach that does address underlying causes of distress could potentially prevent long-term psychiatric careers for some women

(Palmer *et al.*, 1992). Not to offer such opportunities may both fail the individual and risk wasting resources.

Problem 2. Missing current needs

One of the points raised most strongly by women throughout the Stress on Women Campaign was that women often did not feel safe in mental health settings such as psychiatric wards, the very places that should be places of safety and recovery:

> Many felt humiliated by hospital staff and had endured racist abuse from other patients. One young woman said she had been sexually molested by a member of staff. When she tried to report this, she and her parents were told that her illness could have caused her to imagine the incident or that she had even wanted it to happen. Since then she has mistrusted everyone connected with the hospital. Now she feels completely alone with no one to help her.
>
> (Frederick, 1991)

Women can also feel psychologically unsafe for a number of reasons, for instance if they are not able to communicate or understand what is going on:

> I visited someone in hospital and an Asian woman patient clung to me. She told me that Hindi was her first language and none of the ward staff could understand her. She hadn't been offered an interpreter and she kept touching my feet, almost begging me to talk to her. How can they know what someone's mental state is if they don't understand your language?
>
> (Individual surveyed by Southampton MIND)

Practical needs, e.g. housing and money, are often missed. Some women with responsibilities for children or other dependants found that they either could not use the mental health service they needed at all, or only at the expense of perpetual worry about what was happening to their children or relative:

> When I had my baby I stopped going to the day service. It was sad because I used to go every day – now I just sit at home with the baby.
>
> (User surveyed by Southampton MIND)

> Every time I try to find accommodation for a parent with a child, other than in council housing, I meet the 'no pets or children' syndrome of private landlords.
>
> (Liverpool MIND)

Considering that it has been known for twenty years that women with young children are particularly at risk of developing mental health problems, it is surprising that mental health services give so little attention to the immediate childcare needs of women using the services: for instance, less than one in five health authorities can offer places in hospital wards for women with children (Sayce, 1995).

Problem 3. Discrimination repeated

Many women felt that discrimination or oppression had played a part in their distress in the first place, and were devastated to find that experience mirrored in the mental health services. For example, women who had been sexually abused in childhood had often felt oppressed by cultures of silence in their families; when the mental health service did not create safety or make it possible to speak about abuse if it occurred, the experience was anything but healing:

> I was pinned down on my hospital bed by a male patient during the day. He kept following me around. I didn't tell staff because I had been abused before and felt it was all my fault.
>
> (User surveyed by Southampton MIND)

Other women had suffered from racist violence or abuse in their past; if they encountered a white-dominated mental health service, where racist comments went unchallenged, they could not even relax and begin to resolve their problems. Black carers described the anguish occasioned by the choice between seeking no help or seeming to collude with a coercive response from mental health services:

> Many described how relatives they loved had been taken kicking and screaming to hospital by police officers, while they looked on helplessly. Many felt angry that, apart from drugs and detention, there had been no service to help them or their relatives during their times of crisis.
>
> (Frederick, 1991)

We heard from lesbians who felt that the pressure to 'keep quiet' about their sexuality and not to 'ram it down people's throats' was repeated in hospital: they did not feel safe to come out, either to other users, some of whom made anti-gay remarks, or to staff, who appeared to assume heterosexuality. For the few who did come out, the experience had not always been positive: some found staff thereafter assumed their lesbianism was an inevitable part of their distress.

Older women, who in society at large are more likely than other groups to live in poverty and poor housing and to be socially isolated, get less than their fair share of resources from the mental health services. Often they are left in isolated positions at home, prescribed tranquillisers or anti-depressants, but not offered practical help, social and emotional support or counselling.

Our initial findings from the process of consultation with women service users were echoed in extreme form by the conclusions of the inquiry into Ashworth Hospital:

> We conclude that the current regime for women in Ashworth is infantilising, demeaning and anti-therapeutic for women.
>
> (HMSO, 1992)

Selecting the campaign targets

Some of the changes needed would be necessarily long term. To push debate forward we published a policy paper which outlines the 'whole picture' of policy change needed (Wood, 1992). Its recommendations included:

- switch resources to services which meet women's needs (for instance, from mainly physical treatments to a much wider range);
- consult women;
- offer women more choice, for instance of crisis services, self-help and support for women with caring responsibilities;
- implement appropriate staff recruitment and training, including training on gender issues for all mental health staff.

We also believed things would shift faster if we could achieve some specific change in targeted areas within a short time-scale (eighteen months). That way people convinced of the case for change would feel motivated for further action; some of the unconverted would change their position; and public awareness would grow.

We selected four areas for action:

Goal 1. An end to abuse in mental health settings

We wanted to see:

- more awareness that women should have the right to be on a women-only ward, or other women-only setting, if they choose;
- development of policies to tackle sexual harassment, abuse and rape in mental health settings;
- better information and advocacy for users on how to gain support and complain if that is their wish;
- training for staff in implementing the policy successfully and sensitively.

Goal 2. The right for women to choose a woman worker

We wanted to see:

- more recognition by policy makers and professional bodies that choice of a worker, including of a woman worker for a woman, is a key aspect of user choice;
- increased choice of worker under local authority 'care management' and health service Care Programme Approach systems;
- improved strategies for recruitment, training and promotion of health- and social-services staff according to equal opportunities principles.

Goal 3. Childcare for mental health service users

We wanted to see:

- more attention to the needs of parents under stress and their children in the government's health strategy (Health of the Nation) and its Welsh equivalent;
- childcare included in mental health assessments, in health and social services;
- better provision, such as 'parental suites' in hospitals, for parents in crisis; as well as the option for women of being admitted without their child(ren);
- training for magistrates on mental health; and for adult mental health workers on childcare issues;
- more accessible, affordable childcare for all children who need it.

Goal 4. Service provision and treatment monitored by gender

We wanted to see:

- local investigation of different treatments given to women and men;
- regular local action plans to end unfair treatment;
- national targets to end unfair treatment.

IMPLEMENTING THE CAMPAIGN

We decided that this campaign should aim to change policy both nationally and locally. Overt government policy is to devolve much decision-making to local purchasers of health and social services; yet in practice government measures, such as guidance on supervision registers, do change the policy climate in which local decisions are made. We hoped that through our campaign local purchasers and providers would hear about women's needs from documents like the 'Health of the Nation' put out by the Department of Health, as well as from local MIND or women's groups; and that this incremental approach would begin to make women's needs seem an obvious part of the mental health agenda. This strategy clearly worked in some localities: as one psychologist put it, 'suddenly other people in joint planning groups are raising women's issues – they can't write me off as "that feminist" any more'.

MIND produced a Campaign Pack (MIND, 1992), outlining what National MIND would do on each of the four goals and making suggestions for activity at a local level. Local MIND groups, women's groups, rape crisis centres, individual professionals and user groups became involved in different types of local activity.

We also decided to influence public opinion through the media. Recent campaign theory suggests that it can be easier to effect changes in policy if one influences the intellectual climate at the same time as lobbying specific decision-makers (e.g. Whiteley and Winyard, 1987). Previously, it had been thought preferable first to try to exert influence in the 'corridors of power' and only if this were unsuccessful to start embarrassing the government or others through recourse to the media. As it turned out, the Royal College of Psychiatrists made a crucial change in its policy position following the intervention of a TV programme (see below), so the strategy appeared to be vindicated.

EVALUATION: ASSESSING THE CAMPAIGN ACHIEVEMENTS

Evaluation of both successes and failures provides invaluable lessons for a campaign as it is in progress and for future campaigns. Regular bulletins on progress also provide a useful way of building commitment from all involved.

Some achievements of the MIND campaign are highlighted below. A full account of the outcomes was published in 1994 (Darton, Gorman and Sayce, 1994).

Speaking out

When users take action to change their circumstances, it can be both empowering for them and successful as a campaign strategy. One of the lynchpins of the MIND campaign was that it enabled people to speak out, sometimes for the first time. MIND distributed over 40,000 leaflets entitled 'Your Right to Say No', explaining to people using mental health services how to recognise and complain about sexual harassment and abuse. In some hospitals, for instance the Maudsley, this was given to every patient on admission. The media also publicised sexual assault on psychiatric wards: after their coverage of this issue, Radio 4's 'You and Yours' was so swamped by women ringing or writing in with further examples of abuses that they ran a follow-up programme. Numerous people contacted National MIND to tell their story: for instance, one woman told us she had been raped on a psychiatric ward ten years earlier and had never told anyone before, because she felt so ashamed.

Local campaigns

Local campaigning can be effective in raising public awareness of local issues and in creating solid changes in service delivery.

> Now at last I feel I can relax. I feel like I am on holiday.
>
> (Asian woman after transfer to a single-sex ward, following intervention by a MIND advocacy worker who eventually won the argument that the woman could not recover her mental health in a mixed ward.)

In Southampton, a qualitative survey was used to influence local managers. The local press covered the issue of sexual abuse in mental health facilities and the local statutory services began to respond. A clinical nurse was appointed to educate staff on sexual abuse; and the acute services manager, commenting in the *Southern Evening Echo*, said that in the light of the MIND survey, patient observation and security policies had been reviewed:

> Before MIND's national campaign complaints were not getting through.
>
> (*Southern Evening Echo*, 5 August 1993)

The Langbaurgh Campaign Group, involving Redcar MIND, undertook a survey which found that only 3 per cent of over a hundred women users interviewed wanted to be on a mixed ward. The rest either wanted a women-only ward (48 per cent) or a choice, and of those wanting a choice many said their personal choice would be for a women-only ward. This was taken up by the local MP, Marjorie Mowlam, and by the local radio, which broadcast a song written specially for the campaign. This had some success in getting the issue addressed in the local hospital.

In Liverpool, surveys found that women were twice as likely to receive ECT as men, and that there were only 1.5 women psychiatrists for the whole City of Liverpool. The *Liverpool Echo* ran stories such as 'Women Lead in the Figures for Stress'. Results of the local campaign included:

- North Mersey Community Trust formulating a sexual harassment/abuse policy and appointing a female psychiatrist to maximise choice.
- Liverpool Social Services managers receiving directions to consider user choice, and issues of gender and race, when allocating people to social workers.
- Windsor Day Hospital developing childcare provision.

In other areas achievements included:

- South Essex Health's Strategy (1994), following lobbying from South Essex Rape and Incest Crisis Centre and others, stating that 'We accept that single sex areas should be available within residential settings; crèches are needed.'

- West Pennine Health Purchasing Consortium agreeing that contracts they placed with providers from April 1994 would require them to address women-sensitive issues.
- North West MIND being instrumental in getting the practice of 'slopping out' in front of male staff stopped for women patients in Ashworth Hospital.

National campaigning

Influencing national organisations is important in order to influence the message they transmit to their members across the country, to build alliances for lobbying government and other decision-makers and, ultimately, to achieve changes in national policy.

The MIND campaign began by gaining endorsements from a wide range of organisations, including the Royal College of Nursing, Equal Opportunities Commission, Transcultural Psychiatry Society, Medical Women's Federation, British Psychological Society, Royal College of GPs and Save the Children. Some of these organisations gave very active support and went on to publicise their own work on women's mental health throughout their networks. For instance, the Royal College of Nursing produced its own guidelines and called for an 'open acknowledgement of the abuse of women by the mental health care system'.

MIND lobbied MPs and managed to raise some of the problems that women face in parliament. For instance, a motion was put before the House in 1993 calling on the Secretary of State to ensure that women-only wards were available.

National data were not easy to gather, given that there is no requirement to monitor services by gender. Parliamentary questions on issues like how many parts of the country could offer women-only wards, prompted the standard response, 'this information is not collected centrally'. A national sample survey by MIND found that three health authorities out of forty-two had women-only wards within their area. Most said they did offer the choice of a woman worker. However, in one area (Essex) where a survey of women using the services posed the same question, none of the thirty-nine women surveyed said they had been offered a choice of worker. It may be that managers assume a choice is on offer, when both male and female staff are on the books, but that no-one tells the user that choice of worker is available to them. This is particularly anomalous given the evidence that the relationship between worker and user is one of the key issues in the success in any mental health work, and given the supposed commitment to consumer choice in our current health services.

MIND held conferences, built coalitions, lobbied the Department of Health and other bodies, involved prominent individuals (such as Helena Kennedy, QC and Germaine Greer) – with the following results:

- The *Health of the Nation Key Area Handbook on Mental Illness* – distributed to all purchasers and providers of mental health services across the country – included a section on women's needs which repeated MIND's demands for attention to childcare and choice of women-only wards and women workers.
- The government's Mental Health Task Force funded a number of women's projects, including Trent and Yorkshire MIND's 'Stress on Women' development project and Islington's video on preventing sexual harassment and abuse in psychiatric settings.
- The Task Force's own video on day and leisure activities featured women's views on the value of the women-only day at Southampton MIND; it also produced a special International Women's Day edition of its Grassroots newsletter.
- The government's Mental Health Nursing Review included reference to the need for women-only wards.
- A 1993 Association for Metropolitan Authorities' report on mental health recommended that all mental health assessments should include childcare; and that women users should have the choice to see a woman worker.
- Funders (like the Mental Health Foundation) reported increased funding to women's projects.

By 1994, new policy documents were including reference to women as a matter of course. A Task Force Report referred to the need for purchasers to consult with users, including ethnic-minority and women's groups. Two years earlier, women would not have been included in such documents; now they were part of the agenda, even with no active lobbying.

Integrated campaigning

The impact of a campaign is greater than the sum of its parts: it is through the combination of media work, individual action and local and national lobbying, that changes in culture and practice begin to emerge. A shift in thinking on single-sex wards during 1993–1994 provides an example of how this can happen.

One influential organisation in the mental health field that did not support MIND's call for a choice of women-only psychiatric wards was the Royal College of Psychiatrists. Early in the campaign their spokesperson said 'People don't live in monasteries or convents, men and women live with each other.' This view was contradicted by many users, for instance: 'In my home I don't live with strange men, so I don't see why a mentally ill woman in a vulnerable state should have to' (member of Langbaurgh Campaign Group). By 1993 a Royal College spokesperson stated: 'There's very little reason to be worried about this . . . in fact, the justification for fear of sexual attacks is really not there because they are extremely rare; I haven't known of any' (quoted in Altounyan, 1993).

This was an increasingly minority position. Research and consultation around the country showed that once people were asked, they disclosed ample evidence of sexual harassment and assault. For instance, in 1993 the *Health Service Journal* reported a survey of 100 psychiatric patients of whom 60 had been sexually harassed, 10 sexually assaulted and 2 raped (*HSJ*, 1993). Agencies ranging from the Mental Health Act Commission to the Royal College of Nursing were making public comments of concern about women's safety on mixed wards.

In 1994, Esther Rantzen devoted two programmes to this area, inspired by a group of service users in Croydon. One of their members took the cameras round a ward in the local psychiatric hospital, showing where assaults had taken place and how the lay-out was not conducive to safety for women (or indeed for men). On the programme users, Tessa Jowell MP, Liz Sayce from National MIND and the manager of the hospital all said that the lack of choice of women-only provision was unacceptable. The President of the Royal College of Psychiatrists then agreed:

> There was a time when people thought the idea of mixed wards was a good one – that was back in the late 60s, early 70s – but as they actually opened people began to realise that patients were attacked and harmed.

Finally the Royal College had abandoned a position which everyone else thought untenable; even the correspondents in its own *Bulletin*:

> The development of mixed sex wards was part of the drive to humanise psychiatric wards. . . . However, the developments have proceeded without the opinion of patients or their relatives being taken into account. Our results suggest that a substantial number of patients may not be in agreement with their hospital carers.
>
> (Patel, Doshi and Oyebode, 1994)

It was not media work alone that achieved this shift: it was the combination of users speaking out and of lobbying MPs, managers and professionals. This cumulative effect of different campaign strategies led in some parts of the country to a new recognition of women's mental health needs:

> I consider a cultural reassessment, an intellectual explosion is taking place. The Stress on Women Campaign has succeeded in making the invisible visible. Women's previously unheard experiences of mental health services are now out in the open.
>
> (Karen Colligan, Chair, Liverpool MIND)

> The campaign and conference are bringing the hospital walls down. The women know they are not isolated, not on their own.
>
> (Moira Potier, Principal Clinical Psychologist, Ashworth Hospital)

Assessing the campaign's limitations

Taking a cool look at the obstacles and setbacks encountered in a campaign is essential for the planning of future strategy. The MIND campaign was, in part, constrained by the fact that the government has successfully side-stepped all calls for enforceable national policies on women and mental health, as they have more broadly resisted the call for national standards for community care. There is still no absolute requirement for purchasers or providers of services to meet women's needs in the ways that women users have defined to be necessary. There is not even a requirement to monitor services by gender. When we surveyed health authorities and trusts, we found that many could not tell us what proportion of people receiving treatments, such as ECT, were male or female, let alone what the figures were for young women and old women or women from different ethnic groups. It is extremely unlikely that the needs of, say, black women who are receiving disproportionate levels of neuroleptics, or older women getting high levels of ECT, will be met with appropriate alternatives if no monitoring takes place.

The campaign has been successful in changing the 'intellectual climate' and, in some parts of the country, policy and practice. In other parts of the country, however, nothing has changed. Good practice for women, like good practice in mental health generally, is patchy. There are no national standards and very few rights for users.

The legal framework which does, for instance, give users the right to complain about mistreatment, has not been altered through this campaign. There are two problems with this. First, women can only try to seek redress after things have gone wrong; they have no right to have their preference for a woman worker, or a single-sex ward, or decent childcare, respected and met. Second, if things do go wrong, legal redress is not easy to obtain. For instance, if a woman is assaulted on a psychiatric ward by a patient she may want to press criminal charges. During the campaign we have heard of cases where women have been prevented from going through with a case by the Crown Prosecution Service, on the grounds that the testimony of a woman diagnosed 'mentally ill' is unlikely to be believed. If a woman is abused by a member of staff, she may want to take a complaint to the relevant professional body: here again the experience can be difficult. One case heard at the General Medical Council involved a woman facing a panel of one woman and twelve men, and having her entire sexual history brought up (quite irrelevantly). *GP Magazine* (1993) subsequently reported on the terrible trauma faced by the accused doctor under the headline: 'Innocent GP is tortured' and questioned how such cases could be allowed to get to the final stage of a GMC hearing. No reference was made to the trauma experienced by the woman.

During the campaign, MIND produced a briefing for advisers and advocates, to enable them to help people considering taking legal action or making official complaints about abuses. Nonetheless, the system for redress remains stacked against women with a diagnosis of mental illness. Finally, a lack of rights means that even where we have won the argument, for instance for women-only wards, there is no obligation to transform theoretical commitment into action. Some purchasers have said to us that they agree that single-sex wards should be on offer, but that they cannot afford to purchase them.

CONCLUSION

This chapter has shown that in the current political climate a multi-frontal campaign, working nationally and locally, through policy lobbying and through the mass media, can achieve change. The greatest changes achieved by MIND's Stress on Women Campaign happened through influencing the intellectual climate; enabling users to speak out; modifying non-prescriptive national policy (i.e. documents of 'good practice'), and changing some local policy and practice.

Nonetheless, there are constraints on that change, caused by the difficulty of making progress in terms of national standards or rights for users. Importantly, the campaign has shown that different groups of women are very clear about what they want changed and that it is possible to build some consensus on issues such as choice. Choice of a woman worker is of great concern to many Asian women and Jewish women, for reasons that are, in part, different from those for white Anglo-Saxon women; lesbian women may have different reasons again. There is, however, consensus on the objective of choice. Other issues remain specific to different groups and these should be addressed as distinct groups.

This chapter began with a discussion of history. It now seems absurd to us that women could be incarcerated for sending visiting cards to men they were attracted to. In the twenty-first century it will seem equally absurd that women were forced to be 'treated' in mixed facilities, that their experiences of prior abuse and exploitation were paid so little attention, that they were drugged and given ECT on so much larger a scale than men, that black women and Irish women were so often deemed 'mentally ill', that lesbians were not allowed to express their affection for their partners within many mental health settings. The greater the campaigning effort and expertise in this century, the greater the potential benefits for women in the next.

In the course of the MIND campaign we have set out a broad agenda for change, which remains highly relevant. It includes long-term goals, such as switching resources from mainly in-patient physical treatments to a broader range including self-help and rape crisis centres; and more immediate goals, such as improving women's safety and choice within existing mental health services. These goals should be helpful in developing future campaign activity on women's mental health. Any such campaigns should benefit from the success that the Stress on Women Campaign has had in raising awareness of women's mental health needs.

CROSS-REFERENCES WITHIN THE BOOK

REFERENCES

Altounyan, B. (1993) 'Sex on the ward', *Nursing Standard* (3 March).
Darton, K., Gorman, J. and Sayce, L. (1994) *Eve fights back*, London: MIND.
Eichenbaum, L. and Orbach, S. (1983) *Understanding women*, London: Pelican.
Frederick, J. (1991) *Positive thinking for mental health*, London: Black Mental Health Group.
Gorman, J. (1992) *Out of the shadows*, London: MIND.
GP Magazine (1993) 'Innocent GP is tortured' (23 July).
Health Service Journal (1993) 'TV inquiry says sexual abuse rife on wards' (4 March).
HMSO (1992) *Report of the Committee of Inquiry into Complaints at Ashworth Hospital*, London: HMSO.
MIND (1992) *Stress on Women campaign pack*, London: MIND.
Palmer, R., Chaloner, D. and Oppenheimer, R. (1992) 'Childhood sexual experiences with adults reported by female patients', *British Journal of Psychiatry* 160: 261–265.
Patel, A., Doshi, M. and Oyebode, F. (1994) 'Mixed sex wards', *Psychiatric Bulletin* 18: 577.
Sayce, L. (1996) 'Good practice in mental health for women with children', in R. Perkins *et al.* (eds) *Women's mental health in context*, London: Good Practices in Mental Health.
Ussher, J. (1991) *Women's madness: misogyny or mental illness?*, London: Harvester Wheatsheaf.
Whiteley, P. and Winyard, S. (1987) *Pressure for the poor*, London: Methuen.
Wood, D. (1992) *Policy on women and mental health*, London: MIND.

Chapter 18

Developing psychiatric services for women

Elaine M. Gadd

This book has examined many issues concerning the mental health of women and their use of mental health services. In considering what women would like from services, common themes have recurred – women want to be listened to, to have their concerns and experiences taken seriously, and for professionals to understand the culture in which they live their lives; for example, the experiences of those from ethnic minorities or of lesbian orientation. They want to participate in choices about their treatment and to feel safe and comfortable in the setting in which that treatment is delivered. Although it is clear that women have many needs in common, developing appropriate services requires an understanding of the diversity of women's needs and experience.

This chapter considers how we can translate the information available to us into effective service development. From the diversity of concerns expressed in this book, it is clear that there can be no single model of an effective, comprehensive mental health service for women. The discussion in this chapter is about general psychiatric services for adults aged 16 to 64, with particular reference to women. Although service planning for children, the elderly, and particular client groups, such as mentally disordered offenders, will follow the same principles, each group will present different issues to be addressed. Before planning can start, it is necessary to have as accurate a picture as possible of the population for whom services are being developed. Information required will include:

- age/sex structure;
- proportion with marital status single, widowed or divorced (a measure of social isolation);
- proportion and type of ethnic groups;
- social class mix;
- unemployment rates;
- population density (urban, rural, semi-rural);
- Jarman index (a measure of the level of deprivation within an area).

This will need to be supplemented by other locally relevant information, for example on homeless people, refugees, proportion of single-parent families, or particular pockets of high unemployment. Using the data that exist concerning the effect of these variables on mental health, the sociodemographic profile will assist in developing a picture of the mental health of the local population. In Chapter 2, Johnson and Buszewicz have considered some of the data available on the epidemiology of women's mental health problems. They mention the recent national survey of psychiatric morbidity in people aged 16 to 64, commissioned by the Department of Health, which will assist local needs assessment exercises. The first bulletin of the survey, covering national prevalence rates of psychiatric disorder by age and sex, became available in December 1994 (OPCS). A total of eight reports will be available by the end of 1996.

When compared with the community demographic profile, data on use of secondary-care services can provide some information on the extent to which need is likely to be being met; for example, GP referral patterns, use of out-patient, day and in-patient services, contacts with community psychiatric nurses, occupational therapists and psychologists. However, the statistical evidence readily available is strongly biased towards the hospital sector and will significantly underestimate need in the community.

Planning does not take place in a vacuum and an accurate picture of the facilities and services available to meet need is required. As well as disorders unique to women, such as puerperal psychosis, women experience the full range of mental health problems experienced by men and similarly require the full range of services to meet their needs. Central to developing an effective service is the principle of ensuring that resources are targeted and used appropriately.

PRIMARY-CARE SERVICES

In Chapter 14, Corney and Strathdee demonstrated that the vast majority of people who are recognised as suffering from a mental health problem are managed in primary care. So that secondary-care services are able to target their resources appropriately at those with the most severe problems, it is essential that management in primary care is as effective as possible. This will involve ensuring that local GPs know how accurately to recognise and manage common psychiatric disorders, and are involved in the development of policies for referral to secondary-care services. Jenkins (1992) has described a range of initiatives which can assist in GP management of mental health problems. Orton (1994) has reviewed the use of liaison clinics in primary care, pointing out the potential advantages in improved patient care, more efficient use of primary- and secondary-care skills, and convenience for the patient. Such clinics may improve the accessibility of services to mothers of young children (provision of a crèche facility will further assist), and may be perceived as carrying less stigma than attendance at any specific mental health facility. For such clinics to be successful, Orton emphasises the need for clarification of a range of issues, including:

- geographical and practice need for a local clinic
- referral criteria agreed
- agreement reached on clinical responsibility
- specialist–GP equality
- good organisation, including planning, definition of roles, protocols and guidelines, and audit.

In the same way that a population profile informs wider service planning, the age/sex register of the practice and a practice register of those suffering from severe mental illness can assist in defining the specific requirements of a clinic. Examining prescribing patterns can be a fruitful subject for audit; the specialist may be able to advise on prescribing and on alternative methods of treatment. One example is to assist in reducing the use of benzodiazepines, which are prescribed more frequently for women. The Mental Health Foundation has issued 'Guidelines for the prevention and treatment of benzodiazepine dependence', which discusses management strategies in primary care, as well as indications for specialist referral.

The GP is also ideally placed to be proactive in identifying women at high risk of mental disorder and enabling appropriate support and management to be delivered. Particular examples might include young mothers-to-be with little social support who are living in inner-city areas: in Chapter 3, Pound and Abel described the benefits that can be achieved in women with postnatal depression following a brief intervention from health visitors.

SPECIALIST SERVICES

Having addressed appropriate primary-care management, developing effective secondary-care services requires an accurate picture of the range of facilities currently available. This will include information from the NHS, social services, the voluntary sector and the private sector. Information is required on local facilities for:

- treatment
- accommodation
- occupation and training
- recreation and friendship.

Information required will include places available, entry/referral criteria, presence of childcare facilities if appropriate, and suitability for those who do not speak English (e.g. availability of interpreters).

Provision must be made for those suffering with rarer disorders. For such disorders it would not be feasible to provide local services in every district, but planning is required to ensure that those needs are met on a district or supra-district level. An example of particular concern to women is the management of the most severe eating disorders and access to mother and baby facilities; other examples include the management of those with psychiatric problems following head injury and those with presenile dementia.

Although women are very much less likely to offend than men, the needs of those that do must not be forgotten. Women who kill are significantly more likely than men to be found to be suffering from a mental disorder, and imprisoned women have been found to have high rates of psychiatric morbidity. Prison for women is frequently inappropriate, but it may be difficult to find a suitable alternative such as a hostel. Few such hostels cater specifically for women; as many female offenders have been abused by men they may find such a placement very difficult (d'Orban, 1993). The needs of women must therefore not be forgotten in developing forensic psychiatric services (including court diversion schemes), at district, regional and national levels.

Special provision is required for homeless women, who often have high rates of mental illness. In Chapter 9, Cook and Marshall outline the wide range of problems that may affect this group, and discuss setting up appropriate and accessible services for them.

The needs of those in other settings must also be considered; high rates of mental health problems exist in general medical and surgical facilities. Young women have high rates of deliberate self-harm and will present to casualty departments. A particularly important aspect to consider is maternity services; Chapter 3 has discussed the wide range of problems that may present at this time. Thus, service development will need to address both the provision of liaison services, and the training requirements of staff in those settings to ensure that mental health service professionals are used appropriately.

DEVELOPING A COMPREHENSIVE LOCAL SERVICE

The NHS Health Advisory Service (1994) and the Mental Health Task Force (1994) have both given guidance on the range of resources that should be considered in a comprehensive assessment of the service domains for a general psychiatric service described above. Central features include:

Treatment services
- health centres
- home treatment services
- resource centres
- community mental health centres

- hostels
- day hospitals
- in-patient units
- 24-hour emergency services

In addition to examining the treatment settings, the range of therapies available will have to be considered. A particular concern for women is the availability of psychotherapy services and, therefore, the availability of the following should be examined:

- individual psychodynamic psychotherapy;
- cognitive-behaviour therapy;
- group psychotherapy, including availability of women-only groups and groups for those facing particular issues, such as eating disorders or the consequences of sexual abuse.

As well as assessing the availability of such therapies, it is important to ascertain whether they are available to all the population served – for example, those who do not speak English. In Chapter 6, Ismail describes how black women tend to under-use current mental health services, often finding them inappropriate or inaccessible. In particular, they often find it hard to access psychotherapy services. It is important to ensure that the therapies are being used appropriately and effectively; a wide range of information on the effectiveness of treatments is now available, including medication, cognitive and other psychotherapies, and the use of ECT.

Accommodation services

- 24-hour staffed accommodation
- day-staffed accommodation
- supported accommodation
- independent housing
- adult carer schemes
- crisis schemes
- respite accommodation

Wing (1992) has provided an estimate of needs for accommodation (including in-patient care) in an average district of 250,000 residents. The use of the sociodemographic profile enables such global estimates to be interpreted according to local need.

Occupation and training

- workshops
- co-operatives
- employment training schemes

- education
- job clubs

Recreation and friendship

- drop-in centres
- befriending schemes
- self-help and mutual-support groups
- supported use of local facilities, e.g. leisure centres
- clubs

ASSESSING SERVICE QUALITY

Having developed a picture of the needs of the population and the facilities presently available to meet them, it will now be possible to examine to what extent those facilities are meeting the needs of women. Shaw (1986) has suggested that services can be evaluated against the following criteria:

- equity
- appropriateness
- accessibility
- acceptability
- effectiveness
- efficiency.

Using these parameters, how might services be failing women? Throughout this book we can find many illustrative examples, many of which may have a bearing on several of the parameters.

Equity

Equity can be defined as a fair share for all the population according to their needs. Before anyone can receive a 'fair share' it is necessary for the problem to be recognised. Davison and Marshall (Chapter 10) describe the barriers to detection that may exist for drug-misusing women. In Chapter 14, it has been shown that general practitioners may more readily detect mental disorder in women presenting to them compared to men, although they are less likely to refer women on to secondary care. However, not all GPs may be as sensitive to the different presentations of mental disorder that may occur in those from different ethnic groups; this may be particularly so if doctor and patient are not able to converse fluently which may be the case for many Asian women who speak little English. In Chapter 13, Welldon has alerted us to the difficulties that professionals may have in recognising or acknowledging particular difficulties faced by women.

In secondary-care settings, women may be hampered in achieving their 'fair share' for a variety of reasons. If services are failing them on another parameter such as accessibility (as discussed below), they are less likely to engage with the service. The availability of services such as psychotherapy in a variety of languages is often limited.

Appropriateness

Appropriateness can be defined as whether the service or procedure is what the person (or population) actually needs. In Chapter 10, it is pointed out that a drug-misusing woman may present to a variety of services, yet the underlying problem remains untackled because the possibility of drug misuse is not considered. Throughout this book the requirement to ask women what they need has been emphasised. Women may not feel able to express their views easily to professionals; the availability of advocacy schemes, or a befriender, may assist them. The UK Advocacy Network (1994) has produced a helpful guide on the subject. It is important that treatment options are fully discussed with the woman, to enable her to make an informed choice whenever possible. In Chapter 17, Sayce describes how services are often seen to fail in this regard. People are unable to take in a large amount of information in a single interview and information leaflets on treatment are available from a variety of sources. It is often helpful for women to be given such leaflets to assist them in understanding the options and formulating questions for their next visit. However, it is important to remember that information may need to be available in a variety of languages and that not everyone is literate.

An important aspect of appropriateness is to ensure that women are not subject to abuse or harassment, either physical or sexual, by other patients or by members of staff while they are receiving treatment. Chapter 12, by Mezey and Stanko, makes it clear how women users of mental health services may have already been on the receiving end of violent or abusive acts, making it particularly important to avoid any repetition. Clear policies on violent incidents and harassment should be in place, and a complaint of such an incident should always be taken seriously. The woman should be told how her complaint is going to be dealt with.

Accessibility

Access to services should not be compromised by undue limits of time, distance or available information about user rights or the services provided; nor by the services' characteristics, structure, ethos or referral system. In Chapter 17 there was reference to the importance of childcare in allowing longer term users to remain engaged with services after a change in family circumstances, and Nettle and Phillips, in Chapter 15, stress how important it is for arrangements to be made for appropriate childcare, so that women users are able to make full use of available treatments. As well as enabling women to continue to access day services, the availability of childcare can allow women to make full use of their out-patient appointments. If no child-care is available, the child will often be brought into the consultation; this can present difficulties for both mother and professional.

In Chapter 7, Perkins describes the negative effect which the 'heterosexist' ethos of services may have on the treatment of women who are lesbians. The positive approach of Shanti, described by Mills in Chapter 16, in develop-ing an ethos that is acceptable to their client group by extensive local consulta-tion, demonstrates the benefits in improved engagement and outcome.

Acceptability

Acceptable services are provided in a manner that satisfies the reasonable expectations of both users and the community. There are obvious links with this parameter and those described above. Safety within the treatment set-ting is an area that is of particular concern to women. Chapter 7 points out the importance of a range of segregated and non-segregated accommoda-tion and treatment approaches, and of privacy. Lack of privacy, particularly when bathing or washing, may be particularly traumatic to older women. The expansion of the Patient's Charter in January 1995 emphasised the right to advance information before admission if the person is to be placed in a mixed-sex ward, and the provision of a choice between mixed-sex or single-sex accommodation wherever possible. Choice of gender of professional has been emphasised by many authors within this book; it is also clear that women must be told that they have a choice. The sectorisation of services offers many advantages, but it will be important to ensure that procedures are in place for a woman to see a female therapist or consultant, when local staff are male, if required.

Effectiveness

An effective service is one that achieves the intended benefit for the indi-vidual and for the population. Effective treatment begins with correct recognition and understanding of the problem, which will necessitate an understanding of the cultural context in which it arises. Chapter 7 describes the lack of understanding of many professionals of lesbian culture. It is im-portant to look behind the presenting disorder to identify underlying factors such as childhood sexual abuse; unless such underlying factors are addressed treatment is not likely to be effective in the long term. The development of effective services for victims of child sexual abuse and their location, at times within specialist mental health services, but also often within other community-based facilities, is discussed fully by Staples and Dare in Chapter 11. The advantages of early intervention are illustrated in Chapter 3, considering new mothers.

Efficiency

Resources need to be applied to bring the maximum benefit to each service user, without being to the detriment of another. In planning services, it is therefore necessary to have a clear picture of the effectiveness of different treatment options and their relative cost. This will include consideration of the longer term perspective; for example, early specialist treatment for those with severe eating disorders may appear more expensive in the short term, but the benefits in improved outcome may result in longer term savings.

USER CONSULTATION

The illustrations above demonstrate the variety of ways in which services may be, often unwittingly, failing women. In planning a local service, it is important to identify the particular concerns that local women have about existing services. The *Mental Illness Key Area Handbook* (Department of Health, 1994b) gives examples of the range of interest groups that it is important to consult:

- service users;
- patient advocates;
- national and local voluntary-sector representatives;
- Community Health Councils;
- carers and carer groups;
- health and social care professionals in both primary and secondary care;
- housing, education and police authorities.

To involve women service users fully takes time and a variety of approaches. Examples include the use of surveys, focus groups, depth interviews, and consultation with user groups. Some women may find it easier to express their views in a women-only group. Women with young children may find it difficult to participate for practical reasons – holding a session at a play-group or crèche facility can help. The needs of different groups of women – those from ethnic minorities, those with young children, those of lesbian sexuality for example – need to be clarified.

Users may require reimbursement for any costs they may incur by participating and should receive feedback on the outcome of the consultation exercise. The Mental Health Task Force User Group (1994) has produced a training pack to assist service users who may be acting as trainers, speakers or workshop facilitators. Local user groups may find this of benefit.

In the light of the local sociodemographic profile and needs assessment, the profile of current services and local consultation, it will be possible to identify gaps and problems in service provision. A comprehensive service will include a balance of prevention, treatment, rehabilitation and continuing care facilities. It is never possible to develop a service instantly and priorities will need to be identified. All parties (such as purchasing authorities, health authorities, social service authorities) should agree the priorities in the light of the local consultation exercise if services are to develop coherently.

EFFECTING CHANGE

Within each priority, the next task is to identify options for change. There may be a variety of ways in which a particular need can be met and the most cost-effective option should be identified. Some beneficial changes may have no resource consequences – for example, the designation of a particular community accommodation facility as a 'women-only' house. Many of the concerns identified by women in this book reflect the perceived attitudes of professionals, which can be addressed as part of a training strategy. Improving services in the long term will involve a greater emphasis on communication in the pre-qualification training of professionals than has been the case in the past; encouraging examples of this development already exist. It is important to set local targets or objectives for the desired goal, and to ensure that methods are in place to monitor progress towards the target. A simple example would be an objective to ensure that 100 per cent of women were aware that they had a choice of the sex of their keyworker, to be monitored by a survey of users' views at regular intervals.

The staff training strategy will have a central role to play in developing improved services and should form an integral part of the plan. Three aspects will need to be considered:

- information and awareness – this might include sessions to improve understanding of the lesbian culture, as described in Chapter 7;
- training in aspects of service delivery – such as acting as a keyworker under the Care Programme Approach, developing skills in cognitive therapy, or in management;
- supervision – to enhance skill development.

It is essential to remember that services are delivered by people with their own human needs. Staff may also, for example, need facilities for childcare or flexible working arrangements. Being a mental health professional does not render a staff member immune to stress or mental health problems, which can impair their ability to provide care. The World Health Organisation in 1994 reviewed the phenomenon of staff 'burnout', and made recommendations for preventive measures. Factors within the organisation and in job design can themselves promote stress (Warr, 1992). To ensure that high-quality services continue to be delivered, the organisation will need to address:

- action to minimise the chance of stress or mental health problems developing in staff;
- action to ensure that the development of a problem in a staff member is promptly recognised, and that appropriate support, and if necessary treatment, is given;
- action to assist staff who have had a period of sickness absence to return to work.

These aspects can be brought together as the mental health aspects of a unit health policy (Department of Health, 1994a).

This book has attempted to address what women want from services, and the differences between their perceived needs and what they have often received. It is only relatively recently that medicine as a whole has challenged the assumption that what is appropriate and true for men is also true for women. In looking to the future, we need to work towards ensuring that services are equally effective and appropriate for all sections of society.

REFERENCES

Department of Health (1994a) *ABC of mental health in the workplace*, London: HMSO.

Department of Health (1994b) *Mental Illness Key Area Handbook*, 2nd edition, London: HMSO.

d'Orban, P.T. (1993) 'Female offenders', in J. Gunn and P. Taylor (eds), *Forensic psychiatry: clinical, legal and ethical issues*, Oxford: Butterworth-Heinemann Ltd.

Jenkins, R. (1992) 'Developments in the primary care of mental illness – a forward look', *International Review of Psychiatry* 4: 237–242.

Mental Health Task Force (1994) *Local systems of support*, London: Department of Health.

Mental Health Task Force User Group (1994) *Building on experience*, London: Department of Health.

NHS Health Advisory Service (1994) *Comprehensive mental health services*, London: HAS.

OPCS Surveys of Psychiatric Morbidity in Great Britain (1994) *Bulletin no. 1: the prevalence of psychiatric morbidity among adults aged 16–64 living in private households in Great Britain*, London: OPCS.

Orton, P. (1994) 'Shared care', *Lancet*, 344: 1413–1415.

Shaw, C. (1986) *Introducing quality assurance*, London: King's Fund Centre.

UK Advocacy Network (1994) *Advocacy – a code of practice*, London: Department of Health.

Warr, P. (1992) 'Job features and excessive stress', in R. Jenkins and N. Coney (eds), *Prevention of mental ill health at work*, London: HMSO.

Wing, J.K. (1992) 'Epidemiologically based needs assessment', *Report 6: mental illness*, London: NHS Management Executive.

World Health Organisation (1994) 'Guidelines for the primary prevention of mental, neurological and psychosocial disorders', 5. *Staff burnout*, Geneva: WHO.

Appendix
Mental health services for women

Addresses of agencies referred to within the book are listed below in alphabetical order

The Alzheimer Disease Society
National Office
Gordon House
10 Greencoat Place
London SW1P 1PH
TEL: 0171 306 0833

Carers National Association
20–25 Glasshouse Yard
London EC1A 4JS
TEL: 0171 490 8818
Carers advice line: 0171 490 8898

**Drug and Alcohol Women's
Network (DAWN)**
c/o GLAAS
30–31 Great Sutton Street
London EC1V 0DX
TEL: 0171 253 6221

Good Practices In Mental Health
380–384 Harrow Road
London W9 2HU
TEL: 0171 289 2034

Homeless HELP Team
42 Carnegie House
20 Osborn St
London E1 6TD
TEL: 0171 247 7232

Home-Start UK
2 Salisbury Road
Leicester LE1 7QR
TEL: 0116 2339955

Hopetown Hostel
60 Old Montague Street
Whitechapel
London E1 5NG
TEL: 0171 247 1004

King's Fund
11–13 Cavendish Sq
London W1M 0AN
TEL: 0171 307 2400

The Mental Health Foundation
37 Mortimer Street
London W1N 8JU
TEL: 0171 580 0145

National MIND
Granta House
15–19 Broadway
Stratford
London E15 4BQ
TEL: 0181 522 1728 / 519 2122

Nafsiyat
278 Seven Sisters Road
London N4 2HY
TEL: 0171 263 4130

NEWPIN
National Newpin
Sutherland House
35 Sutherland Square
London SE17 3EE
TEL: 0171 703 6326

The Portman Clinic
8 Fitzjohns Avenue
London NW3 5NA
TEL: 0171 794 8262 / 5

St Botolph's Day Centre
Aldgate
London EC3N 1AB
TEL: 0171 283 1950

Shanti Women's Counselling Service
1a Dalbury House

Edmundsbury Court
Ferndale Road
London SW9 8AP
TEL: 0171 733 8581

Tower Hamlets Primary Care Clinical Psychology and Counselling Service
c/o Steels Lane Health Centre
384–398 Commercial Road
London E1 0LR
TEL: 0171 790 7171

WISH
Women in Special Hospitals and Secure Units
25 Horsell Road
London N5 1XL
TEL: 0171 700 6684

Women's Therapy Centre
6–9 Manor Gardens
London N7 6LA
TEL: 0171 281 7879

Author index

Subject index

abuse *see* sexual abuse; perpetrators of abuse
abusers *see* perpetrators of abuse
Admiral Nurse service 60
adolescence: and Asian girls 69; and eating disorders 44–5; parasuicide 41–2; prevalence of psychological disorders 38–9; recommendations for psychological treatment services 44; teenage pregnancy 45–6; *see also* girls
advocacy 74, 253
Advisory Council on Drug Misuse 131
Afro-Caribbean women: lack of understanding of needs of 16; and sickle cell disease 69; and psychotic illness 70; *see also* black women
AIDS *see* HIV/AIDS
alcohol misuse, core services for 140; *see also* substance misuse
Allitt, Beverley 184
Alzheimer's Disease Society (ADS) 56; *see also* appendix 259
anorexia nervosa *see* eating disorders
Asian women: and alcohol 71; and eating disorders 67, 69; lack of understanding of needs 16; and marriage 67, 68; and racism 70; and stigma of mental illness 67; suicide rates among 16, 69; *see also* black women
assessment of service quality 252; effectiveness of 254–5; efficiency of 255; equity of 252–3; and user consultation 255–6
asylum, concept of 86–7, 95, 96

befriending 32, 84, 229, 252
bipolar affective disorder 28, 80
black women: and choice of worker 245;

and counselling 76; defined 65–7; and ethnic factors related to mental illness 68–71; and forensic services 72; and homelessness 113; and interpreters 68, 75, 76, 251; lack of understanding of needs of 3, 16, 67–8, 251; and legitimisation of illness 71; planning services for 72–7; and primary care 71, 198; psychotherapy centre for 219–30; separate services for 74–75; service use of 71–2, 251; and spiritual healers 72; and substance misuse 71, 129, 133–4; and voluntary sector 72
British Crime Survey (1982) 161
bulimia nervosa *see* eating disorder
bullying 46–7
burden of care 104, 105–6; and Expressed Emotion 107–8; and family environment 107; *see also* informal carers

Camberwell Family Interview 107
campaign(ing) for change 231; planning a 232; implementing targets 238;
Care Programme Approach 238
carers *see* formal carers; informal carers
Carers National Association 110; *see also* appendix 259
'Caring for People' (1989) 96, 97
case identification *see* presentation to services
childcare: and community support services 29, 31–3; and drug and alcohol abuse 132, 139, 141; and mothers' vulnerability to depression 13–14; and primary care services 198; recommendations for mental health services 217, 238; social class and